The
EVERYTHING
INVENTIONS
& PATENTS BOOK

Dear Reader:

Bringing a new product to market is not a task for the faint of heart. But if you have something the world is waiting for, you can absolutely beat the odds.

Take us, for example! As two sisters who spent the greater part of our lives as wives and mothers, we are the most unlikely success story you can imagine. We took a very simple idea and developed a product that retails at over $8,000,000 per year. And we continue to repeat this success with more great ideas. If we, with absolutely no background in inventing, could achieve such astounding success, anyone can do it!

With no road map to guide us, we figured out each step as we went along. Throughout the course of this adventure we learned some insider secrets and tips for getting the job done right on a limited budget. Now we want to share it all with you. Are you ready?

Here's to your success,

Mary Russell Sarao

Barbara Russell Pitts

The EVERYTHING® Series

Editorial

Publishing Director	Gary M. Krebs
Associate Managing Editor	Laura M. Daly
Associate Copy Chief	Brett Palana-Shanahan
Acquisitions Editor	Gina Chaimanis
Development Editor	Katie McDonough
Associate Production Editor	Casey Ebert

Production

Director of Manufacturing	Susan Beale
Associate Director of Production	Michelle Roy Kelly
Cover Design	Paul Beatrice
	Erick DaCosta
	Matt LeBlanc
Design and Layout	Colleen Cunningham
	Holly Curtis
	Sorae Lee
Series Cover Artist	Barry Littmann

THE
EVERYTHING®
INVENTIONS & PATENTS BOOK

Turn your crazy ideas into money-making machines

Barbara Russell Pitts
and
Mary Russell Sarao

Adams Media
Avon, Massachusetts

For Jill, Caroline, Valerie, Danielle, Brooke, and baby Margaret,
who give us wonderful reasons to be inventive.

An Everything® Series Book.
Everything® and everything.com® are registered trademarks of F+W Publications, Inc.

Published by Adams Media, an F+W Publications Company
57 Littlefield Street, Avon, MA 02322 U.S.A.
www.adamsmedia.com

ISBN 10: 1-59337-436-4
ISBN 13: 978-1-59337-436-5
Printed in the United States of America.

J I H G F E D C B

Library of Congress Cataloging-in-Publication Data
Pitts, Barbara Russell.
The everything inventions & patents book : turn your crazy ideas into money-making machines /
Barbara Russell Pitts and Mary Russell Sarao.
p. cm. -- (Everything series)
ISBN 1-59337-436-4
1. Inventions--Handbooks, manuals, etc. 2. Patents--Handbooks, manuals, etc. I. Title: Everything inventions and
patents book. II. Sarao, Mary Russell. III. Title. IV. Series.

T339.P53 2006
608--dc22

2005026084

This publication is designed to provide accurate and authoritative information with regard to the subject matter covered. It is sold with the understanding that the publisher is not engaged in rendering legal, accounting, or other professional advice. If legal advice or other expert assistance is required, the services of a competent professional person should be sought.

—From a *Declaration of Principles* jointly adopted by a Committee of the American Bar Association and a Committee of Publishers and Associations

Many of the designations used by manufacturers and sellers to distinguish their products are claimed as trademarks. Where those designations appear in this book and Adams Media was aware of a trademark claim, the designations have been printed with initial capital letters.

This book is available at quantity discounts for bulk purchases.
For information, call 1-800-289-0963.

Contents

Acknowledgments

Our special thanks go to Barb Doyen, agent extraordinaire, whose faith in us never wavered and who made us feel like accomplished authors before we actually were. Barb, you were a gift to us! Thanks, also, to Gina Chaimanis, Katie McDonough, Suzanne Goraj, and the other professionals at Adams who handled us with such kindness through our early mistakes. We also owe a big debt of gratitude to experts in the field who guided us through some of the technical parts of the book. Among these are Jeff Crilley; Mike Clarke; Ron Brown; Chad Yoas; Alan Thiele, Esq. and Alan Beckley. A very special thanks is reserved for our good friend, Robert Wise, Esq., without whom our chapter on patents could not have been written. Bob, your years with the USPTO as a patent examiner and in private practice as a patent attorney have enriched our knowledge and our book. We are grateful.

We'd also like to thank those who were not a part of this book but without whose past efforts the book would probably never have come about. They include our parents, Ira and Blanche Russell, who encouraged inventiveness in us as far back as we both can remember, and our patent attorney, Guy V. Manning, Esq., whose patience with us is never-ending. You are much more than an attorney to us—you are our friend! Finally, special thanks go to those closest to us who believe there is nothing we cannot do. To Charles Pitts, husband, brother-in-law, and best friend: thank you.

Top Ten Most Common Mistakes Made by New Inventors

1. Inventors have a great idea and immediately want to rush to a manufacturer in hopes of getting paid for it. No thought is given to all the steps necessary to determine if the idea is theirs to pursue, how to make a working prototype, or even the steps that need to be taken in order to protect the idea.

2. Inventors fall in love with their idea and insist on going forward even when they receive good advice not to do so.

3. Inventors fail to do a thorough preliminary market search.

4. Inventors fail to do a preliminary patent search.

5. Because their idea solves a problem for them, inventors go forward even though the item has limited market potential.

6. Inventors skip the prototyping step because they *know* it will work.

7. Inventors divulge an idea to others without a nondisclosure agreement and inadvertently start the clock ticking on when, or even if, they can file for patent protection.

8. Inventors present an invention for licensing without adequate preparation or an adequate product presentation.

9. Inventors attempt to invent something with which they have no expertise.

10. Inventors send letters to themselves as a way of protecting their ideas.

Introduction

▶ Everything worth having has already been invented, right? Well, not necessarily. Julius Sextus Frontinus, a highly regarded engineer in first century A.D. Rome, said, "Inventions have long since reached their limit, and I see no hope for further development." In 1899, Charles H. Duell, Commissioner, U.S. Patent Office, said, "Everything that can be invented has been invented." If everyone thought as they did, we would be living in a very different world. There would be no cars, radio, television, airplanes, or computers, to name just a few inventions that have drastically changed our lives since those glum predictions. Thankfully, their opinions were the minority view.

Though corporate invention accounts for a large portion of the patents issued each year by the U.S. Patent and Trademark Office, the patents issued to independent inventors wield a huge impact on our economy and our lives. The car, radio, television, airplane, and computer were all invented by independent inventors!

Inventions need not be highly technical or complicated to positively impact our lives. Sometimes the little things can make a big difference. You may have an idea that will solve an annoying problem faced by millions. For example, upside down ketchup or mustard bottles probably won't save any lives, but they do solve a minor aggravation encountered by millions. This is an example of a simple yet good invention.

Anyone can be an independent inventor. Independent inventors are young, old, male, female, all ethnicities, well educated, and uneducated. There is no requirement to be an independent inventor other than to have a creative way to solve a problem and the tenacity and drive to see it through.

Independent inventing is fun! Even though the independent in independent inventing suggests that you are going at it alone, in fact, you are not. Many independent inventors have blazed the trail before you and have learned the steps and shortcuts to maximize your chances of success. The fact that you have picked up this book indicates that you have the desire and commitment to give your great idea its best shot at making it to the marketplace.

Independent inventing can be very lucrative! If you succeed in getting your product licensed, your work is over. At that point, you simply collect the royalty payments while your licensee manufactures, distributes, and sells your invention. Others work for you while you pursue other activities and interests. If you choose to make a business out of your invention, you have not only created a continuing stream of income for yourself but you have contributed to the economy by creating jobs for others. In America, we are fortunate to have a system that encourages our creativity and rewards our efforts.

Independent inventing is not easy. If it were easy, everyone would be doing it. It takes work, determination, and the ability to ride the emotional roller coaster of the difficulties that are an inherent part of independent inventing. But if you truly do have a better mousetrap or foolproof corkscrew, the rewards can be huge. Make the commitment to follow your dream!

Chapter 1

Me—an Inventor?

Well, why not? Everyone has an inherent desire to solve problems; it's part of human nature. As young children, people begin to devise solutions to the problems they encounter in daily life. The question is, what separates dreamers from achievers? Are achievers just lucky? That famous philosopher, Anonymous, has said that luck is what happens when preparation meets opportunity. This first chapter will introduce you to the world of inventing and give you an idea of whether or not there's a place in that world for you.

What Is an Inventor?

We are all familiar with the names of such people as Thomas Edison, Eli Whitney, and Benjamin Franklin. These, of course, are famous inventors. There are millions of successful inventors whose names are not as well known. Are inventors geniuses? Some are, to be sure. But the great majority of inventors are just ordinary people who thought of a wonderful new product and had the tenacity to see it through to completion. As Thomas Edison said, "Genius is 1 percent inspiration and 99 percent perspiration."

Famous or not, all inventors follow the same steps to get their products to market. While times change and the requirements for getting new products to the consumers vary, there are some basic principles about inventing that determine the success or failure of a project. Here are some secrets that you will need to internalize if you are to be a successful inventor. An inventor needs:

- **Follow-through:** You must develop and sell *products*; you cannot sell mere *ideas*. If you want to make money from your ideas, you will need to develop each idea into a complete invention that you fully understand. You must also take the steps to legally protect each idea.
- **Research:** You must do your homework to be certain the invention can belong to you. A patentability search, including searching the marketplace for existing products and patent searching, is not optional.
- **Knowledge:** A marketability study (also called a marketability evaluation) is also advisable. A large segment of the population must need your invention. If you create something that solves a problem for you, that is a good start. But is it a problem shared by millions of others?
- **Availability:** You must prepare yourself for a long process. Each part of the process will undoubtedly take longer than you expect.

Follow-Through

It is a common misconception among would-be inventors that as soon as they have a great idea they can rush to a manufacturer and sell the idea for millions of dollars. Though it is tempting to get your great idea right into the hands of a manufacturer who you think might pay you for it, manufacturers today are far more deliberate than that and they must go through a set of procedures before making a decision to take on any new product, no matter how good that product appears to be. In fact, taking an unprotected idea for a new product to a manufacturer gives you no way to keep that manufacturer from using the idea without compensating you for it. There is no shortage of ideas; everyone has them. Furthermore, companies are not interested in buying an idea for just any new product. They want developed, legally protected products.

Research

You will need to do some thorough research to determine whether the idea really belongs to you before rushing to market with a new product. A successful inventor knows that just because he has not seen his envisioned product for sale anywhere, the idea may nevertheless already be patented or be on the market in one venue or another. For example, even if you do not find the product in retail or mass merchandise stores, it may be available in catalogs or on the Internet.

FACT

Inventions that have never been patented or on which the patents have expired are said to be in the "public domain." You are free to make and sell your own version of products that are in the public domain, but you will not be able to patent what is already in the public domain.

You will need to search all product sources thoroughly and conduct a patent search before reaching the conclusion that your product idea is truly new and therefore patentable. Literally millions of patents are issued on inventions that never found their way into the marketplace. Also, be warned: No search is perfect; there are always more places to search. A patentability search typically involves searching the U.S. patent databases, and some international patent databases, which include both issued patents and pending published patent applications. A patentability search typically costs no more than $1,000. However, when a large company is sued for patent infringement, it can spend $20,000 or more in an attempt to invalidate the patent that is the basis for the lawsuit.

Knowledge

If your invention solves a problem for you, that's great! Do many people share that same problem? Maybe you have developed a new type of pedal for your unicycle. It works much better than the old type of unicycle pedal and you use it every day. The question successful inventors would ask themselves at this point is, "Are there hundreds of thousands or perhaps millions of unicyclists out there who will feel that they need this product enough to go out and buy it?" Unicycle riding, while it has its devotees, does not appear to be so popular that a product especially for a unicycle could have a huge market. The obvious point here is that in order to be the inventor of a successful product, you will need to do the homework to determine the size of the market for your invention before investing a lot of time and money in it. While it may be worthwhile for you to develop and market that unicycle product, expect the financial returns to be commensurate with the size of the market for the product.

Availability

Being a professional inventor is not a fast-paced job. That is probably the most common misconception about inventing. Even the simplest invention ideas require careful development to ensure that all possible improvements are included. You will need to take the time to work all of the bugs out of your prototype (though a prototype is not needed to apply for a patent). The protection process is slow. According to the U.S. Patent and Trademark Office (USPTO), some patents take three to five years from filing to issuance. Moreover, the marketing of a new product can be the slowest part of all.

Successful inventors know that they cannot take literally the famous quotation by Ralph Waldo Emerson about building a better mousetrap. No matter how good your invention is, the world is not likely to beat a path to your door. Launching a new product can take two to three years or even longer. Overnight success is extremely rare. It is tempting to focus so determinedly on future financial success that you begin spending your money before you have earned it. Even though you have made some sales of your product—or maybe have genuine interest from a manufacturer for licensing it—the likelihood of making large amounts of money in the short run is extremely slim. A successful inventor knows that he must keep his day job until the financial rewards are realized.

QUESTION?

What is the USPTO?

The USPTO is actually two offices, the patent office and the trademark office. All patents and federally registered trademarks in the United States are granted by these offices following a stringent review process and payment of appropriate fees. The USPTO maintains a database of all the patents and trademarks ever issued.

It Starts with a Great Idea

Look around you. Everything you see began as someone's idea. Someone decided that an item of that type was needed and then proceeded to bring it into being. Throughout history, people have had great ideas and they have developed those ideas into the reality that is our world today. So, how do great ideas happen?

Most inventions come about because of an irritation or an annoyance. Sometimes during our routine tasks, we think that something is cumbersome or difficult to do the way that we have been doing it. We find ourselves thinking, "There must be a better way." We begin thinking of better ways to get the job done. Voilà! A great idea is born!

In most cases inventions are improvements to existing products, not a completely new category of product that has never before been seen or thought of. Often, the terms *invention* and *innovation* are used interchangeably. An innovation is an improvement to an existing product.

Problem-Solving as a Profession

Not all inventions are the result of an individual working to solve a problem for herself. Some people deliberately set out to professionally create new and better products for all of us. These professionals, called product developers, have learned the process of thinking creatively so that they are able to repeat their successes. Creative thinking comes naturally to all of us to a degree, but it is an ability that you can nurture and develop into a skill that you can use to make your life easier and to increase your income.

A new use for an existing product or process can also be a patentable invention. Such a new use can create a new market for an item that is already available. Think not only of ways to improve the products you are using, but also of new ways to use the products that everyone is already familiar with. When you make an improvement to an existing product or process, or when you find new and useful ways to use common items, you have a potentially marketable, and possibly patentable, innovation.

Think Like an Inventor!

If you do not already have that great idea but you want to be an inventor, here is the good news: There are ways to train yourself to think like an inventor. When you do, you will find yourself with more great ideas than you can handle. Try this simple exercise: Think of everything you do from the moment you arise in the morning. Then think of what you do that you might do more easily, more inexpensively, more quickly, more simply, more enjoyably, more effectively, or more efficiently than the way you are now doing it. Give yourself the task of thinking of a better way. Now you are thinking like an inventor!

There are places where you can learn inventing and entrepreneurship. A number of universities now offer courses of study in entrepreneurship and product development. Others have inventors' assistance programs. For example, the Academy of Applied Science in Concord, New Hampshire, is a private nonprofit organization that works with teachers to help them encourage inventiveness in children.

Assess Your Ideas

Once you have a great idea for a new product, a new use for an old product, or an improvement to an existing product, do not stop there. Spend some time really thinking about how you would go about accomplishing it. While it is not necessary to know every aspect of how an invention might be developed, it is important to have at least some basic knowledge of the workings or the materials involved. For example, most of us, at one time or another, think of something that we wish existed though we could never create such a thing ourselves. You may think that it would be great to have automobiles that hover over the roadway, avoiding the need for tires. Those kinds of ideas, fun though they may be to dream about, are outside the ability of most of us, as independent inventors, to turn into reality. So, when it is time to decide on the idea that you will pursue, make it something with which you can have a hands-on involvement to fully develop into a product. You can enlist the help of someone who is experienced in building prototypes, but you will need to choose that person carefully and be sure to get a signed *contractor's nondisclosure agreement* before engaging him to work on your invention. This agreement should also include language that assigns any and all intellectual property to you, including patentable ideas, that is created by the contractor during the development of your idea. (See Chapter 3 to learn more about nondisclosure agreements.)

FACT

Alexander Graham Bell managed to beat Elisha Gray to the patent office with his application for a patent on the technology for the telephone by mere hours! Thus began a legal battle over the invention of the telephone, which was eventually won by Bell, who got the credit for the invention.

Go Forward with Good Ideas

Most great ideas occur to more than one person. Often, they seem to occur to many people at around the same time. Alexander Graham Bell, the inventor of the telephone, Thomas A. Edison, inventor of the incandescent light bulb, and the Wright Brothers, inventors of the airplane, received the recognition and credit for their inventions. We might have been recalling entirely different names associated with these inventions had those men not carefully documented their work and promptly filed for their patent protection.

Make Money while You Sleep

Sounds wonderful, doesn't it? It is not a dream. You really can make money while you sleep. Thousands of people are doing it and you can, too. You can learn to program your subconscious to come up with those great ideas during sleep that will translate into money in your bank account. In addition, if you choose to license your invention for a royalty, others will be making money for you while you sleep, lie on the beach, or spend your time dreaming up other moneymaking ideas.

Being a dreamer, whether in sleeping dreams or in daydreams, can pay off handsomely. Paul McCartney, who wrote the beautiful ballad "Yesterday," says that the melody for that song came to him in a dream, together with the lyrics "Scrambled eggs, Oh, my darling you've got lovely legs." Keith Richards, of the Rolling Stones rock band, said that the lyric "Can't get no satisfaction," along with the accompanying guitar riff, came to him as he was waking up in a Clearwater, Florida, hotel room during one of their tours. These gifts appear to have come randomly to these men without any mental preparation. While some solutions do seem to come at random while sleeping, there are ways to program your brain to work on problem solutions during your dream cycles.

Several famous inventors have said that they received the solutions to difficult problems while they were sleeping. Dimitri Mendeleev, a thirty-five-year-old Russian chemist, actually dreamed the periodic table of elements, something he had been puzzling over for several days. And Friedrich August Kekulé had a waking dream while riding on a London bus that led him to deduce the ring structure of benzene.

In both of these cases, the solutions did not come out of the blue. Mendeleev had been puzzling over the elements for days because he knew that there was a mathematical pattern in their occurrence but he could not figure out what it was. He unknowingly programmed his subconscious mind to sort out that pattern. Kekulé had the same kind of experience except that his solution came during a bus ride when he was lulled into a type of hypnotic state and actually dreamed of snakes swallowing their own tails. This vision triggered the realization that carbon atoms can combine to form chains and he concluded that the molecules of benzene formed a ring structure.

Here is another mental exercise to help you use your sleep periods for more than just resting. When you are wrestling with a problem and cannot seem to come up with the right answer, give it to yourself as an assignment just before you fall asleep. Go over the problem in your mind and suggest to yourself that you will come up with the solution. Then put it out of your mind and think of something else. Do not be concerned if you wake up the next morning without the answer. Be assured that your subconscious mind is working on the problem and the answer could occur to you at any time.

The other way to make money while you sleep is to license your invention to a manufacturer who will take all of the responsibility for making and selling your invention. If your product is carried by the twenty-four-hour mass-merchandise stores, people will be buying it at all hours of the day and night. You will literally be making money while you sleep! And, while your licensee is doing all of the work and sending regular royalty payments to you, enjoy those dreams (and daydreams) that could bring you even more enrichment.

Remember to keep a pen and paper handy right beside your bed in case you awaken in the night with the solution to a problem. Your subconscious mind is working while you are sleeping. But if you allow yourself to fall back asleep without writing it down or recording it, you risk forgetting something important.

A Typical Day

There is no such thing as a typical day in the life of a career inventor. Independent inventors are not held to the same stringent rules as are those who work in the corporate world. There is no start time or stop time for the workday. Even though there are no required work hours, many independent inventors find that when they are working on an invention they work longer hours than ever before because their work is no longer work but fun! Each day is different—a blank page on which the independent inventor creates his day as he desires.

There is no commute to the independent inventor's office; his office is his home in most instances. There is no boss to tell her what to do and when to do it. There are no coworkers with whom to compete. There is no dress code. He can work in his pajamas, if he so desires! The independent inventor is her own boss, setting her own schedule and deadlines.

Do not take this to mean that the independent inventor is undisciplined. On the contrary, he may sometimes work in a maniacal manner as he rushes toward the development of his great idea because he is indeed possessed by the need to bring his latest idea into form.

Depending upon the point where the independent inventor is in the inventing process, different activities will be a part of the workday. During the initial steps of inventing, he might spend a portion or all of the day brainstorming. Brainstorming is freeform thinking to which normal restrictions do not apply. It's fun, funny, and sometimes downright silly. The best ideas occur to you when you allow yourself this freedom. If you are lucky enough to have one or more partners, the benefits of brainstorming expand exponentially.

FACT

The ideal size of a brainstorming group is two to five people. During brainstorming the creative juices flow. The inventor spends time dreaming up new products or ways to improve existing products. This is a job in which daydreaming is not only allowed, it is encouraged!

The independent inventor also spends time researching the products of the brainstorming sessions. The research may consist of performing preliminary market studies and patentability searches to be certain that he is not trying to reinvent something that has no demand or has already been invented. It may also involve trips to the local Patent and Trademark Depository Library (PTDL), trips to stores, or use of the Internet to search catalogs, stores, and the USPTO's online database.

Further along in the process, the independent inventor may spend her day experimenting with prototypes, filing for patent and trademark protection, preparing presentations to potential licensees, and scheduling meetings with manufacturers. Telephone calls, e-mail correspondence, and networking with sources of support and help such as prototype designers, patent attorneys or agents, and contract attorneys make up a large portion of the independent inventor's work in his quest to move his product to market.

Love What You Do

There are many things to love about being an independent inventor. It is easy to love a career in which every day is different, interesting, and challenging. It is easy to love a career that offers complete independence from workaday routine. It is easy to love a career in which your creativity is not only encouraged, it's a requirement. It is really easy to love a career that does not require 100 percent of your time, allowing you the time and flexibility to pursue other interests. And it is most easy to love a career in which, once the work is finished, a project continues to generate income in the form of mailbox money. Mailbox money is income that comes to you at regularly scheduled intervals without further effort on your part. These are just some of the things that are easy to love about being an independent inventor.

Set aside a specific time on a regular basis to work on your invention. Put it on your calendar and consider it an important appointment with yourself. Your unwavering dedication to this time commitment will help you to keep daily distractions from intervening while you progress toward your goal.

Not everyone can embrace some of the other things that you must love about being an independent inventor in order to succeed. For example, you must have a passion for it. If you do not, you will never succeed. You must have a burning desire to see your product on the store shelves. If you do not, it is unlikely that you will have the tenacity to stick with it through the difficulties that will come. There are always things that do not work as you thought they would. Product development is not a straight, smooth road. It is full of surprises and disappointments. You must be able to weather these times and continue to move forward toward your goal. Your invention idea must nag at you so that you cannot fail to pursue it. Finally, you must commit yourself totally and completely to setting goals for making progress with your invention and holding yourself accountable for achieving those goals.

It is easy to have a great idea only to allow your everyday life to consume all of your time and energy and let your invention languish on the sidelines of your life. In order to be a professional inventor, you must make the commitment of time, energy, and resources to give your invention idea the opportunity to succeed.

Inventing as a Profession

Are there professional independent inventors? You bet there are! Professional inventing is a job that allows complete flexibility. You can do it on a full-time or a part-time basis, depending upon the other financial and time requirements present in your life. It naturally follows that the more time and effort you devote to it, the more likely you will be to achieve success in the shortest amount of time.

Many independent inventors have no other job. Inventing, also known as product developing, is their job. They develop one product after another for specific companies with whom they have formed a relationship, or they develop products for a variety of companies. Most independent inventors specialize in developing products for specific industries with which they are most familiar. For example, some product developers develop products for the home maintenance category, or the school and office supply category. The list of categories of inventions is truly endless.

Specializing in a category of inventions can make the process move more smoothly and quickly. Once you have developed trust-based relationships with a group of manufacturers within a specific category of products, it becomes much easier to present and license products to them, and most independent product developers prefer to work this way. Once you have shown manufacturers how creative you can be and how responsive to their product lines you are, it is common for them to give you their wish lists for the type of products they are seeking for the coming season.

Professional inventors have an assortment of products in various stages of development at any point in time. While they are stuck in a holding pattern on one invention, they are moving forward and making progress on another. You will find that, as you get into the mode of creating new products, ideas seem to spawn other ideas, keeping the process going. Overall, being a professional inventor is an interesting, challenging, and fun way to make a living. It is a job that is never dull because each day is different from the day before and each day will be different from the days to come.

Chapter 2

Do You Have What It Takes?

What does it take to be an inventor? Lots of people have good ideas, but not everyone has the potential to be a good inventor. Those who successfully make that leap from idea to invention must know something that the rest of us don't, right? Well, sort of. But inventing is something that, once you know the secrets, you can definitely accomplish if you are willing to put forth the effort. This chapter will give you the inside scoop on what it takes to enter the world of inventing.

Mental Preparation

Turning an idea into an invention is similar to other endeavors in which you will go from idea to finished product, whether it is writing a report, assembling an item from a kit, or cooking dinner. With each of these jobs, you will first need to visualize your goal, the steps you will follow to reach that goal, and the materials and/or education you will need to accomplish it. If you are cooking dinner, for example, you will first need to have a clear idea of just what the dinner will consist of and gather the ingredients. You may also need a cookbook in order to follow the recipe.

The above example is intended to show that inventing, complicated though it may seem, is really just another cognitive adventure in which you will follow a pattern of mental steps in order to achieve the desired results. This seems to be the downfall of many inventors who fail; they have the idea but the thinking stops right there! Successful inventors continue with the thought process to actually develop the idea, and then they proceed through the steps until they see their products actually on the market.

FACT

The successful inventor sees inventing as a set of logical steps she will follow with each new idea. Inventions can be vastly different, but the basic steps for developing, protecting, and marketing are the same whether the invention is simple or complex. Learning these steps can help to ensure success.

The next time you have a good idea, consider it an assignment that you have been given and begin your mental preparation for developing that new product. Think about where you will begin your research to make certain that the idea is yours to pursue. Think about the materials that might be used to create it and whether it is something that is within your capability to develop. Even if it turns out that you cannot continue with your first idea, consider the experience mental exercise for when that perfect idea occurs.

Think Outside the Box

Inventors learn to approach problems from every possible angle. They are likely to take a problem and mentally turn it over and inside out to figure out how best to solve it. While both the successful and the unsuccessful inventor are annoyed by the problem, and while both might think, "There ought to be a better way," the unsuccessful inventor is likely to work on another way that is so similar to the current one that he cannot come up with anything really innovative. The clever inventor thinks of several other ways in which he might achieve the same result and some of his ideas may be vastly different from the way that the task is presently accomplished. He considers what might be the easiest, fastest, or least expensive way to reach that result. It is in thinking outside the box that some of the best innovations have come about.

If you do not already think that way, is it possible to learn to think outside the box? Of course! How does one do it? It just takes practice and a conscious effort to allow your mind to roam free when seeking solutions. Most of us are afraid of appearing ridiculous if we come up with off-the-wall solutions to problems, but that is exactly the type of thinking that has brought about the development of some of our most innovative products.

When brainstorming for a solution, allow your mind to go wild with possibilities. Do not use your critical left brain at all—do not evaluate the ideas or think of practical considerations in the early phase of brainstorming. Just allow your right brain to roam free. This is necessary in order to create a mental environment that will open up your creativity. Evaluate the ideas for usefulness and practicality only after the creative session is over.

Just imagine how different our lives might be today if some of our earlier inventors had not allowed themselves to approach problems from directions that must have seemed amazing for their time. One example of someone who thought outside the box and created wonderful innovations is George Washington Carver. This former slave, one of the most prolific inventors in

American history, developed hundreds of new products including adhesives, dyes, bleach, linoleum, talcum powder, and even a rubber substitute from peanuts, soybeans, sweet potatoes, pecans, and other items that were previously considered to be foodstuffs only. His contemporaries probably had a good laugh if he shared with them that he was attempting to create paint from soybeans!

A Light Bulb Moment

We have all had those moments when it almost feels as if a light bulb has switched on in our minds. A solution just suddenly appears, apparently unbidden, to something that has been a problem. Although it seems unbidden, remember that your subconscious has been working on it for a while. When you mull over a problem and then go on about your routine without consciously thinking about it further, your subconscious picks up where you left off.

An idea does not have to be a technological marvel in order to be a great, moneymaking invention. Some of the most useful and lucrative inventions have been so simple they could have been invented by children. In fact, some of them were!

FACT

The USPTO does not keep statistics on the sex or age of patent applicants, so it is impossible to determine how many children have applied for or been awarded patents, but there are many inventions that are known to have been invented by minors—such as the technology for television!

Chelsea Lanmon, a Texas child, received a design patent on a disposable diaper with pockets for holding baby wipes and a powder puff that she invented when she was five years old! The kindergartner was helping her mother care for her baby brother when she thought of the innovation in diapers. Chelsea's light bulb moment must have come when her brother needed a diaper change and the accessories for that task were not handy. Chelsea and her mother, Ginger, reasoned that if a diaper of that sort would be helpful to them, it would also be helpful to millions of others who had infants in their homes. Mrs. Lanmon collaborated with Chelsea to obtain patent protection on her great idea and Chelsea found herself listed in the USPTO database as a patent holder at the ripe old age of eight.

Here's another example. The Popsicle was invented in 1905 by eleven-year-old Frank Epperson, of San Francisco, California, who accidentally left outside some powdered soda pop and water that he had mixed up. The next day he discovered it frozen solid with the stirring stick standing straight up from it. This was Frank's light bulb moment! Frank could have looked at that frozen concoction, said, "Oh, well," and thrown the whole thing away. But in his little accident he saw a new product. One hundred years later, Popsicles are still a popular snack.

Inventions often happen in just this way. The inventor who sees the possibilities in these accidents finds a place in history for his discovery. If you can look at your everyday experiences through the eyes of an inventor and consider the possibilities in the things that do not turn out as you expect them to, you will see that you can create light bulb moments. We often hear people speak of turning lemons into lemonade. That lemonade can be the result of your light bulb moment.

Are You a Dreamer or a Doer?

If you are thinking that you have to choose between being a dreamer and being a doer, know that to be a successful inventor, you must be both! We all dream up good ideas at times. Those who are only dreamers go no further than the dream stage. Doers take that dream and work at making it into reality. This does not mean that every new product dream that is pursued ends up in the marketplace. Actually, very few of them do. Doers also know that if one dream is not something they can bring into reality, they should simply move on to their next dream. Doers realize that dreams and great ideas are not in short supply. Most successful inventors have chased a dream until they found that it was already patented or even on store shelves. This has happened to just about all of us at least once, and to some of us many times.

Finding that someone has beaten you to your idea is not cause for giving up. When you see something on a store shelf that you thought was your invention idea, it should make you realize what good ideas you have. Your good idea made it all the way to market! This should serve only to reinforce the determination in you that when your next good idea comes (and it will come), it will reach store shelves because of *your* efforts.

Realize that you do not have to commit to the entire invention process in the beginning of your mission with a new idea. Commit to one step at a time during the early stages and build on your good results. Each step successfully accomplished reinforces your motivation to continue.

The difference between dreamers and doers is that dreamers are content to just dream while doers dream and then do it. There must be reasons why dreamers do not continue on to become doers with their ideas, but what are they? Are their ideas bad? Is it because the very thought of attempting a process that they do not understand intimidates them? The truth is that it's probably different for everyone. But the only way to make success a possibility is to try for it. Do your best to suspend your doubts and assume that you can learn to do something that is entirely new to you. Whether you realize it or not, you've done this many times before. When you learned to walk, speak, and read, you were traversing brand-new territory.

Doing something that you have not done before and do not know exactly how to do can seem scary, but if you never step out of your comfort zone, you will never achieve anything of value. A comfort zone is not just comfortable—it's boring. Doers experience the excitement of reaching for a place in history, or at the very least for the satisfaction of creating something that makes life better for themselves and others.

Go for It!

Fear of failure is one of the greatest hindrances to creativity known to man. All of the great inventors in history, the ones whose stories are recorded, have experienced failure. They regarded failure not as an ending, but as a steppingstone to the success they later achieved. Failure is a learning experience that inventors go through as they proceed along the path of product development. This is not to say that you are doomed to fail with your first invention. Many inventors make home runs on their first attempt. But if you could visit with those who were successful on their first attempts, they would tell you that they had setbacks and difficulties on their way to success.

FACT

The claims portion of a patent, which is a series of one-sentence paragraphs at the end of a patent, is the portion of the patent that describes what the patent holder owns. It determines what constitutes infringement. Accordingly, in patent litigation, the claims are the primary focus of attention.

The course from idea to marketplace is never smooth. Obstacles that you may find yourself challenged with along the way may come in the areas of market research results, patentability search results, prototype failures, or patent application claim rejections. While any of these *can* ultimately shoot down that particular invention idea, don't be in a hurry to give up. Many times these seeming failures are only temporary setbacks.

Failures that you overcome along the way will reinforce the knowledge that difficulties are a part of the experience. There are ways around most of those difficulties. This, again, is part of being a creative thinker.

For instance, in your research you are likely to find other inventions on the market or in the patent database that serve the same purpose as your invention. Some of them may even appear to *be* your invention! Before you panic and give up, look carefully at the other product to see if your idea is superior in some way. Sometimes, making sure that your invention is superior in the way it is made or in ease of use can get around what seems like an insurmountable problem that would prevent you from getting your patent. Also, the other inventions may appear to render your invention legally unpatentable. However, patentability is a legal judgment, based on factors that a layperson isn't qualified to analyze. Be sure to consult with a patent attorney before jumping to any negative conclusions based on other patents or products found on the market.

ALERT!

The USPTO approves only a small percentage of patent applications on the first office action. This means that the majority of applications have claims rejected at first. It is critical for new inventors to understand that patent claim rejection is usually not the end of the road for their inventions. A good patent attorney is skilled in negotiating with the patent examiner, and can often overcome the claim rejections, resulting in an issued patent.

One area where new inventors often become frustrated and are tempted to give up the effort is in the prototyping stage. It is almost guaranteed that your invention will not end up being exactly what you envisioned when you first had the idea. During prototyping, it is common to find that your first idea will not work or that it will be far better if you make certain changes. If you give up on your first attempt, you will never know what you might have achieved!

The third area where a new inventor is often tempted to throw in the towel is during the prosecution of his patent application. It is important for you to know that it is a rare patent application that is approved on the first office action from the USPTO. When your patent application comes back from the USPTO and the examiner has rejected most or all of your claims, it is a frightening situation for you if you are unfamiliar with the way the patent office works. Many inventors feel that it is all over at this point. In most cases, it is simply a matter of having your patent attorney or agent rewrite the claims to make them acceptable without diluting the strength of those claims.

ESSENTIAL

Doers take their dreams and, after determining that they have a good chance to succeed, chart a course toward that success. Remember: If you never start, you can be sure that you won't finish. Giving it a try only increases your chances of getting there. Be a dreamer *and* a doer!

That said, if you are considering taking on the challenging role of a would-be inventor, one of your first tasks is to familiarize yourself with the steps you'll be following. Inventors complete these steps in various orders, and sometimes they even leave out a step or add a new one. Each step will be described in greater detail later in the book, but the following is a basic description of each in a suggested order:

1. Think of an idea.
2. Conduct a preliminary market search. The inventor does this at stores and on the Internet.
3. Conduct a preliminary patent search. The inventor does this on the Internet or at a patent library.
4. Build a prototype. If the invention idea is simple and inexpensive enough, the inventor can create this on his own at this point. Otherwise, prototyping can be delayed until a later time.
5. Obtain a professional patentability search.
6. Get a marketability evaluation. This is a professional evaluation that includes a preliminary patentability search unless the inventor has already had a professional search performed and provides her results to the evaluators.
7. Have a formal prototype made.
8. File a patent application.

Reality Check

Though you absolutely want to be a person who does something with her dreams, you also want to be at least pretty sure that the dreams you choose to pursue are worth pursuing. There is that Eureka! moment of excitement when that idea first occurs. During the euphoria of the moment, it is difficult to imagine that the whole world will not fall in love with your invention idea, just as you have. Without dampening your enthusiasm too much, you will need to come back down to earth and look at it as objectively as you can in order to determine if it really will be worth your time, effort, and money.

You came up with this great idea because it solves a problem for you. Now is the time to look objectively at the problem and to look at how others are dealing with that problem. If you have come up with a solution to a widespread problem for which there was previously no solution, you may indeed have a great idea. If you have a solution to a problem for which there were solutions but your idea is superior in some respect, you still may have a great idea.

Your reality check will include being brutally honest with yourself in several areas before you can conclude that this is the big one that deserves the expense and effort needed to bring it to market. Judge your idea against the seven criteria below to measure its chances for success in the marketplace. You can succeed with a very good product even if your invention does not fit all seven of these standards for marketable products, but the more check marks you can place by these statements, the greater are your chances for success.

- ✔ The chances of obtaining a good, strong patent are excellent.
- ✔ There is a huge market for it. Millions and millions of people will want to buy it.
- ✔ The benefit of your product is obvious.
- ✔ It will be inexpensive to produce.
- ✔ The spread between manufacturing cost and selling price is great.
- ✔ The item gets used up and consumers will purchase it repeatedly.
- ✔ The manufacturer already has distribution channels in place.

If you plan to license your invention, a good, strong patent is highly advisable. Since you plan to create a business around your invention, you will want a good patent to discourage competition.

Your product will need to be something that large numbers of people will have a strong desire to own. In order for a product to sustain itself in the marketplace, sales must be frequent enough and in a large enough quantity to cover all of the normal costs of manufacturing, advertising (if necessary), sales, shipping, insurance, and miscellaneous costs and still leave a healthy profit.

It is a real plus if the benefit of your invention is obvious enough that it will not require a great deal of consumer education for the buying public to understand. If consumers can look at your product and immediately realize what it is and why it is needed, it has a far better chance of being successful quickly. Products that must be explained and advertised are very costly to successfully place on the market.

In order to cover manufacturing costs and allow for a profit at each level along the way, a product must retail for at least four to five times the manufacturing cost. In other words, if the manufacturer can make the product for $1, the product should sell at retail for $4 to $5 at a minimum. It is important to look objectively at your product to assess how much the buying public would be willing to pay for it. New inventors often have a tendency to overrate the retail value of their inventions, but manufacturers are very much in touch with what the public will pay for the products they make. If your product can be made so inexpensively that the spread is even greater than four to five times the manufacturing cost, this will make it much more attractive to a potential licensee.

If you are going to license your product to a manufacturer of similar products, there is a distinct possibility that the manufacturer will already have the equipment in place to add your product to his line. It may require very little time or expense for him to tool up to add your product. Manufacturers are always on the lookout for wonderful new products that are so similar to their current line that they will fit right into their current manufacturing capabilities with little or no additional expense.

If your invention is something that will get used up and the consumer will be returning to the store to buy it repeatedly, that is a real benefit for you and for the manufacturer. Sometimes a very inexpensive product that must be purchased again and again will make more money for the inventor than an expensive item that a consumer will need to buy only once. Think of all of the disposable items that we buy constantly, such as facial tissues and writing paper, and you will see how this works to the advantage of the lucky developer of such products.

Products that you plan to license for a royalty will be easier to place with a manufacturer if you are careful in the selection of the manufacturers whom you approach. Manufacturers that already have similar items in large retail chains will already have the distribution channels (shelf space in retail stores) available and waiting for that new product.

The last part of your reality check involves your commitment to what could be a long process. The new inventor often believes that he can take his wonderful idea straight to the manufacturer who would make it or to the retailer who would sell it and then see his product on store shelves within a matter of weeks or months. Wouldn't it be wonderful if it did work that way? By now, you know that it does not.

FACT

Shelf space in retail stores is plotted out on a planogram and allotted to manufacturers. Competition among manufacturers is strong for retail shelf space. When a manufacturer places a new product on the shelf, he must displace a product that was in that space. New products must be better sellers than the previous ones to merit shelf space.

If you have determined that your invention has an excellent chance of being a viable product, your only decision at this point is whether you are willing to go the distance to make it happen. While you will be going through steps that will seem to be plodding at times, your enthusiasm for what you are creating should carry you over the rough times. You will need to be prepared for setbacks and disappointments during the development, legal protection, and marketing of your idea. The key to getting through these situations is to keep your goal in mind at all times. If your family or friends are not supportive, you must accept that and continue toward your goal. If your idea is important enough to you to find the time and money to make it a reality, you could be among the group of people who can call themselves successful inventors.

Chapter 3

Protecting Your Idea

If you think inventors never have to be clock-watchers, think again! Some aspects of inventing are extremely time sensitive. Failure to follow the rules could result in your losing all rights to your great invention. So, as soon as you have your great idea, start protecting it by documenting its history in an inventor's journal. Nondisclosure agreements and the USPTO's Disclosure Document Program are also great tools at your disposal. While the USPTO's Disclosure Document Program is very helpful to independent inventors, it is certainly not a requirement.

First to Invent Rule

The United States and Canada are unique in the world because they are First to Invent countries. The First to Invent rule holds that if the independent inventor can prove that he was the first person to have the idea and develop it into an invention, he is the only person who has the right to file for patent protection on that item.

QUESTION?

Who enforces the First to Invent rule?
The inventor enforces it by presenting his case and documentation to the USPTO, proving that he was the first to work on an invention. If he is successful the USPTO will reverse its ruling and award the patent to him.

The rest of the world operates on the First to File system. The differences between these two approaches to determining the ownership of an invention are enormous. In First to File countries, it is a race to the patent office. Whoever files for the patent first is considered to be the inventor of the product whether or not she was the first to come up with the idea. The First to File system creates an atmosphere where stealing ideas from others is rewarded, if not outright encouraged. Our First to Invent system does not prevent those determined to try to take someone's idea from her, but it does discourage it.

Our First to Invent system is very fair and independent inventor–friendly. It means that if little independent inventor Joe Blow comes up with an invention and can prove the date that he started working on it and he has proof of his continuing work on it, he would be awarded the patent even if some gigantic corporation filed for a patent stating a later conception date. This evens out the playing field between independent inventors and companies with more personnel and resources for product development.

First to Invent does not mean first to have the idea. It is a good deal more than that. An individual could have a great idea and do nothing with it. That person has no right to claim that idea as her invention because she did nothing further. In order for her to be considered by the USPTO to be the rightful inventor, she must follow up the idea with action. She must work on reducing the invention to practice. That means making a working prototype, or diligently pursuing the preparation and filing of a patent application, without creating an actual prototype. It means working consistently on the development of the product and documenting her progress.

ALERT!

It is often tempting to omit building a prototype when you are sure that your idea will work. This can be a costly mistake because you will inevitably make improvements on your first concept that will make your patent stronger. However, a prototype is *not* needed to file a patent application.

How often have you seen one of your good ideas in the marketplace and thought to yourself, "I thought of that!" It has happened to all of us. It is a fact that in most cases, the same great idea has occurred to more than one person at around the same time. It is common for several people to be working on the development and protection of the same idea at the same time. This means that when you have one of those light bulb moments, it is vital that you work as quickly and efficiently as possible in order to be the one who reaps the benefits. Do not rush to the point that you become careless in the handling of the details of researching, documenting, protecting, and prototyping your idea, but allowing time to pass without moving forward could mean that you will see your product brought to store shelves by some other inventor. In the world of new product development, timing is indeed everything.

Product developers have a plan in place for each good idea and they are prepared to move immediately when their light bulb moment occurs. They know the steps they need to take and they are ready to spring into action when a great idea comes along. Once you have gone through the steps with your first invention, the steps will become automatic to you. These basic steps are listed below and will be elaborated on later in the book:

1. Marketability study
2. Preliminary online patentability search
3. Prototype
4. Professional patentability search
5. Disclosure document

While some of the steps outlined above will be time-consuming, they are too important to your invention for you to be anything less than meticulous in each area. You will not be involved in the professional patentability search, but most product developers handle the other steps themselves. The marketability study should cost you little or nothing. The preliminary online patent search is also fairly inexpensive or even free.

Depending on your invention, the prototyping can be very inexpensive. It is not necessary to spend a lot of money on that first prototype if you can put something together from materials you find around the house or in local stores. At this point, the prototype is optional, but you may want to prove to yourself that your idea works as you envision it will.

ALERT!

Some companies, as a condition of employment, require employees to sign documents stating that anything the employee invents during his employment, whether related to his job or not, belongs to the company, not to the employee. Other companies are more specific, limiting the restriction to work-related inventions. Make sure you (or your attorney) read and understand your employment agreement to know how it affects you and your inventions.

One-Year Rule

The USPTO has a very strict One-Year Rule relating to the filing date for your patent application. It also relates to the circumstances under which you may disclose the idea without adversely affecting when or even if you can file for patent protection. That sounds scary, doesn't it? It is. It is no joking matter. If you tell someone about your invention or show it to them or offer it for sale without proper protection in place, you could be jeopardizing your rights to ever file for patent protection in the United States or internationally.

The One-Year Rule of the USPTO states that you have exactly one year from the first publication or first *public use, sale, or offer for sale* of your invention in the United States in which to file for patent protection or forfeit your rights to it forever. It is considered an offer for sale of your invention if you offered it for sale to a business by actually quoting a specific price.

What is a public use? Public uses occur in several ways. A public use may be a demonstration of the invention at a trade show. Or a public use may be the operation of your software invention at a local corporation. The one-year clock starts ticking on your invention the moment you make the first public use or publication of it.

Discussing your invention idea with just your spouse or immediate family is not considered a public disclosure. However, discussion of your idea with anyone, other than your immediate family, without the protection of a nondisclosure agreement could be considered to be a public disclosure of your invention, and thereby result in the loss of the trade secret status of your invention and the loss of your foreign patent rights.

In the course of developing your invention, it may be necessary to discuss your invention or even get help from others in developing the product. You can do that without jeopardizing your trade secret protection, or your foreign patent rights, by judiciously using nondisclosure agreements each time you divulge your invention. If you are getting assistance in the actual design of your invention or your prototype, you will need to use a special type of agreement called a contractor's nondisclosure agreement.

ESSENTIAL

It is not necessary to have intellectual property attorneys (patent attorneys) or patent agents sign nondisclosure agreements before you disclose your idea to them. The ethics of their profession require them to keep confidential any information you share with them. In other words, disclosing your invention to a patent attorney will not "start the clock" of the USPTO's one-year rule, as such a disclosure is not a public disclosure.

Create an Inventor's Journal

Because the United States is a First to Invent country, it is of vital importance to begin documenting your invention at the earliest possible date. The reasons for this have been detailed earlier in this chapter. Your inventor's journal is your first step in documenting exactly what your idea is and when you first conceived it. Here we will explain how to create your journal and how to keep it updated.

E⚡ ALERT!

Do not keep your inventor's journal as a computer file or typewritten document. In order for it to serve as legal proof of important dates and details, it is vital that your notes are kept in the proper way and in the proper type of laboratory notebook.

Your inventor's journal is a diary chronicling every detail of your invention from when and how the idea occurred to you to the materials you purchased for the prototype to the changes you made as you worked with it. Begin by writing your idea in detail in the book, including drawings. Date the top of the first page and date the beginning of each new entry. Fill in the pages completely, writing in ink from top to bottom and side to side, ignoring the margins. Do not white out or erase anything. Just cross out any mistakes. You must not leave any spaces that could be filled in later. This is why it is important to cover each entire page. Do not skip any pages and do not tear anything out. Write on both the front and the back of each page. These things are very important as this journal establishes when you first got the idea and exactly what your idea is.

After you have thoroughly described your invention in your journal, ask a friend who was not involved in the invention process, and who will have no financial interest in your invention, to sign a nondisclosure agreement that you will keep for your files. Then ask your friend to read, understand, and sign and date the book, including language to the effect of "Read and understood by" followed by your friend's printed name. Date each subsequent entry and continue to keep the journal of your progress with your invention. Staple receipts for materials, etc. to the pages. Periodically, ask a friend to read, sign, and date the journal. It does not have to be the same friend each time as long as you get a signed nondisclosure agreement from each person with whom you share the journal. Some inventors elect to have their journals notarized as further legal documentation, but it is not required. Notarizing a journal is *not* sufficient authentication, since notarization only authenticates a signature, and is *not* a statement that the material was read and understood as of a certain date by the Notary Public.

You may never need to use your journal for anything more than just to look back and reminisce about your adventures along the way. We hope you do not! But if you should ever need to prove when you got your idea and began working on it, your journal becomes a legal document that could make the difference between keeping your patent and losing it.

FACT

Books that can be used as inventor's journals are available at office supply stores, drugstores, and grocery stores. They are often called composition books. Be certain the pages are stitched in. Pages that are sewn into the book are very difficult to remove without leaving evidence of the removal. A binder filled with loose-leaf paper is unacceptable.

File a Disclosure Document

Your next step in documenting your invention is to file a Disclosure Document with the USPTO. This document is not a patent and the date of its receipt will not become the effective filing date for any subsequent patent that you may file. Those are the things a Disclosure Document is not. So why should you send anything to the patent office at all? The Disclosure Document, not to be confused with the nondisclosure agreement, is another important part of your documentation of when you conceived your idea and exactly what the idea is.

ALERT!

Begin protection measures for your invention as soon as you have the idea. Start by creating your inventor's journal. Be sure to use nondisclosure agreements when revealing your idea to others as well.

Years ago, the most common first step that independent inventors took to protect their ideas was something that became known as a poor man's patent. It was simply a matter of writing a description of the idea, sealing it in an envelope, and mailing it back to oneself. Many people are still doing this today with the mistaken notion that they are protecting and dating their ideas. The problem with using this method is that the United States court has ruled that it will not be accepted in a court of law as proof of ownership of an idea. It was stated that an individual could mail an unsealed envelope to himself, thereby getting a dated postmark, and then at a later date enclose the information. The

USPTO has a program in place that accomplishes the same thing that inventors are attempting to do with the poor man's patent. It is the Disclosure Document program, and it is a very simple part of your documentation to do.

Disclosure Documents are kept on file at the USPTO for two years. They are never looked at by examiners and only become important if the inventor finds it necessary to prove the invention's date of conception.

While the filing of the Disclosure Document is simple and inexpensive to do and is something you can do without assistance, you will need to carefully follow the directions as to how the USPTO requires it to be done. The patent office requires that you use a standard format for your Disclosure Document because of their data storage methods. The Disclosure Document (including drawings or sketches) must be on white letter-size (8.5 by 11 inch) or A4 (21.0 by 29.7 cm) paper, written on one side only, with each page numbered. Text and drawings must be sufficiently dark to permit reproduction with commonly used office copying machines. Oversized papers, even if foldable to the above dimensions, will not be accepted. Nor will the USPTO accept any type of attachments to the Disclosure Document, such as videotapes or prototypes of any kind. If you send any such materials, they will be returned to you.

The Disclosure Document must be accompanied by a separate cover letter signed by you, stating that you are the inventor and requesting that the material be received under the Disclosure Document Program. The USPTO suggests that your request take the following form: "The undersigned, being the inventor of the disclosed invention, requests that the enclosed papers be accepted under the Disclosure Document Program, and that they be preserved for a period of two years."

Be sure to follow the instructions exactly when preparing and filing your Disclosure Document with the USPTO. This is a simple step but it can be very important if you should ever need to prove when you conceived and developed your idea.

If you prefer, instead of the cover letter you may use the USPTO's cover sheet to accompany the Disclosure Document that you have prepared. You will find in Appendix D in the back of this book a sample blank Disclosure Document. A link is also provided for the actual cover sheet blanks in PDF form that you can print for your use. You will need to fill out the requested information on the cover sheet and send it along with your Disclosure Document and a check or money order for $10.00 made payable to Commissioner for Patents. Make copies of everything you have enclosed in your mailing to keep for your files. Send the packet to:

Mail Stop DD
Commissioner for Patents
P. O. Box 1450
Alexandria, VA 22313-1450

The USPTO will return a notice with an identifying number and the date they received the document. Then they will keep your document on file for two years. This document, together with your inventor's journal, becomes the basis for any future proof of ownership of an invention idea. Again, this document is not required, and many choose to rely solely on an inventor's journal that is read, understood, and signed by two witnesses. The inventor's journal is essential and sufficient. However, a Disclosure Document is still a valuable tool for the independent inventor.

Keep It Hush-Hush!

It seems that novice inventors often fall into one of two groups. The inventor in the first group is so paranoid that he can barely share the idea, even with those closest to him. The one in the second group feels the need to tell everyone he meets about his great idea. Do you recognize yourself as one of these two? It is quite normal to be nervous about having a great idea stolen. It is also quite normal to be so excited about your idea that you want to shout it to the whole world.

By now, you know the reasons for keeping your idea secret until the invention is protected and ready to be unveiled. To repeat the basics: There are two main reasons for discretion when you have a great idea. The first is the possibility that someone who hears about the idea might try to claim it as her own and beat you to market with it. The second is that some kinds of public disclosure create a time-sensitive situation where you must be prepared to file your patent application within a year.

Another, possibly more important reason for maintaining discretion about your invention idea is to preserve your right to file for foreign patent protection if you want to sell your product in foreign markets. You must file for your foreign patent within one year of filing for your U.S. patent or lose all rights to ever file for foreign protection. Also, you should keep in mind that your invention should be maintained as a secret until the patent issues, if at all possible. Inventions are disclosed when they are manufactured and sold to the consumer. Other inventions, such as some software programs, do not reveal the algorithms "under the hood" when they are commercially used. In such cases, trade secret status for the algorithms should be maintained until the patent issues. One way to preserve trade secret status is by careful use of nondisclosure agreements. There are ways in which you can share the idea with those who may be able to assist you in the development or those who can guide you to the resources you will need along the way. Whatever your reason for disclosing your invention idea, unless the person you disclose to is a patent attorney or a patent agent, you will need to make good use of nondisclosure agreements.

ALERT!

Many inventors begin to seek publicity for their new product once the patent is filed. Although the "patent pending" designation affords some protection, there is still an element of risk in taking an unpatented product public to the extent that your competition can reverse engineer the product. The product is fair game until the patent issues, unless certain aspects of the product can be maintained as a trade secret.

Although most inventors who plan to license their inventions begin marketing to manufacturers as soon as they have patent pending status, discretion is also a good idea at this point. As long as your patent application has

CHAPTER 3: PROTECTING YOUR IDEA

not been published, the entire patent application, including the claims within that application, are held secret by the USPTO. This could be important in the event that a manufacturer who is less than honest decides to attempt to find a way to make your product without benefit of a license agreement by "designing around" the claims of the patent application. This is a strong reason not to share the claims portion of your patent application with manufacturers. Even if the claims are maintained in secrecy, until the patent actually issues, anyone can make and sell the product.

Nondisclosure Agreements

Nondisclosure agreements, also called confidentiality agreements, are documents used by inventors to protect their inventions by maintaining the trade secret status of the invention and preserving the foreign patent rights of the invention. Note that a sale or an offer for sale under a nondisclosure agreement is still a sale or offer for sale, and so in this case, a nondisclosure agreement would not keep the USPTO's clock from starting to tick on when the invention's owner must file for patent protection. A nondisclosure agreement usually consists of one page on which the inventor briefly describes the invention and the recipient of the information agrees that he will hold the information he receives about the invention in total confidence. The nondisclosure agreement is for the inventor's records and serves two purposes. First, it serves as proof of when the inventor divulged her idea and to whom. Second, it serves as a deterrent to anyone who might be inclined to try to take the invention and pursue it as his own idea. Once he has signed a nondisclosure agreement, the recipient of the information would be hesitant to try to claim the invention as his own because the actual inventor would have proof of when he saw the idea. Each nondisclosure agreement should be kept in a file with other records pertaining to the invention.

Standard Nondisclosure Agreement

There are two basic types of nondisclosure agreements. The first, a standard nondisclosure agreement, is to be used in ordinary circumstances between the inventor and the person to whom he shows his invention. For example, this type of nondisclosure agreement should be used when the inventor is discussing his invention and seeking advice from friends, neighbors, or colleagues. This is also the type of nondisclosure agreement that should be used if he wishes to divulge his invention to members of an inventors' club or association or in any other group setting.

ALERT!

Unscrupulous people or companies may sign a nondisclosure agreement and then choose to ignore it. Even when using nondisclosure agreements, use caution in choosing to whom you disclose your invention.

Contractor's Nondisclosure Agreement

The second type of nondisclosure agreement is designed to be used when seeking the help of professional prototype designers or others in developing your invention. This contractor's nondisclosure agreement is very important because when a professional is helping you build or improve the design of your product, that person is in a unique position. He may come up with ways to make your product better and in doing so may become a co-inventor, and therefore will be considered a co-owner of the invention unless you have had him sign the contractor's nondisclosure agreement. This agreement says that you are hiring him to help you with your product and he is doing it for a fee. It also states that he understands that the invention is to be solely yours, and consequently he agrees to assign any rights that accrue to him as a co-inventor to you, ensuring that any improvements or suggestions he makes become your intellectual property. He thereby relinquishes any claim to the invention when he signs this type of nondisclosure agreement. Again, this agreement is to be kept by the inventor as proof of when and to whom he showed his invention or from whom he sought help with it.

Chapter 4
Join the Club!

Are you feeling all alone in your quest to develop and market the next great new product? Then join the club—literally! There are inventors' clubs and organizations all across the United States that can offer the support and guidance you're looking for. These groups of people who've "been there and done that" are among the best resources for the lone inventor. These people understand what you are feeling and can help you on your journey. This chapter will fill you in on inventors' clubs and organizations available to you.

Benefits of Joining a Club or Organization

When is the right time to join an inventors' organization? Yesterday! Well, almost. Generally, a would-be inventor knows where he would like his idea to end up, but he hasn't a clue as to how to get there. The time to align yourself with those who have already been down that road is before you make some of those common new-inventor mistakes.

There are numerous benefits from joining an inventors' club. Read on to learn about some of the biggest pluses.

QUESTION?

Whom will you find at your local inventors' club?
Generally, you will find individuals who have successfully marketed their ideas, patent attorneys and/or agents, other novice inventors, prototype designers, people with experience in manufacturing or in having products made offshore, and people experienced in creating business plans. Perhaps you'll even find a product scout!

Free Professional Advice

While the professionals who are there are undoubtedly hoping to gain new clients from their association with inventors, in almost every case they give freely of their advice and assistance at the meetings. Their solicitation for business, if done at all, is decidedly low-key. They realize that the meetings are not the place for pressure tactics. They know that most independent inventors have to find the funds to develop their ideas from a budget that does not normally include such items as legal advice and prototype design. These goodwill gestures on their part usually do come back to them in the form of paid business and referrals from the club members. Some new patent professionals have even built up a practice from their association with these organizations.

Sharing of Resources

While the benefits of having free professional advice at these meetings is difficult to overstate, another great benefit of membership in inventors' clubs is the networking and interaction among new and seasoned inventors. Just realizing that one is not alone is worth the price of membership to many product development novices. The novice inventor often finds that, even though she is new to this arena and has limited experience, the resources she has located are exactly what another member is seeking. Sometimes she can provide information about a person or company that provides necessary services at a cost that is lower than the going rate for such services.

FACT

Inventors' organizations often have tables set up with helpful articles on the different aspects of inventing and marketing as well as information on classes and services in your area. Look for bulletins on inventors' seminars around the country. You also are likely to find necessary forms for USPTO filings and people who can assist with completing them.

Avoiding Mistakes and Scams

Because product development is not something that one normally learns in school, the person with a great idea for a new product often feels the need for help in the form of guidance as to what early steps to take. The smart novice inventor will seek early help to avoid mistakes that can be costly. Inventors' club members can teach those early steps and they usually even have printed materials outlining those steps. Often you will also find the forms you will need and instructions on where to file those forms.

Since product development services offered to inventors are largely unregulated, the industry is rife with unscrupulous people who prey on the naïve would-be inventor who is especially susceptible to their offers to get his idea on the market. These organizations can help novice inventors understand the methods of these dishonest companies. They can steer the inventor toward legitimate assistance and away from swindles.

Locating your nearest inventors' club and joining it can be a wise move whether you are a new or a seasoned inventor. Membership fees are usually extremely reasonable and the assistance and contacts you can gain could make the difference between the success and failure of your invention.

Hearing from Experts

Another great benefit of inventors' organizations is the speakers they bring in for their meetings. Attendees at these meetings will get the opportunity to hear patent attorneys, legitimate marketing agents, prototype specialists, successful inventors, authors of books on inventing and marketing, representatives from the patent office, and others who have the kind of information the novice inventor really needs. The variety of experienced people who offer advice that can save time and money for the independent inventor is a definite bonus of membership.

FACT

One intangible but very real benefit of membership in inventors' clubs is the sense of accountability you will get just from the association with the people in these groups. You will not want to attend the next meeting and report that you have done nothing to move forward with your invention. The motivation and need to show progress is a genuine benefit of membership in an inventors' organization.

Inventors' Associations and Clubs

There are local, national, and international inventors' clubs and associations that provide services and information for independent inventors. National and international inventors' associations sometimes have panels of experts who field questions from independent inventors. They often post free newsletters and information important to the inventor community on their Web sites as well as articles on inventing written by experts in various aspects of the process. In the United States, there are two national clubs, the United Inventors Association of the USA and the National Congress of Inventor Organizations. The United Inventors Association of the USA provides an online bookstore with books and supplies that meet the needs of independent inventors. They also provide marketability evaluation services for a reasonable fee.

ESSENTIAL

Networking and sharing of information, inspiration, and encouragement are essential for most independent inventors. You can find a list of local clubs and organizations in each state on the United Inventors Association Web site: *www.uiausa.org*. If you do not have a club near you, join the UIA itself. It is not quite the same as joining a local club but it is the next best thing!

Inventors' clubs and associations are not uniform in their makeup, their procedures, or the information and services they provide. They are as different as the people who make them up. Some clubs are very structured and each meeting features a speaker who addresses various aspects of the inventing process. Other clubs are more informal and consist mainly of friends who get together to brainstorm and share resources. Still other clubs combine both approaches, having speakers on occasion but primarily attempting to address the needs of the independent inventor, wherever she is in the process, by providing patent attorneys, patent agents, prototype designers, and successful inventors to whom she can address her questions and concerns.

The inventor is usually concerned about divulging his idea to people he may not know well. This is a legitimate concern. Inventors' clubs address this concern in one of two ways. Some clubs ask the inventor not to divulge his idea at all, but to speak only in generalities when seeking help. This is certainly possible. For example, an inventor who has invented a new type of three-ring binder notebook may say that he needs help in finding someone who can help him with a "spring mechanism" made of metal or plastic. He has not specifically stated what his invention is but he has stated the exact type of help he is seeking. Other members of the club can direct him to possible sources of help. If an inventor feels that she must describe her invention in some detail in order to get the help she needs from a specific source, she should get a signed nondisclosure agreement from that person for her files and meet with him in private.

Other clubs address the problem of confidentiality by having all members and visitors sign, as they enter the meeting, a group nondisclosure agreement stating that they will all hold any information shared at the meeting in total confidence. This type of agreement is often referred to as a blanket nondisclosure. It does not appear that there have been any problems with this method, such as having an idea stolen by someone at the meeting, but it is a matter of discretion. If you are at all uncomfortable with this "blanket nondisclosure" method, it is always prudent to maintain the secrecy of your invention.

If you find that you are not in an area that already has an active inventors' club or association, start one! Build your own network of support and help. Contact local patent attorneys, local universities, or the Small Business Development Center (SBDC). Inform them of your intent and ask them to let their clients know about the new association that is being created. The USPTO's database allows you to search issued patents according to the patent owner's city. Get the list of local inventors from that online database and contact them about becoming involved in an inventors' club. People who have already patented, and in some cases marketed, their inventions can be valuable sources of information for novice inventors. Finally, the United Inventors Association of the USA offers a free guide on how to establish your own club.

How many inventors' associations and clubs are there?
There are approximately 135 local inventors' associations and clubs in cities and communities across the United States, Canada, and Puerto Rico.

Inventors' Seminars and Workshops

The field of product development for independent inventors has been evolving into an industry of its own for the past few decades. New companies have appeared on the scene specifically to serve the needs of independent inventors, such as invention marketability evaluation and prototype designing services.

ALERT!

Unscrupulous companies are known to host seminars that purport to offer inventor education and assistance. These functions are designed to mimic the seminars given by legitimate organizations but they are offered for a different purpose: to lure unsuspecting inventors. Carefully check out the sponsors of any seminar before enrolling.

Because product development by individuals has become such a force in the economy, many of the large manufacturers are actively working to incorporate designs submitted by independent inventors into their product lines through licensing. Another route commonly taken by the individual inventor is to create a business by handling the manufacturing and distribution of his own product. Whatever decision you make regarding the disposition of your new product, you will greatly enhance your chances for success if you take the time to learn everything you can about this new endeavor.

One of the best ways to do this is to attend the seminars and workshops that are held around the country for new product developers. Local inventor groups or universities usually sponsor these events. They often schedule them to last through a weekend, during which classes will be offered on every aspect of product development, legal protection, and marketing. Top experts in the field serve as teachers, such as patent attorneys, product agents and representatives, prototype designers, catalog representatives, and authors of books on everything from funding your invention to writing your own legal protection documents. These seminars often have one large room with booths that an inventor can rent for a small fee to show off his invention. At this point, he is attempting to license or sell the invention. He would obviously want to have some protection in place, such as a filed patent application, before making a public display of the invention.

Two of the largest annual seminars are the Minnesota Inventors Congress, held each June in Redwood Falls, Minnesota, and the Yankee

Invention Exposition, offered each October in Waterbury, Connecticut. These two events have Web sites where you can learn about past seminars and what is scheduled for upcoming ones. In addition, there are a number of similar but smaller meetings in all areas of the country. All of these inventors' seminars are open to the public and many of them have no admission fee, charging only for workshops you attend. You can obtain an updated list of these events by checking the Web sites of *Inventors' Digest* magazine or the United Inventors Association.

Mark your calendar for June and October! The Minnesota Inventors Congress is held each June in Redwood Falls and the Yankee Invention Exposition is held each October in Waterbury, Connecticut. These meetings are attended by inventors and experts from across the country. If you can possibly go, these events will be tremendously helpful to you.

The USPTO has sponsored large seminars in the Washington, D.C., area and at the Franklin Pierce Law Center in Concord, New Hampshire. These two- or three-day seminars have included classes in all areas of product development, protection, and marketing. More frequently, they have small workshops in Patent and Trademark Depository Libraries (PTDLs) around the country. These workshops are devoted to specific areas related to patents and trademarks only, and licensed patent attorneys, agents, or USPTO employees teach them. And they are free! This is a service provided by the USPTO for the benefit of independent inventors. Another free service from this agency is periodic online chats with examiners and others who provide answers to the many questions that all independent inventors seem to have. This interactive workshop is a great opportunity for the independent inventor to get a better understanding of the USPTO and what happens to his patent application once it has been filed. You can find information about when to log on to these chats on the USPTO Web site or from your nearest patent library.

ESSENTIAL

Become familiar with the USPTO Web site. Its section of frequently asked questions is a good way to educate yourself on all aspects of intellectual property protection. You will also find notices of upcoming opportunities for online chats with examiners and other patent experts there and on the Web site of Ask The Inventors!™

Still another educational resource for independent inventors is that provided by the Small Business Development Center (SBDC). Your local office has a wealth of information; some of them offer classes at no cost to the attendee. The SBDC offers courses with weekly classes, usually running for two or three weeks, for a reasonable fee. Among other offerings, you can get a crash course and some individual help in writing your business plan and learn the different options you have for setting up your business.

Why should you attend these events? The reasons are as varied as the people who attend. For the new inventor, it is a quick and inexpensive way to get the education you need. People who know their subjects well provide these classes. For those who already know the basics, it is a chance to learn some tips that can smooth your way to success. And, for everyone who attends, it is a chance to network. These events draw the creative people, the movers and shakers, of the product development world together. You just might meet someone there who can give you a major boost toward your goal.

Trade Associations

Regardless of the category of your invention, there is undoubtedly a trade association that serves professionals in that industry. There are trade associations for everything and those associations have listings of all the members of their group as well as all the news and information relating to their industry. For example, if your invention has something to do with preparing food in a clean and hygienic way, there is an association for that. It is the Society of Food Hygiene Technology. If your invention has something to do with dispensing dressings or sauces, there is an association for that. It is the Association for Dressings and Sauces! According to the U.S. Department of Agriculture, there are sixty-two trade associations related to various aspects of the food industry. On the other hand, if your invention is an improvement on a bicycle, there are national, international, state, and local bicycle associations. The same is true for virtually every other category of invention.

The trade associations that relate to your invention can be extremely valuable sources of information for the independent inventor. They provide a list of all the manufacturers who make products in the category of your invention and the manufacturers who have the distribution channels in place and the ability to get your product on the market. Those are the very companies that may be interested in licensing your product.

FACT

Your local reference librarian can direct you to trade magazines for virtually any trade category. Check with her for assistance in finding the association that would be appropriate for your category of product. If your library does not have the trade magazine you need, get the names of the associations from the library and check online for information.

Obviously, as a product developer, you will not be able to join any professional trade association as a manufacturer. Most trade associations have a category of membership called associate members. Associate members are not manufacturers but they offer products and services that benefit the members. For example, companies that provide packaging for particular types of products may belong to the trade association as an associate member. Or—and this is where the independent inventor comes in—product developers for a specific industry also often belong to the trade associations as associate members. Membership fees for associate members are often substantially less than the fees for regular members. Consider this an investment in your invention and one well worth the cost.

When you join, you become an instant insider. Being an insider in the industry of your invention can make the difference between getting your product to market and not. It is just human nature for a company's representative to be more willing to talk to you if you are a member of that industry's professional organization. That automatically elevates you to being someone who understands the industry. If you are an association member, you are more likely to get the appointment to talk to the manufacturer and he is more likely to take you seriously as a product developer.

Trade Shows

A wonderful resource for the individual who is developing a new product is the trade show. There are trade shows for every imaginable product. To find out about trade shows in general, check with the reference librarian at your local library. If you use the Internet, just type the keyword "trade shows" into a search engine such as Google or Yahoo!. This will bring up numerous links that will lead you to trade shows of all kinds. If you are looking for trade shows in a specific area for your own invention, just add that word to your keywords, such as "craft trade shows." You will find links leading to the exact trade shows you are seeking with information on when and where they are scheduled.

Why should you go to a trade show when you are just in the early development stages with your invention? The name of the game here is to learn as much as you can as quickly as you can. If you expect to succeed in marketing a product, it is vital that you know as much as possible about the products in that category and those who make and sell them. You can learn a great deal by visiting trade shows in your area of interest. If you are interested in licensing or selling the patent rights to your invention to a manufacturer, you will find most, if not all, of the relevant manufacturers under one roof. This is where these manufacturers go, usually once a year, to show off their products and make sales to retailers.

A visit to a trade show exhibiting the companies that make products that are in the same category as your invention idea will be a great learning experience on several levels:

- You will be able to familiarize yourself with the products of every company represented there.
- Each manufacturer's booth will show you virtually the entire product line of the company in one small area.
- The trade show will be an excellent place to get ideas for your next inventions as you wander around, looking at all the new products.
- You will have an opportunity to introduce yourself to the product development people who are representing their companies in the booths.

As you wander among the booths, you will be able to find the companies that make the products that are most similar to your invention. Since these manufacturers have their booths filled with essentially everything they sell, you will be able to see firsthand which companies' product lines are the best fit for your invention. These companies will become your "targets" if your goal is to license your invention for royalties or to sell it outright. If your goal is to create your own business, it will be helpful to know which manufacturers make the products that are the most like yours. These will likely be your competition.

Having the opportunity to get up close and personal with almost the entire product line of every company at a trade show is an experience that will be valuable to you, no matter what direction you decide to take with your present invention. It is a virtual certainty that you will not be a one-hit wonder. That is, once you have successfully marketed your product, you have effectively broken into the industry and made your mark as a product developer for that category of products. If you developed one product for that industry, chances are good that you will think of other innovations for that same market. When you are ready to begin work on your next new product, you will already have scoped out the products within that category and the companies that make them. If you do choose to invent again, you will find the marketing to be immensely easier as a product developer who has established credibility.

When you have seen how lucrative product development can be, you will be eager to develop new products for your chosen category. What better place to get ideas for your next inventions than where you can view essentially everything that is being marketed in this country in your category?

As you walk around the trade show floor, be sure to stop by the booths and meet the manufacturers' representatives. Give them your business card and be sure to pick up their cards. This will give you an easy access to these people when you are ready to submit a product to their company. Even though they are unlikely to remember you, they will respond to your mention of having met them at the trade show.

Attending that first trade show will be a large part of your introduction to the industry and will make you feel like the inventor you are!

Trade Magazines and Journals

Trade magazines and journals are a valuable resource for you as an independent inventor. Most trade associations have a magazine subscription that goes to all members of the association. If you are not a member of the trade association for your category of invention, you can find some of the magazines and journals at a city library or university library. Becoming familiar with and studying these publications can give you, as a product developer for a specific industry, an edge. With these magazines, you can stay apprised of the latest news and trends that may influence the type of products you choose to develop. Additionally, these trade journals feature advertising for products and services related to the industry. You can often find sources for assistance specific to your invention, such as prototyping or parts.

Not all industry-related magazines and journals are the publications of specific trade associations. Some are merely magazines that are directed toward a specific interest group. To find the magazines that may be appropriate to the area of a particular invention, look in the Bacon's Directories, a set of books that are available at some, but not all, libraries. It may be necessary to go to the main branch of a city library or to a university or college library in order to find them. The Bacon's Directories list magazines according to subject category. There are magazines for every imaginable interest and activity.

In addition to the magazines that are industry specific, there are magazines that are written especially with the independent product developer and entrepreneur in mind. *Inventors' Digest* is one such publication. It keeps the inventor informed about issues important to independent inventors. It is a trustworthy resource for information and services needed by product developers, and it features encouraging and inspiring independent inventor success stories. There are four issues each year, with newsletters in the intervening months. Back issues of the magazine are also available to order.

FACT

Inventors' Digest magazine is available by mail or online. It is the only magazine in this country that is specific to inventing. With articles written by various experts in product development, protection, and marketing, this magazine could prove to be worth more than the price of the entire subscription with your first copy!

Another magazine that you will find helpful is *Entrepreneur*, particularly if you plan to build a business around your invention. Unlike *Inventors' Digest*, it directs its message primarily toward those who wish to create a business. Both magazines are valuable resources that, as a serious inventor, you should check out.

Chapter 5

Whom Can You Trust?

Are you afraid someone is going to steal your great idea? Most independent inventors are. Some have a fanatical belief that everyone is out to take the idea from them. Others are too trusting of anyone who expresses belief in the idea. The wisest position lies somewhere between these two extremes. When you have a great idea for an invention, a little paranoia can be a healthy thing. There are guidelines and resources to help you determine who can be trusted and who cannot.

How to Tell the Good Guys from the Bad Guys

There are ways to determine if the company or persons you are dealing with are legitimate or not. How many of the inventions that they have evaluated in the past five years received positive evaluations? How many of them received negative evaluations? Far more positive evaluations than negative evaluations are a red flag that you may be dealing with an unscrupulous invention-marketing company.

The following are the USPTO's Top Ten Scam Warning Signs:

1. The company runs slick ads on TV and radio and in magazines (these are the first hooks).
2. The company refuses to respond to your questions in writing, signed by a company official. (Legitimate companies will provide the answers in writing.)
3. Salespersons want money right away.
4. They tell you to describe your idea in writing, mail it to yourself, and not open the envelope because that will prove the date of your invention. (This is worthless advice.)
5. You are promised a patent search but with no legal opinion of patentability signed by a patent attorney or patent agent. (This should be provided to you.)
6. You are guaranteed that you will get a patent or else get your money back. (Legitimate sources will make no such guarantee.)
7. You are advised to apply for a design patent. (This type of patent has limited applicability to most inventions, though not all.) Design patents are based only on how an invention looks and do not address any possible use for the invention.
8. You are unable to reach company employees without leaving many messages. (Maybe there is no real office or location for the company.)
9. You are told that your idea is a sure-fire hit. (It is likely that every client of this company is told that exact same thing! Be skeptical.)
10. The company refuses to provide client references or blank copies of their forms and agreements for your review. (Get at least five names of their clients in your area to contact and take their blank forms to an attorney for a legal opinion.)

How many inventors helped by the company have actually made more money from the invention than they paid to the company? How many of their clients have gotten license agreements for their invention? The bad guys often make more money from the inventor than the inventor will ever make from his product. If they have managed to obtain license agreements for less than 5 percent of their clients it would indicate that they take on inventions that are unworthy simply to get the money or they are not aggressively marketing their clients' inventions.

The scam artists move from one company to another, or simply change the name of the company to start anew. They do this in order to conceal complaints or legal problems with the Federal Trade Commission, Better Business Bureau, any consumer protection agency, or the Attorney General's Office under the previous company name. The inventor should ask for the names and addresses of all previous invention-promotion companies with which the company or its officers have been associated within the previous ten years. They should also ask what other names the company has used in their state or in other states, and whether those companies or they individually have ever had complaints filed against them with any government or consumer protection agencies. After receiving answers to these questions it is a good idea to visit inventor-friendly Web sites, such as *www.inventored.org* and *www.uiausa.org*. They maintain lists of complaints against invention marketing companies and individuals. The Federal Trade Commission also has records on companies that it has received complaints about, investigated and/or prosecuted.

FACT

Legitimate invention-marketing companies have a very low acceptance rate; they accept 5 percent or less of the inventions submitted to them for development. This is because they have a good eye for what can successfully be marketed and because they often bear some or all of the up-front marketing expenses.

Legitimate companies and scam companies may both charge an up-front fee to represent an invention. The difference between the two is what the inventor gets in return. Legitimate companies may charge relatively small development, prototype, and promotional material fees. They may also require reimbursement for travel expenses related to presenting the product to manufacturers for potential licensing. The legitimate companies are happy to provide an accounting of all these costs so that the inventor will know exactly what he is getting for his money. The unscrupulous companies are more likely to charge a substantial fee up-front and provide only generalities as to why the money is necessary and how they plan to spend it.

On rare occasions, when a legitimate company is extremely excited about the marketability of an invention they may agree to take it on for absolutely no up-front fee and make their earnings by sharing in the eventual royalty payments. It is a lucky inventor who finds herself in this unique position.

Legitimate marketability evaluation services provide detailed reports with documentation on how they reached their conclusions; the con artists write reports consisting of vague generalities with no documentation regarding the research on which the reports are based. They speak about the thousands or millions of potential customers the invention might have. Their reports are designed not to provide the inventor with useable information but rather to excite him about the tremendous potential of his product.

ESSENTIAL

Most legitimate sources of help encourage the inventor to be involved in the process by selecting and employing her own patent search firm and patent attorney. The scam artists, on the other hand, promise the inventor that they will do it all for her. The old saying "If it sounds too good to be true, it probably is" certainly applies here.

Legitimate companies provide a variety of services, some more than others. Some simply evaluate the idea. Others will help to prepare a prototype (virtual or actual) that can be used when presenting the product for possible licensing. The expertise of licensing agents who also evaluate ideas is substantial. They may also provide brochures and a first-rate product presentation. They may present the product to potential licensing partners and negotiate license agreements. Their expertise at presenting inventions for licensing and their many manufacturing contacts are both of tremendous value to independent inventors.

Big-Time Crooks

Invention promotion is big business! The FTC estimates that independent inventors spend hundreds of millions of dollars each year with companies who advertise that they can help them get their products to market. According to R. J. Riley, inventor and scam company watchdog, one company that is currently being investigated by the Federal Trade Commission has provided financial records showing that they have an income in excess of $2.5 million dollars per month from unsuspecting novice inventors. And, this is not even the largest company of this type! Unfortunately, most of the companies who advertise on television and radio and in print media seldom, if ever, live up to their hype. It is the business of those companies to make money, not to develop inventions. And make money they do!

How Do They Do It?

These scam companies lure unsuspecting independent inventors using slick professional ads placed with respected media outlets. For instance, their ads may appear on cable television networks and channels such as CNN, MSNBC, the Discovery Channel, the Learning Channel, and others as well as regular network channels CBS, NBC, ABC, and Fox. Their commercials may appear during news programming, lending more credibility and authenticity to their claims. After all, if they advertise on CNN they must be legitimate, right? Wrong! Those networks sell advertising; they do not screen the companies to be certain that the companies deliver what they promise.

How can these scam artists make promises they cannot or will not live up to and stay in business? Isn't that unfair advertising? You would think so, but it is not. The reason it is not unfair advertising is that they do what they say they will do, but they do it in a very haphazard, inadequate way. They stay just inside of the law to keep from getting into legal trouble. They will perform a market search, but it is an inferior and undependable search. They seldom find anything that would conflict with your invention idea. It is, after all, not in their economic interest to find anything to prevent you from pursuing your idea. They want to keep the money coming from you, not to cut it off. They also will do a patent search, but again it is substandard. Part of keeping you on their hook is to keep you enthused about your product.

Producing prior art (items similar to yours that have been previously marketed or patented) that will impact the patentability of your product will not do that, so they are unlikely to come up with anything that would indicate difficulty in obtaining patent protection. Even if their search uncovers a utility patent (a patent on the way an invention is made or how it is used) on your exact invention, they are unlikely to inform you of that fact.

These irresponsible companies will also live up to their promise to get a patent on your product. What they do not tell you, however, is that they will get a *design* patent, not a utility patent. If they have discovered a utility patent on your invention, they get around it by simply making some very small change in the way the product looks, such as painting a stripe or a flower on it, and filing for a design patent. Design patents are relatively easy and inexpensive to obtain (though it will not be inexpensive if you have them do it!) but the usefulness of a design patent is limited. The independent inventor is rarely able to get a company to license a design patent because design patents are extremely easy to circumvent by simply making a minor change in the design or look of the product.

ALERT!

If your design patent is the same invention as one that is already in the patent books as a utility patent, you will most likely be infringing the utility patent if you market that product. Obviously, you would not be able to license such a patent. In all, these types of firms provide very poor basic services for exorbitant fees and obtain worthless patents that are overly narrow and virtually useless in the marketplace.

The big scam invention-promotion companies have a well developed formula for luring you into their trap:

- They advertise that they will send you a free inventor's kit.
- They begin calling persistently to sell you an invention evaluation.
- The evaluation inevitably comes back positive.
- The report consists of a nicely bound book, sometimes with your picture in it.

- They pressure the inventor for still more money in order to patent and market the invention.

The free inventor's kit that these companies send out is nothing more than free information you can get for yourself from the USPTO. At *www. uspto.gov/web/offices/com/iip/index.htm* you will find brochures with all of the basic information you need. They lead you to believe that it is something that they have put together to assist you. The impression they want to give you is that this information is available only from them.

A short time after you have received your free inventor's kit, the telephone calls begin. Very friendly and professional-sounding sales representatives urge you to send them money so they can perform an invention evaluation. They rush you, telling you that you will lose out if you do not act quickly. These pressure tactics are one of the main clues that you are being hustled. Legitimate invention promotion companies will not phone you to pressure you to sign up for their services. Legitimate companies have more business than they can handle; they do not need to hustle prospective customers.

If you send money for the preliminary evaluation and patent search (usually under $1,000), the company invariably comes back with a positive, often glowing report. They seldom, if ever, come back with a poor evaluation on a product. They usually indicate that they are very excited about your idea. At this point, they recommend that you have them prepare an in-depth report on your invention. This second report, of course, will cost more money.

When your in-depth (second) evaluation report arrives, at a cost to you of well over $1,000, it comes bound with many official-looking sections. The company may pander to your ego by including your photo if you have sent them one in previous correspondence. The novice inventor is often impressed that he has gotten something of value that will help him to market his invention. This official-looking portfolio (the in-depth report) is nothing more than a lot of useless filler documents and a statement that, in their opinion, your invention is patentable and marketable. They are setting you up for the next stage, where they will offer to get your patent for you (for another large payment).

The marketing that these companies do consists of including your invention on a massive list of other inventions that is sent unsolicited to an undisclosed number of manufacturers. Obviously, most if not all of the companies that receive these unsolicited lists immediately throw them away.

They know that the inventions listed are not protected by utility patents and they are, therefore, simply not interested.

Often the company also promises to show your invention at international trade shows, shows that are inconvenient or impossible for you to attend. If you speak with one of these companies and they mention this, see if you can pin them down on exactly what trade shows they will be attending, how they will show your invention, and what proof you will have that they actually did it.

FACT

A company may advertise that it is the biggest or the oldest invention-help company in the United States. While this may be true, there is no guarantee of honesty or ethics here. It only means that a lot of people have paid them a lot of money for a long time. You could potentially be just another inventor they lure into their scheme.

How Do They Get Away with It?

A few years ago, the FTC set up a sting operation to catch some of these scam companies in the act of their unscrupulous behavior and expose them. In Operation Mousetrap, as the sting was called, someone professing to be an inventor contacted one of these marketing companies. He told them that he had an idea for an insulated bag for pizza delivery companies to use in order to keep the pizzas hot. Who has not seen these items for years and years? The invention-promotion company, however, told the inventor that he had a dynamite idea that would make him millions of dollars. They urged him to send them money for market and patent searches. Operation Mousetrap sent them the money. Lo and behold—the market and patent searches came back with the report that there was nothing even close to the inventor's idea. At that point they urged the inventor to send them still more money, thousands of dollars this time, so they could begin patenting and marketing his idea.

According to the Federal Trade Commission, Operation Mousetrap resulted in a law-enforcement sweep that leveled federal and state charges in seven actions against companies and their principals involved in schemes supposedly to help independent inventors who tinker away in their garages late into each night in the hope of "building a better mousetrap." The FTC, which brought five of the cases, said the defendants in its actions generated in excess of $90 million for their own pockets by exploiting the ideas, hopes, and dreams of tens of thousands of consumers.

Many independent inventors who have had the unfortunate experience of dealing with them are afraid that these companies will steal their ideas. This seldom, if ever, occurs. These scoundrels are after the inventor's money, not his idea. Actual inventing, protecting, and marketing an idea are work and these organizations have no interest in actual work. They just want the money.

We'll never know how many useful and inventive products never make it to the marketplace because of these unscrupulous companies. Many inventors are so discouraged, disheartened, and financially exhausted after their experience with them that they fail to pursue their ideas further.

ESSENTIAL

Legitimate companies are eager to provide you with contacts and references because they do not want to be confused with the scam companies. So, if you're considering getting the help of a company whose credentials you cannot absolutely verify, remember the old adage: "When in doubt, don't!"

According to R. J. Riley, inventor and scam company watchdog, a new type of scam has recently appeared on the scene. He says that two companies in particular are "chasing issued patents" by contacting the owners of recently issued patents and promising to help them promote their invention. Riley says these companies are taking their victims for between $10,000 and $14,000 each! Beware of companies that contact you once your patent has issued. If you are concerned about a company's legitimacy check on Riley's InventorEd Web site (*www.inventored.org*) before using its services.

If you have fallen victim to these unscrupulous companies, don't beat yourself up. Many intelligent people are sucked into their trap—these companies are slick! They sound legitimate. They advertise in the most respected publications and on highly respected news and information shows. Intelligent people are accustomed to delegating tasks; in the case of their invention idea, they believe that they are delegating it to a company that will handle it for them in a professional and competent manner. It is easy to understand how this happens once. Now you are forewarned. Don't let it happen to you twice!

Small-Time Crooks

Big-time crooks spawn small-time crooks. The fact that the major scam companies are raking in literally hundreds of millions of dollars each year from independent inventors who are seeking help inevitably attracts other opportunists wishing to get a slice of the pie. They are not as big and do not have huge advertising budgets, but their practices have the same results for the novice inventor. They take her money and deliver few legitimate or valuable services in return.

Often they are simply a Web site that an inventor finds while surfing the Internet looking for help with his idea. They make claims of expertise that is nonexistent. They have even been known to claim that they were attorneys when they were not! They copy the methods of the big companies and sell virtually worthless inventor help kits. They claim successful records of accomplishment in marketing products. Most often they claim that they are currently in the process of negotiating licensing or marketing for a variety of products but due to confidentiality they cannot divulge what the products are or with whom they are negotiating. These claims are impossible to either prove or disprove.

Like the better known invention-promotion companies, these con artists' only goal is to relieve the inventor of her cash. Generally, they are not as slick as the big companies are, so they get into problems with the legal system or the Better Business Bureau more often than the larger companies do. Does that stop them? No way! They just change their name and open up a new business in a different location. Speaking of their locations, if you can locate them at all you will often find them doing business from a post office box with no actual business office. Their Web sites usually do not list a physical location.

These small operators are just as lethal to the independent inventor as the big ones. Their practices and appearance may be slightly different but the result is the same. They will tie up your invention and keep you from doing the necessary work to get your product to market yourself or they will prevent you from finding legitimate help.

Patent Attorneys and Patent Agents

The new inventor often wonders if a nondisclosure agreement is necessary when the invention idea is shown to a patent attorney or a patent agent. This document is not necessary when disclosing inventions to these professionals.

Patent attorneys, also referred to as intellectual property attorneys, and patent agents are ethically bound by their professions to keep your conversations private. If one of these professionals disclosed information that he received in confidence, he would lose his license to practice. You may fully and openly discuss your invention with these professionals and show them your drawings, photos, or actual prototype in total confidence that the information will not be shared, nor will it trigger the One Year Rule for the filing of your eventual patent.

ALERT!

Remember that the Internet is not regulated. Disreputable people and companies can make any claim on Internet Web sites. Minor crooks often have very professional-looking Web sites offering a variety of needed services to unsuspecting inventors. If you are unable to check them out through legitimate sources, use extreme caution.

Prototype Designers

Prototype designers come in all kinds of disguises. They may advertise themselves as just that, prototype designers. Or they could be a carpenter shop, a welding shop, or a manufacturing company. Your own prototype designer could be a tailor. A prototype designer is whomever you need to help you with your particular prototype.

Professional prototype designers (the ones who identify themselves as such) are accustomed to working with independent inventors and they usually know the ropes regarding the protection of an invention idea. In fact, they usually already have the specific nondisclosure document that will protect your invention in this situation and they are prepared to sign it for you before seeing your idea. This document is usually called a contractor's non-disclosure form and it is more restrictive than the type of nondisclosure agreement (confidentiality agreement) that you would use with anyone else to whom you disclose your invention.

Even if your prototype designer already has such a document, it is a good idea to take your own form for him to sign. This is because the wording of these documents varies widely and there are certain phrases that you will want to be sure are included in your document. It is important that this document clearly states that the designer agrees that this is your invention, he is being paid to do certain work for you, and any suggestions, changes, or improvements he makes belong to you, the inventor, alone. If a prototype designer refuses to sign such a document, then you should refuse to disclose your invention to him. Find someone else to do the work for you.

You may find yourself seeking out assistance with the development of your invention from someone who is experienced in a particular area and has the ability to create your prototype but who has never been involved with the creation of a new product. A nondisclosure agreement may be something with which she is completely unfamiliar. In most cases, these individuals will gladly sign your document after a simple explanation that this is a routine legal document that you, as the inventor, must have signed for your own protection. After all, she wants the work order and she will probably have only a passing interest in it as an invention. But here again you must get her to sign before going any further.

Even though it is normal and even healthy to be a bit paranoid about your great invention idea, product development and marketing are not as simple as they sometimes appear to be to the uninitiated, so idea thieves are not as prevalent as we often fear them to be. It is only necessary to select your assistance carefully and be sure to get the forms signed before commencing.

Legitimate Marketability Evaluation Services

As is the case with other services for independent inventors, evaluation services come in all forms. Offers of evaluation services come from numerous sources and in all price ranges. How can you tell which are the legitimate services and which are the wolves in sheep's clothing? It takes some vigilance, but there are ways to ferret out the truth.

ALERT!

Carefully check out invention evaluation offers that you find on Internet Web sites, on television, or in print media. "Free evaluations" are often just the bait in a carefully prepared trap to entice independent inventors to use their so-called services. Offers of "free evaluations" are often more costly, in the long run, than legitimate evaluations that are provided for a fee.

The first thing you will need to know is what is included in the evaluation, how the information is derived, and how it will assist you in making critical decisions regarding your invention. You will also want to know who is gathering the information, how long the evaluation will take, and what the cost will be.

Legitimate evaluations services *do not* offer to take your invention to trade shows or send information on the product to manufacturers. Legitimate evaluation services *do* provide you with signed nondisclosure documents, and they carefully guard your privacy and your intellectual property rights.

QUESTION?

How much does a legitimate marketability evaluation cost?
Costs vary from service to service but they generally cost significantly less than $1,000. Obviously, evaluations that are more time-consuming and require more expert advisors will cost more. Evaluations that evaluate products according to a specific list of attributes are even less expensive.

Some of the evaluation services that you can be sure are legitimate are connected with universities around the country, and at least one is offered by the United Inventors Association, one of the two national inventors' organizations in the United States. A good way to find legitimate evaluation services is to ask a source that you already trust, perhaps your local inventors' organization or one of the national inventors' organizations.

Chapter 6

Your Idea—Your Responsibility

Someone might get a great idea for a new product and then immediately want to hand the idea off to other people and let them do all the work of researching, developing, legally protecting, and marketing it. The originator might think that having the idea is enough of a contribution on his part and someone else should jump at the chance to develop the idea. That is not the way it works. It is your responsibility alone to pursue your own idea. If you do not have enough faith in your idea to do the work involved, you can't expect anyone else to.

Preliminary Searching

Remember that your idea is your idea, and it is up to you to take all the necessary steps to determine whether you may pursue that idea. The first step is an online patent search. There is no legitimate service that will do it for you. The USPTO provides Internet access to their patent database through their Web site, *www.uspto.gov*. You must search both issued patents and pending patents if the pending patents have already been published.

FACT

The USPTO publishes all applications for U.S. patents eighteen months after the filing date unless the inventor has specifically requested, by checking an appropriate box on the application, that it *not* be published until the patent issues. This option is not available to inventors who are applying for international patent protection; their applications will be published eighteen months after the filing date.

Expect your online patent search to take three to five days, at a minimum, and probably much longer. Consider the time you invest in performing the search to be your investment in your idea.

Most independent inventors perform their own online patent search of the USPTO patent database soon after having their great idea. This is a wise course of action. When you have a great idea for a new product, chances are excellent that someone else is having that same idea at about the same time. There is also the likelihood that someone has already had your great idea and patented it. If you do find your envisioned product in your online patent search early in the inventing process, you can save time, effort, and money by stopping further efforts on that invention and, instead, moving on to your next great idea.

Wise independent inventors don't take it personally when they find their invention already spoken for. Every independent inventor has had the experience of finding his great idea either already on the store shelves or protected by a patent, whether it is in the stores or not. You may still proceed with the idea if the others who have come up with the same basic invention that you have thought of have done nothing with it. If they have not developed and patented or sold the invention, you still will be the inventor if you actually make a working product of your idea and take the necessary steps to protect it.

Is Your Invention Worthwhile?

Immediately upon having a light bulb moment about a great idea for a new invention, independent inventors get very excited. If they think their idea is terrific, other people will undoubtedly feel the same way, right? Not necessarily. Consider the inventor with allergies who created a hat that holds a roll of toilet paper. Who wouldn't want to just pull a piece of tissue down to wipe his nose? A lot of people. Perhaps she didn't feel ridiculous wearing a roll of toilet paper on her head, but most people would. Needless to say, that invention, though a perfect fit for that particular inventor, does not hold mass appeal. It is extremely unlikely that you will ever find it on the market.

Countless would-be inventors have come up with ideas like this. For example, did you know that you can now get a portable safe for your valuables? Now the thieves can simply take your valuables with them and open them later at their convenience. Also, did you know that there are fruit-flavored pencils, for people who chew their pencils? There are also vibrating ketchup bottles for people who are too lazy to shake the bottle. Most people have never felt the need for these products. They appealed to their inventors but not to the mass market.

Large companies are not exempt from coming up with inventions that aren't worthwhile. Nike, the extremely large and successful athletic shoe manufacturer, missed the mark with their spring-in-the-heels tennis shoes. Sound clever? Think again. Who jumps from their heels? The shoes look nifty, but they don't work.

The point of this discussion is to encourage you to think critically about your ideas. Successful inventions are products that are needed or desired by millions. They are also products that are easy to manufacture and distribute in a cost-efficient way. Be sure that your invention fits these guidelines, no matter how fun or unique it is. If it does, your chances of success will be greatly enhanced.

FACT

Sometimes inventors come up with great products that solve specific problems, but the problems are shared by so few people that it makes the cost of developing and marketing the invention insurmountable. For example, one inventor came up with a special lens for suffers of a rare eye condition. The lens was too expensive to produce and had too small a market to make it attractive to a manufacturer.

Steer Clear of Assumptions

Assumptions are big dangers in the business of inventing. Just because you would like to have your invention doesn't mean others would, too. And just because you have not personally seen your invention in the stores does not mean that it is not available from any other source. Also, do not assume that your invention is the greatest thing since sliced bread simply because your friends and family tell you it is. Your friends and family love you and they may tell you what they think you want to hear, not what they really think. These are dangerous but very common assumptions that first-time inventors often make.

On the other hand, don't let yourself be swayed by friends and family who tell you that your invention is not a good one or that they have already seen such a product. Some family dynamics are such that members constantly put one another down. They might even say something like, "You are not an inventor. It can't be a very good idea if you came up with it." Sometimes they may intend to tease you but could inadvertently dash your hopes. Your product may be such an obvious solution to a common problem that they actually think they have seen such a product.

When Jelane Honeysuckle, the inventor of Size-Ables, children's clothing that grows with the use of zippers, told family members about her clothing idea, they told her that they had seen such a product on the market. "It's out there," they said. It wasn't. She immediately went on a search of stores to see if her idea was already sold in the marketplace. She searched everywhere and to her great relief, she did not find her invention. What they had seen were the pants with the zippers around the legs that remove a portion of the fabric to make long pants into shorts. That product actually removed some of the fabric. Jelane's invention with the use of separating zippers just made the clothes grow! She proceeded with her invention and it went on to be selected as one of the finalists in the CBS television network's New Product Hunt in 2003. If she had listened to the naysayers in her family, none of those wonderful opportunities would have come her way. It is your job, as the inventor, to do the necessary research to determine whether you should proceed.

One mistake many beginning inventors make is trying to think only of products that serve a completely new or obscure purpose. However, the most successful products often address problems that others have already tried to solve or those that most people encounter on a regular basis. Perhaps you have seen the infomercials for the pans that are designed to let you flip a pancake by turning the pan over rather than flipping the pancake with a spatula. Before that invention came along, everyone just flipped pancakes the old-fashioned way, possibly getting batter all over the stovetop. The new product solves the same problem of turning the pancake in a new way. That is not to say that the new way is necessarily better than the old way. Whether it is better or not, though, the folks who are selling the pancake-turning pans have sold huge numbers of their product. The point here is that the annoyance your product solves has probably been previously solved using other products or methods.

ESSENTIAL

You will have greater success with your product if it solves a common problem in an easy, convenient, and economical way. In order for people to want to purchase your product, they must perceive that it will make their life easier or more convenient in some way. It must offer more than just a different way of solving a problem.

Doing the Preliminary Market Search

It is your job, as the inventor, to thoroughly search the market for any existing product that fulfills the purpose of your invention. Not all products are sold by the large mass-merchandising stores, hardware stores, or craft stores. Some products are sold in a limited venue to specialty stores or specialty markets. Other products are sold only through Web sites on the

Internet. Also, special category items or very unique items are often sold only in catalogs. Catalogs are a niche market for many unique items that appeal to buyers with very specific interests. For example, there are catalogs that are directed to candle makers and beadwork projects. There are catalogs for nearly every special interest group. You must thoroughly explore each one of these sources. Your preliminary market search should consist of three distinct parts: retail store search, Internet search, and catalog search.

When doing your preliminary market search of stores, you must look beyond the big chain companies that immediately come to mind. Be certain to search small independent stores too. The idea is to check every retail store that could conceivably carry your product.

Searching Stores

When it is time to do the retail store portion of your preliminary market search, it is important that you actually go to the store. A telephone call to the store is inadequate. Often the people answering the telephones do not even know what products the store has or does not have. Even worse, these people often don't care! They may say they have the product in an effort to get you to come into the store. Or they may say they don't have it if they are busy and don't want to take the time to look. All in all, talking to clerks or office personnel who happen to answer the phone will often result in incorrect or inadequate information. There is no substitute for actually going into the store and looking at the products on the shelves. Go to the section where your product would be displayed. If your product could be used for more than one purpose, look in every possible section of the store where your invention might logically be sold.

Go to every type of store where your product might be found. For example, if you have invented a new type of utility knife you would need to check the mass merchandise stores such as Wal-Mart, Kmart, and Target as well as hardware stores such as Home Depot and Lowe's. Your utility knife would probably also be carried in hobby stores such as Hobby Lobby or Michaels, and in sporting goods stores such as Academy or Oshman's. Finally, your knife might even be carried in large grocery store chains or home goods stores

ALERT!

Even though Americans, British, and Canadians all speak English, the words we use, and their spellings, are not always the same. You can miss large sections of the possible market if you fail to use all possible words and spellings. When performing your catalog search, be sure to check the search engines for listings using the British and Canadian spelling of catalog, which is *catalogue*.

Searching the Internet

When you have completed the retail portion of your preliminary market search and have not found your product, it is time to move on to the Internet search. The Internet search must also be exhaustive. Using various search engines, search for your product using any possible word that might be used to describe it.

On the search engine Google, there are nearly a million and a half listings for *utility knife*. Obviously, you would need to refine your search; it would be an impossible task to look at each of those listings. If your invention were a utility knife with a serrated edge, for example, that would reduce the listings to less than 50,000. If your serrated-edged utility knife had a pearl handle, you could further refine your search and reduce the number of listings to less than 3,000. That is still a huge number but it would be possible to look at each and every one of them within a reasonable amount of time. Doing your Internet preliminary market search is a tedious and time-consuming job, but it is a job that *you* must do. Many inventors have found their product offered for sale on the Internet after having been unsuccessful in finding it in a thorough store-to-store search.

Searching Catalogs

After completing the retail store search and the Internet search, it is important to do a catalog search. Many catalogs are now listed online and it is possible to do a thorough catalog search right at your computer. You may simply type in the word *catalog* in several search engines. For example, if your product is a home and garden tool, type in *home and garden catalog*. Google shows more than five million listings when you type in this search criteria.

If you find your product listed for sale in a catalog, even if it is a foreign catalog, the USPTO would consider that prior art and it would likely prevent you from getting patent protection on your idea. Sad as it is to find your product, it is better to find it in your preliminary market search of stores, the Internet, and catalogs than to invest your time and money developing and attempting to protect something that is either in the public domain or already patented.

Put It on Paper

As you go through your preliminary market search, keeping accurate and detailed records can help you further down the line in the inventing process when you are preparing to license or market your invention. Make a list of all the stores you go to in the course of your preliminary market search. If they don't have your product now, they may be likely retailers to carry it in the future. Get the information on the stores. Where are the headquarters? Get the contact information. How many stores are in the chain? While you are in the store, ask the manager for the names of the distributors they work with for the products that are in the same category as your product. If you eventually choose to manufacture your product yourself, the distributors who already place products in the stores would be valuable allies to have when the time comes to get your product into those same stores. Don't be afraid to ask for specifics: locations, phone numbers, etc. And always put the date at the top of each page of your notes.

As you look at the products most similar to your idea, write down the names and contact information of the companies that manufacture those products. Those companies may eventually be your target licensees. They obviously already manufacture products for that sector of the market into which your product fits. They also already have an established relationship with the retailers and have store shelf space already assigned to them on the store's planogram. If one of those companies were interested in licensing your product, it would be an easy matter for them to place it in the stores.

During your Internet and catalog searches, you should do the same. Keep detailed records of the companies and catalogs that carry similar products as well as the manufacturers of these products. Many independent inventors who choose to manufacture their products themselves find that selling through catalogs is one great way to market their products. Identifying potential catalogs for your product can prove extremely valuable.

ALERT!

Failure to keep accurate records of retail stores you visited and manufacturers of similar or competing products during your preliminary market search will result in a duplication of work and effort as you reach the licensing or manufacturing portion of the inventing process. Don't create more work for yourself!

The *independent* in *independent inventor* means that you are researching and developing your idea for an invention on your own. You may have help from others from time to time, but the bottom line is that it is your idea and your invention and you must be willing to do the necessary work to be certain that you have the right to proceed. You cannot expect anyone else to do it for you. So, if this information hasn't scared you off and you're still committed to your idea, get to work!

Chapter 7

E Your Own Patent Search

Doing your own preliminary online patent search can save you time, effort, and money. However, this is a preliminary search only, not a replacement for your eventual professional patent search. The purpose of your online search of the USPTO patent database is to determine, to the best of your ability, if your invention has already been patented. If you do find your invention already patented, your time, effort, and finite financial resources can be directed toward your next great idea rather than spending it unnecessarily on someone else's patent-protected invention.

What Is a Patent?

The USPTO defines a patent as a property right granted by the government of the United States of America to an inventor "to exclude others from making, using, offering for sale, or selling the invention throughout the United States or importing the invention into the United States" for a limited time in exchange for public disclosure of the invention when the patent is granted. In effect, this means that the inventor is granted a limited monopoly on the invention for a set period of time.

During the time in which the patent is in effect, the inventor, or the assignee or licensee of the patent, is the only person who has the right to manufacture and distribute the product. As the owner of the patent, the inventor may sell or assign the rights to its use to another party, such as a licensee. In exchange for receiving the patent, the government requires that the invention be fully disclosed, without retaining any trade secrets on how to best practice the invention. This means that when the patent issues, the government will publish the patent and it will be available for anyone to look at in the patent books at the USPTO offices in Washington, D.C., the PTDLs, or on the USPTO's online database.

A patent gives an inventor the right to stop anyone else from either manufacturing and distributing the product or importing it from another country for distribution in the United States. Usually, if a company can be shown to be an infringer, the company will pay damages to the inventor in a settlement out of court. About 2 percent of the time, a lengthy and expensive lawsuit in federal court may be required to stop an infringer from selling your product.

QUESTION?

Will the USPTO make an infringer stop?
No. Once a patent holder or his assignee detects patent infringement in the marketplace, he must use the federal courts to attempt to stop any infringing company from producing, importing, and/or selling the product. The burden of proof is on the patent holder, and the patent holder must also bear the expense of litigation.

Many inventors have misconceptions about what a patent can do for them. In addition to being aware of what it can do, it is equally important to know what it cannot do. A patent does not guarantee that your product will make it to the market. It does not guarantee that your product will make money if it does make it to the market. And finally, it does not attest to the quality or superiority of your product over similar or competing products. It is simply a grant of exclusive rights regarding the manufacturing, sale, and distribution of the product for a set period of time. Furthermore, a U.S. patent only protects the U.S. market for the invention. To stop others from making, using, and selling in other countries requires a patent in each country where such protection is needed.

However, a patent can be used as a way to enhance the marketing of a product, by providing evidence of its uniqueness. A patent, or even "patent pending" status, also tends to suggest that a product has unusual intrinsic value.

Why Search?

The preliminary patent search is a make-or-break point in the decision on whether to move forward with your invention idea. Many products that have had or now have patent protection never made it to the market at all or were marketed on such a limited basis that they are relatively unknown to the buying public. Other products have been marketed without patent protection. Even an expired patent is prior art. And a patent that is valid and enforceable might become the basis of a patent infringement action against you, even if the inventor has never sold a product that includes his invention. A thorough patent search is essential before moving forward.

According to the USPTO, only 3 percent of the patents issued to independent inventors make it to the marketplace. As a result, the patent books are full of patented inventions that were never commercialized. Even if they never made it to market, however, they are not available for anyone but the inventor to pursue during the life of the patent. Your great idea may already be patented, but you will not know that until you do a search. To disregard an issued patent prior to its expiration date is to invite a patent infringement lawsuit against *you!* It can cost a million dollars, or more, if you lose or must settle an infringement lawsuit. Not many independent inventors have the resources or inclination to do so.

If you have a patent and find that someone or some company is infringing your patent, it can be equally daunting to enforce your own patent. Most independent inventors do not have the resources to fund such a lawsuit. If, however, you have taken all the necessary steps to document your invention (inventor's journal, Disclosure Document, use of nondisclosure agreements, etc.) and the potential rewards are significant enough, you may be able to find an attorney who will take your case on a contingency basis.

Internet Searching

The easiest and most convenient place for many independent inventors to search is online from the convenience of their home or office. The USPTO has an online database (the link for the patent office is listed in Appendix B at the back of this book) that lists the full texts of all patents issued since 1976, as well as all U.S. published patent applications since March 15, 2001. Patents from 1790 through 1975 are searchable only by patent number or current U.S. classification. There are also databases of foreign patents and foreign published patent applications available from vendors, such as Delphion, for a fee. In addition, searching of databases of other technical literature is also useful and possibly important, depending on the invention. These services, however, are not free. A thorough search may also include searches of one or more of these databases.

There are four basic ways to do an online patent search. To do a thorough search, you should do all of them. At a very minimum, you should do the key word search, classification search, and the prior art search or reference cited search.

Key Word Search

First, search the database for issued patents and published pending U.S. patent applications. To do a key word search, you must think of terms that would undoubtedly be listed in any patent describing your invention. For example, if it is a baseball cap with a battery-operated fan mounted on the bill of the cap you might choose words like *hat* and *fan*. You could also use words like *cap, head covering, headgear, headwear, battery-operated,* and *cool* or *cooling*. When you are doing a key word search it is important to think of every possible key word that might be used in describing your invention. If you need to, get out the dictionary or thesaurus and look up synonyms. Keep in mind that a term may consist of more than one word. You are allowed to enter two terms at a time for each search. For example, Term 1 in the search might be *battery-operated*. It could be hyphenated, or not. Term 2 could be *head-covering*. A key word search is tedious but essential. If you find your exact invention during this search you need go no further.

If you find inventions that are similar to yours but not your exact invention, you should print them out in their entirety, including the images. When printing the images, you must click on the little printer icon at the top of the patent image page, not on your toolbar at the top of the computer screen. If you have difficulty accessing the patent images, it may be because you do not have a required program. InterneTIFF will solve the problem. You can locate the free download for it from any search engine by simply typing in "InterneTIFF". There are links that sell this program, but the free download works just fine. Any patents that are at all similar to your invention should be set aside and taken to your patent attorney when that phase of the inventing process begins.

As you go through the key word search, make a list of all the patent numbers that are listed among the "References Cited" on any patents that are similar to your idea. Make a list also of the classification numbers listed on those patents. All of those patents and classifications must be searched before determining that your idea is available to pursue.

The USPTO always has staff on duty available to help you and to answer your questions. They can be reached twenty-four hours a day, seven days a week so you can always call on them for help. For twenty-four-hour technical and general support, call them at (800) 786-9199 or (703) 308-4357.

Prior Art Search

After completing the key word search you should do the prior art search. Using the patent numbers listed on the most similar patents as prior art, pull them up one by one. Look at them carefully. Again, if any are particularly close to your invention, print them out in their entirety and set them aside to take to your patent attorney for a legal opinion. It's important to note that you as the patent-seeker have an obligation to bring any references that are similar to your invention to the attention of your patent attorney, who is required by law to cite these references to the USPTO. If this is not done, the patent, even if it issues, could later be deemed invalid due to inequitable conduct.

FACT

There is no definite stopping point in a patent search and as a result you may never feel finished. But when you keep coming across the same patents repeatedly and you are not encountering patents you have not previously seen, you have probably searched as thoroughly as you can.

Pay particular attention to the classifications and patents listed under "References Cited" on those patents. If this seems like you are going around in circles, you are! Patent searching is time-consuming and tedious but it must be done before proceeding with developing your invention.

Classification Number Search

The third and possibly most important search you should do is the classification search. In the key word search and the prior art search you will undoubtedly keep seeing the same classification numbers appear repeatedly. Choose the classification numbers most often listed on the patents closest to your idea and perform a search using them. It is very common to find patents that are close to or identical to your invention when doing a classification search that were completely missed when doing the key word or prior art search. That is why a classification search is essential when doing an online patent search.

Hybrid Search

The fourth type of search is a hybrid search. This is a search using both a key word and the closest classification number to your invention. This type of search will bring up fewer patents for you to wade through.

Once you have completed the search for issued patents it is time to start all over, this time searching patent applications. The patent applications list is not a complete list of all patents that have been applied for but not yet grant-ed. Not included in the USPTO database of published patent applications are those patent applications that have not yet been published (applications to be published are published at about eighteen months from the filing date) and those patent applications that will not be published until the patent is granted. Also not included are Patent Cooperation Treaty (PCT) applications that have designated the United States. These applications are also published at eighteen months from the filing date (see Chapter 11 for more on PCT applications).

The Published Applications database is much smaller than the Issued Patents database since it lists patents that have been applied for but not yet granted, and because it goes back only to 2001. Also, the Published Applications database is incomplete. An inventor applying for only a U.S. patent may specifically request that his application not be pub-lished until the patent is granted.

The United States Patent and Trademark Library

For those who live near the Washington, D.C., area or are willing to travel there, the USPTO provides a public search facility in Alexandria, Virginia. It is open to the public Monday through Friday, 8 A.M. to 8 P.M. (closed weekends and federal holidays). There, the inventor will find state-of-the-art computer workstations as well as trained personnel who can assist and direct her in her search, at no charge. In addition, a history of all patents issued by the USPTO since its inception in 1790 can be searched using the computer data-bases, microfilm, optical disc format, the Official Gazettes, Annual Indexes (of Inventors), and the Manual of Classification and its subject matter index.

The inventor can also access records of patent assignment and transac-tions that affect the ownership of patents such as microfilmed deeds and indexes. In all, you can perform a more thorough search at the public search facility than at any other location. Moreover, sitting in the room where many great inventors have sat and searched before you is a great thrill!

FACT

At the USPTO public search facility, you can also look at patent file wrappers. File wrappers include the original application, actions by the examiner, amendments made by the patent attorney, and any supporting affidavits and arguments by the applicant or his representative. It also includes correspondence between the applicant (or his representative) and the examiner.

The Patent and Trademark Depository Libraries (PTDLs)

Throughout the United States there are eighty-four PTDLs. According to the USPTO, PTDLs are libraries designated by the USPTO to receive copies of patents, CD-ROMs containing registered and pending marks, and patent and trademark materials that are available to the public free of charge. The libraries also actively disseminate patent and trademark information and offer Internet access to the USPTO's online collections. You will find a list of all the PTDLs in the United States in Appendix C (page 267).

At the PTDL, the inventor has access to the library personnel who have had special training from the USPTO in patent and trademark searching. They are there to offer free advice and literature on how to conduct a thorough search. It is not necessary for the inventor to divulge his idea to the librarians in order to get their help. The PTDL librarians are able to help the inventor do a search without ever knowing what the invention is. If you feel you must disclose your idea to the PTDL librarian to get her help, have her sign a nondisclosure agreement beforehand in order to prevent your discussion from being considered a public disclosure. Many of the PTDLs have subscribed to a special program called WEST that allows the inventor to access more information than is available to home patent searchers through the USPTO online database.

In addition to being available to the public free of charge during normal library hours, the PTDLs frequently offer classes or seminars that are also free on various aspects of patent and trademark searching and related subjects.

What if You Find Your Invention?

A patent search is one of the few times that you will search and search for something while hoping and praying that you do not find what you are looking for! But if you do not find anything even remotely close to your product, you are doing something wrong. The USPTO database has postings of more than 6,800,000 patents. Those patents are in every category and subcategory imaginable. It is nearly impossible for you to find absolutely nothing that could be considered prior art. If you do not find anything at all, you should revise the key words you are using in your initial search. Perhaps you could be more precise or more descriptive.

During your patent search, you will undoubtedly come across patents that are similar to your invention. You may encounter patents that sound like your invention based on the descriptive words in the title of the patent. Do not jump to conclusions! While the descriptive titles do describe the inventions, they can also be misleading.

One of these might be your exact invention, but they certainly can't all be even though the words used to describe them sound so similar. These are numerous patents granted over a time span of several years. They sound quite similar but they must not be similar or they wouldn't have been granted patent protection. If you come across a description that *sounds* like it could be describing your invention, take a close look. Be certain that it *is* your exact invention before giving up. Since patent terminology is often difficult to understand, it is suggested that you take copies of such patents to a patent professional for advice.

Moving Forward

If you do come across that heart-stopping patent that appears to be your invention, slow down! It may or may not be your invention. You must read the patent specification to know if the patent anticipates your invention. You should also read the claims to see whether your invention infringes the patent. That invention may serve the same purpose as your invention, but is it accomplished in the same way? Do the claims of the found patent cover your method of making your invention? Perhaps they do not, and your method of making the invention is a significant improvement over their way of making it. In this case, you can patent your improved method even if the claims of the found patent cover your method. However, to practice the invention, you'll need to get a license from the owner of the found patent.

Patent claims can be difficult for nonprofessionals to understand. Before abandoning your idea, take the troublesome patent reference to a patent professional (i.e., a patent attorney or patent agent) and have them determine, by examining the claims closely and comparing them to the embodiment of your invention, whether or not it would be wise for you to proceed.

The lesson here is don't jump to conclusions. Be certain that you know where you stand before assuming that you have found your invention and have lost out. Undoubtedly, many fine inventions have been abandoned before they had a chance because their inventor, who was not trained to understand the nuances of patent language, gave up without seeking legal advice. Don't let this happen to you. Be certain you know what all your options are before throwing in the towel. And if this one's a no-go, move on to the next idea.

Chapter 8

Professional Patent Search

You have already done your own online preliminary search, ideally a thorough one. Now you are wondering if it is truly necessary to pay for a professional search. The answer is a resounding "Yes!" The professional search is much more exhaustive than your search could ever be. Professional searchers have many more resources at their disposal, not to mention years and years of patent-search experience. Even the most thorough novice searcher cannot approach their expertise.

What Is a Professional Patent Search?

Professional patent searchers are professionals who are experts at finding any and all relevant prior art. Prior art includes any patent that is in any way pertinent to your possible patent. It may be something quite close to your invention or it may be an invention that has one or more specific parts of the design that are relevant to your patent application. Prior art can also include products that have been marketed or shown in public that were not patented. You can ask your searcher to search for nonpatent prior art as well, using the many nonpatent databases that are now available.

QUESTION?

Does the USPTO require a professional patent search before filing for a patent?
No. If you choose to file without having a professional patent search you may do so. It is not the USPTO's job to stop you or to make sure that you have done your due diligence. They will be happy to accept your filing fees whether or not you've done a thorough search.

Professional patent searchers have very expensive computer software and access to professional Web sites that help them do a thorough job in as short a time as possible. They do not use the USPTO patent database that the rest of us use. Their professional databases and software programs allow them to do key word searches encompassing the entire history of the U.S. patent system all the way back to 1790! The USPTO database will only allow a key word search back to 1976. Patents issued prior to 1976 are only available by patent number or by classification number in the USPTO database.

The professionals' resources also allow them to pull up any foreign patents that would also be considered prior art. Searching for years has given them the experience and vocabulary to do a thorough search. They may be able to find your exact invention in as little as fifteen minutes or they may spend two to three weeks searching. It all depends on the category of the product and its specific design features. On average, they will probably spend three to four hours on a search. You may spend as much as four to five days on the USPTO's Web site and still not find the entire list of relevant prior art.

ALERT!

Say you have an improvement to a bicycle and do a key word search using the terms *bicycle* and *two-wheeler.* It's likely that you won't come up with anything that resembles your invention. However, a professional patent searcher knows to also search using the term *velocipede.* This search could turn up a number of products just like yours that you never found on your own.

A number of professionals are qualified to do patent searches, including patent attorneys and sometimes their staff members, patent agents, and professional patent search firms. Not many intellectual property attorneys or patent agents perform patent searches themselves. Their hourly rates would make it prohibitive for most of them to do patent searches even if they had the interest in doing them, which most of them do not. Many, if not all, patent attorneys and patent agents hire professional search firms to perform patent searches for their clients. Nearly all professional searches are performed by firms that perform this service as their only business.

Many of the professional search firms are located in and around the Washington, D.C., area. This is because until recent years the only way to perform a thorough search was to actually travel to the USPTO's physical site and search in the public search rooms by opening drawers of patents and looking through the actual patents. Now, of course, it is no longer necessary or even possible to do these searches at the patent office by going through the actual paper copies of the patents. Thorough searches can be performed on the Internet with specially designed software.

Choosing a Professional

A professional patent search firm should do your patent search. Twenty years ago, there were probably 100 or more professional search firms. Five years ago, there were probably thirty firms. Ron Brown's firm, Patent Search International, one of the oldest and most trusted firms, has been in business for more than thirty years. He says that there are probably as few as five legitimate search firms in existence now. Notice the word *legitimate*. Anyone with a computer can claim to do professional searches, usually for a ridiculously low price. Most times those people have not had any professional training, and it is unlikely that they have had much experience. For the extremely low prices they charge, you can be pretty sure that they have not purchased the very expensive software programs that the true professionals use. You can also be fairly certain that you will not receive a legal opinion of patentability from a patent attorney when you entrust your great idea to one of these "professional" searchers.

ALERT!

You can find the legitimate patent search firms through trusted sources such as *Inventors' Digest* magazine, the United Inventors Association, or Ask the Inventors!™ Do not confuse the legitimate search firms with the invention promotion companies that advertise on television and radio.

As recently as 2002, most of the legitimate professional patent search firms were located within driving distance of the USPTO offices in Washington, D.C. (actually Arlington, Virginia). This is no longer the case. Until the fall of 2004, most professional searchers made daily trips to the public search rooms at the USPTO, after they had completed their computer searches, where they pulled actual paper copies of patents to examine before issuing their opinions. In the fall of 2004, the USPTO removed all of the paper copies. They are no longer available for viewing. This is a shame, for there was nothing quite like being able to view the actual patents. Professional searchers were so experienced and accustomed to searching it is said that they could walk into the public search room at the USPTO and walk directly to the stacks of relevant patents.

The legitimate search firms provide a legal opinion of patentability. That is, they will have a patent attorney look at your completed search results and give her opinion of the likelihood of your being granted a patent on your invention. This is essential. A patent search without a legal opinion of patentability is worth little to you. The patent searchers can tell you if there is a patent on your idea and they can give you a list of all the patents they find during the course of the search that may be relevant, but they cannot tell you if your idea is something that can be patented. Only a professional patent attorney or patent agent is qualified to do that. Some of the legitimate search firms, such as Patent Search International, will even include a trademark search for no additional charge, if you have selected a product name for your invention at the time of your patent search.

Steer clear of patent search firms that do not provide a legal opinion of patentability. Legitimate patent search firms will have a patent attorney examine the results of your search and render a legal opinion on whether your invention is patentable. They will also provide you with copies of any patents that they consider to be prior art.

The name for your trademark is not the same as a descriptive term for your invention. For example, Coca-Cola is the trademarked name for a soft drink. *Soft drink* is the descriptive term that describes what the product actually is. If your invention is a new type of pancake turner, you may call it the Incredible Flap Jack Flipper as you market it. On your patent application, it would probably be referred to as a pancake turner or cooking utensil. But the Incredible Flap Jack Flipper is the name you would like it to be called when it is offered for sale. The trademark search is for the name your product would be called in the marketplace. The trademark search offered by some search firms is an extra value and you should take advantage of it. Invest the time to come up with a name for your product in order to take advantage of this bonus.

Calculating Search Value

Searches that cost more are not necessarily worth more. In fact, the search you have your attorney arrange for you at a cost of $1,000 to $1,500 or more is, without a doubt, the same search you could have gotten yourself for around $250! Your attorney hires one of the professional search firms to perform the search and tacks on a substantial fee for himself in the process. You can cut out the middleman, your attorney, and save a bundle in the process. When you hire the professional patent search firm yourself, rather than going through a middleman, you can expect the cost of a thorough professional search with a legal opinion of patentability to be in the $225 to $500 range.

Even though searches that cost more are not necessarily worth more, beware of "professionals" offering bargains. With the advent of the Internet, patent search firms began popping up offering searches for as little as $25! These firms usually consist of a guy and his computer and the USPTO database. There are no licensing requirements for patent searchers, so anyone can claim to be a professional patent searcher. We can say unequivocally that any search you pay only $25 or $50 for will *not* be adequate. In fact, it may end up being a *very expensive* search in terms of its eventual cost to you if you file for a patent only to have it rejected when the USPTO examiners find prior art that the patent search firm should have found.

What a Searcher Needs from You

Beyond your name and basic contact information, the patent search firm you hire will need a general account of the evolution of your idea. If you fail to provide the firm with all the relevant information you have, it may result in an inadequate search that is your fault, not theirs. You should cover all points on the following checklist before submitting your idea for the search:

- ✔ Name you've given your invention
- ✔ Description of the invention
- ✔ Drawings of the invention
- ✔ Date of conception of the idea for the invention

✔ Dates the idea was shared with others

✔ Date the first drawings were made of the invention

✔ Whether a working prototype has been made

✔ What problem the invention solves and how the invention solves it

✔ What special molds or tools, if any, are required to make the invention

✔ Whether any previous patent searches have been done on the invention

✔ Patent numbers of any pertinent prior art located in previous searches

Patent search firms do not need to know how terrific you think your product is. They only want to know what it is, its purpose, and how it works. Some beginning inventors have the mistaken idea that they need to sell the search firm on what a great idea they have come up with. They may even believe that the searchers may want to invest or partner with them on their invention. Wrong! Search firms search patents—that's it! They are not in the business of investing in the inventions that come their way.

What if They Find Your Invention?

When you send your invention idea off for a patent search, the last thing you want to hear is that they have found your exact invention—and it is already patented! You don't want to hear that they have found something even close to your invention. But if it happens, does it mean you've reached the end of the road? Not necessarily. Obviously, if it is the exact embodiment of the invention that you have developed, you may not proceed any further on that particular design. To do so would make you an infringer of that patent. However, if it is a different method or way of accomplishing the same goal as your invention, you may have a little wiggle room.

If their claims are narrow (very specific) in the materials and methods used to make the product and your product can be made of different materials or in a different way, you may still be able to adjust your product enough to get around the existing patent. On the other hand, if their claims are broad it may, indeed, be the end of the road as far as this particular invention is concerned. Broad claims may describe the product in such general terms that it could be made in a variety of ways with a variety of materials. Such claims are much more difficult to design around. However, you should not jump to any conclusions regarding claim interpretation. Claims must be interpreted by a patent attorney, who may want to consult the "file history" of the claims to determine their scope more precisely.

If your patent search comes back with copies of several patents listed as relevant prior art and you have any question about what exactly they are describing, your best course of action would be to take your invention idea, as well as all the prior art, to an intellectual property attorney. He can evaluate and advise you on whether or not it is feasible to proceed with the development of your invention.

ESSENTIAL

> If you make changes in the design of your product after the results of your patent search are returned, you must have another search performed on the improved invention before starting the patent application process. Any time significant changes are made in the design of your invention, a new patent search should be performed.

Too many people think that if their idea comes back as not patentable it is all over. They fail to see that they can use the prior art as a tool. Ron Brown of Patent Search International says, "They can look at the patents found and use them to improve the idea to the point where they might have a patentable idea." It can be a new beginning, not an end.

Does a Positive Result Guarantee a Patent?

A positive result on your patent search means that the prior art that was found does not seem particularly relevant to your invention idea and the legal opinion of patentability states that it is likely that you could receive patent protection for your invention. Great news, right? Yes, it is great news, but it is no guarantee that you will receive a patent on your invention. Some novice inventors incorrectly assume that if they get a positive result it will automatically result in a patent. A few even think that the positive result of the patent search is a patent. It is not.

FACT

Patent claims that are too specific may result in overly narrow patent coverage. This is a common mistake made by inventors who write their own patent applications. The result of narrow claims is that the patents are often easy for competitors to circumvent, resulting in a virtually worthless patent.

There are still many variables involved that can potentially derail the eventual issuance of your patent. The quality of your patent application is of paramount importance. Whether you have it written by a professional such as a patent attorney or patent agent or whether you write it yourself, it must be written with precision, attention to detail, and an adequate understanding of patent applications and their requirements and language. If it is not written properly, it can result in your patent being overly narrow in its coverage or even being denied altogether. There is also the possibility that the examiner assigned to your patent application will find prior art that was not located in the patent search. This possibility is unlikely if you have had your search performed by one of the legitimate professional search firms. In fact, some of them will even give you your money back if the USPTO patent examiners turn up any relevant prior art that they missed. The top firms seldom, if ever, have to return a client's money. They are that good!

Finally, there is the possibility that the patent examiner assigned to your application may not understand your invention. If the examiner does not understand your invention and how it differs sufficiently from prior art, it is the job of your patent professional to overcome that. He may accomplish it by rewriting the claims, or he may even discuss it on the telephone with the examiner. In all, a positive result on your patent search is definitely a good thing, but it is by no means a sure thing.

Negative Legal Opinion

Receiving a negative legal opinion on the patentability of your product is disheartening. But is it the death knell for your invention? Not necessarily. It is simply one patent attorney's opinion. If you just cannot let go, you should get a second legal opinion.

The bottom line is that you should not give up until you have exhausted all possibilities. One negative legal opinion is just that; it is *one* opinion. Most likely, if you were ill and were unsatisfied with one doctor's diagnosis, you would seek a second opinion. This situation is no different. If you have faith in your idea, get a second and even third opinion before giving up for good.

A team of Texas inventors was told by three patent attorneys that their invention was not patentable because the attorneys simply did not understand the specifics of the improvements that made the product patentable. These inventors went on to find an attorney who understood what made their product patentable and they eventually received not one, but *three* strong patents! They have since licensed the product and made a great deal of money.

Chapter 9

Your Prototype

Developing your prototype will help you achieve a number of important things. In addition to allowing you to express your creativity, it will prove that your idea is viable. You will need to know right away if it will work as you believe it will. Creating your prototype will also allow you to determine improvements that you can make on your original concept.

What Is a Prototype?

Simply put, a prototype is a working model of your invention. It is as simple or as complex as your invention idea. If you are wondering whether you must have a prototype in order to file for a patent, the answer is no. The majority of patents are issued on applications filed without the patent examiner ever seeing the actual invention. They make their rulings based on the application and the patent drawings only.

ALERT!

The USPTO does not require, or even encourage, you to send a prototype with your patent application. On rare occasions, if the examiner refuses to believe that the invention will work as the application states that it will, it is helpful to send a working model to prove your point.

If you will be licensing your invention for royalties, you will need a prototype to show to your potential licensees. Manufacturers who are considering adding a new product to their existing line of products will want to pick up the prototype, turn it over, open it, close it, and just generally see how it works. While they can see what it would look like from a drawing or a computer graphic, potential licensees want to handle the product and visualize how they might make it and how it would fit into their line. Of course, there are exceptions, such as items that are very large or very complex, but even in those cases they will likely want to see the actual item to verify that it does work as intended before committing to a license agreement.

ESSENTIAL

If you plan to build a business around your invention and manufacture it yourself or have it manufactured, you will need a prototype as a starting point. You will probably go through several prototypes before you arrive at the final model that is ready for commercialization. It is essential that you settle on your final model before investing in the equipment, tools, or molds that will be necessary to mass-produce your invention.

Additionally, prototyping is important because it is during the creation of the item that you will discover changes and improvements that will make it better. This is very important because you will need to make it the best that it can be and find all of the ways you can improve on your original idea. If you do not, you can be sure that someone else will come up with those improvements and make your invention obsolete. Remember, if your product is highly marketable, once your patent issues—if not before—any competing manufacturer may look at exactly how your product is made by examining your published patent. At that point, if they can, they will think of ways to improve your product and get around your patent. Or they could surround your patent with numerous improvement patents. Improvement patents are those that improve on an already patented invention. If the improvement is unique and useful, the patent will be allowed.

Look at each prototype with a critical eye.

- Does it work the way I envisioned it would?
- What can I do to make it work more efficiently?
- What can I do to make it easier for the consumer to understand how it works?
- What can I do to make it more attractive?
- What can I do to make it easier to package?
- Is there something I can do to make this product useful for additional purposes and thereby increase its potential market?
- Is there another material it could be made of that would reduce manufacturing costs?

Project your thoughts into the future regarding what might be included in future embodiments. Include it now, at least in the patent application!

Sometimes, even with very simple ideas, once prototyping begins you will discover reasons why it will not even work the way you first envisioned it. Many novice inventors will say, "I don't need a prototype; I know it will work." Famous last words! On the other hand, you may discover that it can cost less to manufacture or be made more attractive by the use of other materials. Prototyping is very much a learning process and you will become intimately acquainted with your product by becoming involved in its physical creation.

While inventing the incandescent light bulb, Thomas Edison tried over 6,000 materials to use as the filament before finding the one that did work. He did not give up; you shouldn't either! If you are unable to make your first idea work, keep on trying. And if you have to abandon an idea, move on to the next great one.

Developing a Prototype

A prototype has three basic functions: It embodies what an idea is, shows how the idea works, and proves that the idea does work. Your prototype does not have to look shelf-ready (ready to be displayed on a store shelf). You do not even have to make it from the materials that you envision would be used in the finished product. All you have to do is prove that the idea works.

If your invention will have moving parts, your prototype should also have moving parts. It can be crude in appearance, but it should be capable of doing what it is intended to do. A prototype, by definition, is a working model, so your prototype needs to work.

An independent inventor should *not* go to the substantial expense of having a plastic injection mold made in order to create a prototype. Injection molds are used for mass-producing a product at the manufacturing level. It is costly and risky for the independent inventor to allot such a significant portion of his capital investment to the development of a plastic injection mold. Inventors who have done this are often chagrined to learn that their investment was for naught since the manufacturers will probably have their own plastic injection mold made to their specifications before starting production. Manufacturers understand that if they license a product that requires a plastic injection mold, the expense of making it is their responsibility.

Can You Make Your Own Prototype?

You definitely can and should make your own prototype if it is at all within your ability to do so. You can probably build most of your prototypes on a limited budget. Even if you expect to make the final product from an injection-molded plastic, you can often make a working prototype from some other material that you can find at your local hardware store, grocery store, craft store, or even around your house. This is when you really want to think outside the box. At the very least, your first prototype, when you are proving to yourself that you have a viable idea, should be something in which you have invested as little as possible.

A few years ago, a couple of product developers came up with some ideas for improvements in plastic portfolios, the type used for school report covers, among other things. They bought plastic portfolios and cut them apart. When they tried to attach sections of the portfolios back together, they discovered that no adhesive would bond the plastic. Finally, when they could not attach the parts in any other way, they sewed them together on their sewing machines! When they went in for their licensing appointment, they felt the need to explain their dilemma as the reason for the stitching. They felt embarrassed to show such homemade-looking prototypes to a major manufacturer of office and school supplies. As they began to explain that they knew that the manufacturers would not be sewing the products together, one of the vice-presidents interrupted them to say, "No need to explain; that's how we do it in our prototyping room!"

FACT

It is not necessary to have professionally made prototypes for licensing appointments. Manufacturers know that independent inventors do not have the ability to make shelf-ready prototypes. They only need to see what the product idea is, how it works, and how it fits into their product line.

Rapid Prototyping and Molding

Injection-molds are extremely expensive, sometimes costing hundreds of thousands of dollars to create. This has been a huge obstacle for the independent inventor because it was only practical to create such a mold for a product that would be in production, not for a single prototype. Wonderful new prototyping methods arrived with the advances in the use of computers that result in beautiful prototypes that look exactly like injection-molded items.

Rapid prototyping and layered manufacturing are just two of several names for a group of computer technologies that are used to fabricate prototypes directly from CAD data sources. The process is sometimes also called desktop manufacturing because, through the use of 3-D stereolithography, plastic material is layered on and bonded to form any type of object. These technologies are also used for a number of purposes other than independent inventor prototyping. They are beginning to be widely used in the medical field to assist surgeons with preoperative planning and by researchers in several medical disciplines.

Some of these technologies are called additive and others are subtractive. The type we refer to here, the type most used for prototypes, is additive, where the layers are built up in areas to create the shapes needed. Different materials can be combined if necessary to create the desired finished product. The prototypes developed by these methods are not durable enough to be used as the eventual product would be used, but they are certainly durable enough to show what the product would look like. Although the methods vary in some respects, they are very similar and they all produce beautiful prototypes for very reasonable prices. The prices may vary in different parts of the country, but the cost can be as low as $14.00 per cubic inch of material used in the object.

This technology has mushroomed within a short period of time. A few years ago it was a technology that was usually associated with universities, and that was where inventors were referred to find this service. Within the past three years, prototype designers have acquired the computers and the training so that it is now very easy to find someone in any area of the country who can do this type of work. You can find them through search engines on the Internet by typing *rapid prototyping* or you can find them in your telephone directory under *Prototypes*.

Another choice for the inventor who wants a good-looking plastic prototype but would like to create it himself is the method developed by Randall Landreneau, an inventor in Tampa, Florida. After watching his video, you will be able to create professional prototypes with very basic tools and materials that are inexpensive and widely available. You can find information on this method on his Web site, *www.reproduce100s.com*.

Professional Prototype Designers

Who can you consult for help turning your idea into a product? Thanks to the growing number of independent inventors and the increased demand for assistance with building prototypes, professional prototype designers are now relatively easy to locate. These are people, artists at their trade, who can work with you to develop your idea into a working prototype. Your invention may be something that you need welded or otherwise created from metal parts. It may be made of wood, rubber, fabrics, or flexible plastics. A good general prototype designer has equipment and training in all types of materials and many of them also do rapid prototyping. Most of them are trained and talented in a number of areas.

Many inventors are so excited about their product that they believe the prototype professional will jump at the opportunity to trade their services for a share of any eventual profits. However, such participation is the exception, rather than the rule. Do not count on making your prototype designer a partner in your project.

ALERT!

Be sure to get a signed contractor's nondisclosure agreement before sharing your idea with anyone who is going to help you with your invention. This special agreement requires her to acknowledge that it is your invention and that the intellectual property related to any improvements she adds will belong to you.

What do you do if your idea is for something that is somewhat complicated, perhaps with mechanical or electrical parts? Matthew Smithers, a well-known prototype designer in the Dallas, Texas, area, says that the inventor should think in terms of what other already existing object has similar workings. He suggests buying an inexpensive item with similar parts in order to have the parts that you need for your prototype. Why reinvent the wheel if you can get what you need from another item? If you can do that yourself, you will save some money, too. If you need a prototype designer to build it for you, check with him to see if you can bring the item that you believe could contribute the needed parts.

Other Sources for Prototyping

Prototype designers may not be doing business under that title, but anyone who is proficient in the area that you seek is a possible prototype designer for your purposes. Listed below are some of the professions that you may call upon for assistance with creating a new product.

- Sheet metal shop
- Tailor
- Carpenter
- Ceramics shop
- University students
- Computer programmers
- Craftsmen in the area specific to your invention (jewelry, chemical, plumbing, electrical, etc.)

There is always the issue of trust when sharing your idea with a stranger. And, you are right to be concerned, especially when that person will be taking an active role in the actual development of your invention. It is wise to be cautious in your choice of assistance, particularly if the person you select is not a prototype designer by trade. The reason for this is that prototype designers are accustomed to working with inventors and confidentiality is a part of their business. Workers in other fields may have had no previous experience in working with inventors.

This is where a nondisclosure agreement comes in. What is a contractor's nondisclosure agreement and how does it differ from an ordinary nondisclosure agreement? A nondisclosure agreement that you would use when sharing your idea with anyone other than the person assisting with your prototype covers two areas for the inventor. The first thing most people think of is the fact that it puts the recipient of the information on notice that the idea belongs to you. He is acknowledging that you shared the information with him. This is obviously a deterrent against his stealing the idea. The other important function of the nondisclosure agreement is that it protects the inventor from having made a public disclosure of the idea. Remember, once you have made a public disclosure, you can lose your foreign patent rights, and you can lose your trade secret protection.

ALERT!

The problem with sharing your idea with someone is not so much the likelihood that she would steal the idea. It is more likely that she would not handle the product with the privacy that you require. When dealing with workers who can help you but who are not professional prototype designers, go over the contractor's nondisclosure form with them and have them sign it before disclosing any information.

The contractor's nondisclosure agreement functions in the same way that the regular nondisclosure agreement does, but it goes further to cover the relationship between you and the person who is assisting you. This document also states that the worker acknowledges that the invention belongs to you and any changes or improvements that he makes also belong to you. He acknowledges that he is simply working for hire. In other words, he will not be the co-inventor of the item. In the alternative, if the worker is deemed to have contributed to the invention as a co-inventor, then he must agree to assign any and all of his rights to you. Deeply regretful is the inventor who fails to use the contractor's nondisclosure agreement only to find that the contractor is now considered, by a court of law, to be a co-inventor of the product, without any obligation to assign his rights to you, and thereby permitted to commercialize the invention without needing a license.

ESSENTIAL

When choosing a prototype designer to assist you in the development and refinement of your product, it is important to select him carefully. You should interview him as to the types of products he has developed in the past. As in any profession, prototype designers tend to specialize in certain areas. If he has primarily worked with metals and your invention is to be made of molded plastic, you probably need to keep looking.

Most prototype designers already have such forms available that they are happy to sign. To be certain that you have the type of nondisclosure agreement that includes the exact wording you require, we suggest that you take your own contractor's nondisclosure agreement with you. Obviously, people who work in other disciplines and who are assisting you with a prototype are not likely to have these forms or even to be familiar with them. So be prepared with the forms when you approach anyone for help with your prototype. Most people have no problem with signing such forms, but if you do encounter resistance, take your invention and find someone more cooperative.

Chapter 10

Invention Marketability Evaluation

Invention marketability evaluation is an important, but optional, step in the inventing process that the wise inventor will utilize. Independent inventors are already at a commercial disadvantage when compared to large corporations that have plenty of resources. A complete and competent invention marketability evaluation can help level the playing field by giving independent inventors the same market evaluation information that large companies have access to in-house.

What a Marketability Evaluation Tells You

An invention marketability evaluation of your product is a thorough analysis of its chances of success in the marketplace. An invention marketability evaluation is not your opinion of how good your idea is. It is not what friends, family, or colleagues have to say about your idea. It most definitely is not what one of the invention promotion companies you see on television or in print ads has to say about your idea. It is what one of the professional legitimate invention marketability evaluation services has to say about your product after doing an extensive assessment of its market viability. They will primarily assess the technical feasibility of your invention. Is it really possible to create this invention using current technology? A technical consultant can make a determination on whether or not the item will perform as intended. It may also include a preliminary search of existing patents that could interfere with your ability to proceed with your invention.

The preliminary patent search that is part of the product assessment provided by the more thorough marketability evaluation services will list any patents they found that appear to be close to your invention. This is valuable information that will be extremely helpful if you have not already had a professional patent search prior to the marketability evaluation. It will help the professional searcher to do a more thorough search in the shortest amount of time. In a race to market, time is money! The size of the market for your invention will probably be determined as well as how competitive the market will be for your invention.

The marketability evaluation services will provide you with their signed nondisclosure agreement and they will protect your idea by having anyone to whom they divulge the idea, in order to get an expert opinion, sign a nondisclosure agreement. Submitting your idea for evaluation in this way is not a public disclosure of the invention.

Will there be competing products that will make it difficult for you to get a foothold in the market? Is your product unique enough to overcome competing products that are currently used to address the problem your invention solves? How aggressive will your competitors be in protecting their turf from new competition? As part of the determination of how competitive your product will be in the marketplace, the marketability evaluation team will compare the manufacturing cost and retail selling price of your product with the manufacturing cost and retail selling price of competitive products. They do this in order to assess whether your product will be priced competitively enough to break into the market. You can have a terrific product, but if the manufacturing cost is significantly higher than that of your competition, it will be nearly impossible to attract a manufacturer for licensing or the end consumers for purchasing at the retail level.

The more extensive marketability evaluation reports will include a description of the distribution channels of competing products as well as market sectors or distribution channels for your product that you may not have thought of.

A professional marketability evaluation assesses the marketability of your idea using the following methods:

- It takes into account the trends in the particular sector of the market your product will enter. This is done using trade association reports, published market studies, and other sources as needed.
- It determines how difficult or easy it will be to get distribution for your product.
- It reports new laws or regulations that could affect the size of the potential market for your product.
- It considers the size of the potential market for your product and whether that market is growing or shrinking. It may also describe who the typical user of your product will be.
- It may give you a report on customer satisfaction with your product by surveying potential purchasers with questions that do not reveal what the product is, but rather the problem that it solves. Potential purchasers respond as to whether or not they would buy such a product.
- It may make an assessment of how needed your product is based on research that indicates the size of the potential consumer market for a product of that type, whether your product can be competitively priced, and an evaluation of competing products that address the same need.

QUESTION?

What types of products should you submit for marketability evaluation?
All products—whether household items, sporting goods, automotive accessories, biotechnological breakthroughs, software programs, or hair and fashion accessories—should be evaluated by a professional marketability evaluation service. There is really no category of product that should *not* be evaluated.

When you get one of the more thorough professional marketability evaluations, it may even include information on possible licensees for your product. During preparation of the report, major manufacturers who may eventually be target licensees are contacted to assess their interest in a product that would solve such-and-such a problem. (The evaluation service will not divulge the specifics of your invention unless the manufacturer signs a nondisclosure agreement beforehand.) The service will get the manufacturers' assessments of your product. For example, one might say that she would be interested in your product if it were a different size; another might ask whether the manufacturing cost could be reduced or if the retail selling price would be feasible within a specific range. The reports usually include all the pertinent information on whom to contact within each company. This alone could make it easier to find a licensee, since you will have a preliminary idea of how receptive specific companies are to your invention. Finally, a thorough marketability evaluation can even give the inventor direction by suggesting the next steps he should take in order to move forward with his product.

FACT

Professional marketability evaluation services do not require that the items they evaluate be patented prior to their evaluation. Inventors may submit inventions for evaluation at any point in the process, from a picture drawn on a napkin to a granted patent. Even so, you might save yourself some money if you do your own preliminary market and patent searches before submitting.

Benefits of a Marketability Evaluation

Professional marketability evaluations will give you vital information that will help you, the independent inventor, to determine which of your many inventive ideas to pursue. Independent inventors are idea factories. In most cases, they have more ideas than they have the financial resources or time to pursue. Professional marketability evaluations give them the information on which to base informed decisions. They can help the independent inventor focus on the ideas that are most likely to generate income and avoid spending time, energy, and limited resources on products that have little chance of success.

In addition, positive marketability evaluations from reputable services can be very useful when seeking financial backing for your invention. Investors or bankers are much more likely to grant your request for funding if your invention has been evaluated by a reputable service and they have assessed the product as having a likelihood of success in the marketplace.

The following are *not* required in order to submit your idea/product for marketability evaluation:

- A preliminary patent search
- A professional patent search
- A working prototype
- Professional drawings
- A pending patent
- A granted patent

According to the Wisconsin Innovation Service Center, considered one of the best marketability evaluation services in the country, the average cost of introducing a new product has quadrupled over the last ten years. That fact, in combination with the fact that the majority of new product ideas are not successful in spite of the money and effort invested in them, makes it crucial that independent inventors use all the resources at their disposal to ensure that their idea has a good chance of success before investing time and money on any particular idea. Investing in a professional marketability evaluation is like hiring an entire team of consultants to help you to make informed product and market development decisions.

A marketability evaluation service will not make the determination as to whether or not you should proceed with your idea. It will provide you with the information that you, the inventor, can use to make an informed decision. Some services will give you a viability ranking on a sliding scale of one to ten, with ten being a positive recommendation that you move forward with taking your invention to market and one recommending that you reassess your commitment to this particular project. Other services may provide you with a written report assessing the strengths and weaknesses of your product and its chances of success in the marketplace.

Where Can You Get a Marketability Evaluation?

You can get a legitimate marketability evaluation from many different sources in the United States. Many universities have marketability evaluation services as a part of their business and entrepreneurial programs. The university marketability evaluation services are often among the most thorough, complete, and detailed marketability evaluations available.

There are other legitimate sources of marketability evaluations. Many of them are associated with SBDCs, individual companies, licensing agents, or inventor help groups. Consider the following list:

- **Small Business Development Centers:** These are most often affiliated with community colleges. Check with a community college near you to see if they offer marketability evaluations in cooperation with the SBDC.
- **Individual companies:** Individual companies such as Wal-Mart also offer evaluation services. The Wal-Mart Innovation Network (WIN) offers two different evaluation services from its Innovation Institute. The first is the Product Assessment Service (PAS) and the second is the Preliminary Innovation Evaluation System (PIES).
- **Legitimate invention services:** Legitimate invention services such as Patent Café and the United Inventors Association of the U.S. also offer marketability evaluation services to independent inventors. Patent Café offers an Internet evaluation service where the inventor inputs pertinent

information to get a report. The United Inventors Association (UIAUSA) offers the Innovation Assessment Program based on the PIES system.

- **Licensing agents:** Licensing agents or companies also offer marketability evaluations. They perform legitimate marketability evaluations, but these may be less extensive than the evaluations performed by either university or not-for-profit groups. These independent companies assess the invention based on their industry contacts and their ability to secure a license agreement for the product.
- **Canadian Innovation Centre:** Canadian inventors may choose to have the Canadian Innovation Centre, a not-for-profit company associated with the University of Waterloo, perform their marketability evaluation.
- **Scam companies:** Do *not* go to a company that advertises on television or radio or in print ads for your marketability evaluation. Generally, those companies offer worthless marketability evaluations. After all, they want you to sign up for their patenting and marketing services and you would not do so if you received a negative evaluation.

FACT

You can call the business or entrepreneurial departments of universities near you to find out whether they offer professional marketability evaluation services to independent inventors. If they do not offer these evaluations for a fee, check with the dean of the business college to see if marketing classes perform market searches as class projects.

Cost and Duration of Marketability Evaluations

The cost of professional marketability evaluations varies depending upon the time spent and the resources accessed as well as the number of people involved in doing the necessary research. Obviously, the more thorough the evaluation is, the more time, research, resources, and experts will be involved in performing it—and the more the marketability evaluation is likely to cost. That is not to say that less expensive professional marketability evaluations are not also very useful and appropriate. The less expensive evaluations provide less information but, depending upon the product, this may be all the information necessary for the inventor to make a decision about whether he should proceed. The most thorough marketability evaluations generally cost well under $1,000 but it is possible to get a competent professional evaluation for far less. The cost of the marketability evaluation includes all the experts and sources they contact regarding your invention. There are no extra fees above and beyond the standard cost of the evaluation. Check the Web sites for these services or phone them to get pricing.

University Evaluations

The cost of the university evaluation varies according to the depth of the investigation, the research involved, and the network of contacts utilized. University evaluation programs often have state or federal funding that helps to keep the cost down for a first-rate marketability evaluation.

Each university determines the extensiveness of its marketability evaluations as well as its cost. Baylor University in Waco, Texas, offers an evaluation service through its John F. Baugh Center for Entrepreneurship that evaluates each invention based on thirty-three different criteria. This is one of the less costly marketability evaluations.

For-Profit Evaluations

The cost of for-profit *limited* marketability evaluations performed by individual companies such as the one offered by Wal-Mart are to determine if your product is appropriate for their stores. Those offered by for-profit *invention-marketing companies* such as Harvey Reese & Associates or Lambert & Lambert are often considerably lower than the services of some university services. These evaluations are simply meant to determine whether they would be interested in marketing your product for licensing. Be aware, however, that if the invention-marketing companies go on to obtain a license agreement for you, they will take a share of your royalty as part of their payment for their services. These for-profit evaluations are different in scope from the more expensive marketability evaluations. Check with the evaluation services to compare what is offered and costs for each.

Invention Services Evaluations

The costs for the Internet evaluation program offered by Patent Café and the PIES evaluation offered by the United Inventors Association of the U.S. are at the lower end of the pricing scale. This in no way reflects on the value of the services. What it does reflect is the exact features of the evaluation and the methods used. They evaluate your invention based on a pre-set formula and set of questions. They do not consult experts or do extensive research. It is basically a test your product is given with a resulting score. It is a more subjective evaluation than the ones based on research and expert consultants' opinions.

It usually takes between four and eight weeks to obtain the results of your marketability evaluation. If your invention is in a very technical or unusual area, the marketability evaluation may take a little longer than normal in order for the inventor service to locate the appropriate experts or technical advisors.

Marketing Class Evaluations

If you are operating on a really tight budget, you may be able to get a competent and thorough evaluation performed by a local university or college. The marketing departments often will take on evaluating a product as a class assignment. The students will do the work under the supervision and guidance of their professor. The advantage to taking this route is that it will be absolutely free to you. The disadvantage is that it will probably be a semester assignment and you may have to wait until the end of the semester to get your results.

To have an evaluation done this way, you will need to contact the head of the marketing department of the college or university, then sit down with her and pitch your case as to why your product would be a good one for her class to study. Many independent inventors have taken this route and been delighted with the results. If you can afford the time, you should consider this alternative to the more costly marketability evaluations.

In the Event of a Positive Marketability Evaluation

When you receive a positive marketability evaluation for your product, it is time to move forward, and quickly! Time is of the essence. It is safe to assume that other people are working on ideas or inventions similar, if not identical, to yours. As a result, you must take all the necessary steps to claim the idea as yours and get patent protection in place. Your next step depends on where you were in the inventing process when you submitted your idea for marketability evaluation.

If you were just at the idea stage, then you should begin by making sure that your inventor's journal has been witnessed and signed.

If you have not done so, it is time to submit your idea for a professional patent search. If you already have either a pending patent or an actual granted patent, it is time to move to the marketing phase of inventing.

Some marketability evaluation services, such as the University of Wisconsin Innovation Service Center, provide additional services to inventors who have had them perform the initial marketability evaluation for an additional fee. For example, WISC offers licensing partner searches, potential and current distributor surveys, competitive intelligence insights, and customer satisfaction assessments. If you are shy or timid about moving to the marketing phase of your invention, these services may be exactly the kind of help you need to continue moving your product to market.

FACT

Legitimate professional marketability evaluation services will not market your invention for you. They will direct you to legitimate sources of marketing help but they will not usually collaborate with you or do it for you. Their services are limited to new marketability evaluations and they do not get involved in anything that could be considered a conflict of interest.

In the Event of a Discouraging Marketability Evaluation

If you get a discouraging marketability evaluation on your invention idea, you may follow one of three courses of action. You can move on to your next idea, get a second opinion, or proceed anyway.

Move On to Your Next Idea

You may accept that this is not the best idea to pursue and move on to developing your next great idea. Remember, a poor marketability evaluation is not a rejection of you; it is only an assessment of that idea. This is why you paid for the marketability evaluation in the first place: to find out things you did not already know about the market for the idea. All inventors have ideas from time to time that may be good but are not feasible for some reason.

Get a Second Opinion

If you still have faith in your idea in spite of the negative marketability evaluation, you may choose to get a second opinion by sending your idea to another legitimate professional marketability evaluation service. It is not common, but occasionally an inventor may get a negative marketability evaluation from one service and a positive one from another. Keep in mind that the marketability evaluation services are staffed by people with subjective opinions.

Proceed Anyway

Finally, it is your idea and your invention; you can choose to proceed in spite of the poor review. If you choose this course of action, do so at your own peril.

Most marketability evaluation reports are not an absolute negative or an absolute positive. They generally fall somewhere in between the two extremes. You may receive a somewhat positive review, in which case the service may recommend that you do additional research or make modifications in your design before proceeding. At that point, you must decide whether you will follow their suggestions or stick with your original plan. You have paid for their expert opinions; we recommend that you heed their advice in order to maximize your chances of success. If, on the other hand, you receive a generally negative opinion, you must determine whether it is possible to make the changes necessary to make your product viable in the marketplace.

Chapter 11

Patenting Your Invention

When you first have a great idea you want to pursue, your first thought should be to patent it. A patent is the best way to protect your idea and move forward with it at the same time. Many novice inventors know the terms *patent pending* and *patented* but do not understand exactly what they will have once they get a patent, or even how to start the process. This chapter explains how and why you should get a patent.

An Overview of the Process

A patent is your own little government-sanctioned monopoly for a set number of years. During the term of your patent, the government grants you the exclusive right to manufacture, distribute, and sell your product. Anyone else who makes or sells your product without your permission can be sued for patent infringement. Using your patent, you have the potential to stop anyone else from making, selling, or using a product that is described by the claims in your patent.

Before you file for a patent, it is important to understand a little about the process. It is possible that someone has had your idea, patented it, and not done anything with it. It is also possible that someone may have already filed for a patent on your invention but it is still in the patent pending phase, and so it has not yet issued. If it has already issued, or if it has been published as a patent application at eighteen months, you can find out about it by searching an online patent database, such as the free one at *www.uspto.gov*. If a patent application has been published that closely or exactly describes your invention (verify this with a patent attorney), you must decide whether you want to proceed with your own patent application. It's also possible that a patent application is pending, but not published, on exactly what you've invented, but you will not be able to know until the pending patent issues.

Patent pending applications are published after eighteen months unless the inventor or her attorney has specifically indicated that she does not wish to have it made public (this option is available only if she does not intend to apply for foreign patent rights). For the first eighteen months after a patent has been applied for, the patent pending applications are not made public so there is no way to find out if one is already in the system.

FACT

The exclusive rights to your patent begin on the day the patent issues and end on the day it expires. Many inventors mistakenly believe that their patent protection begins when they file for a patent and receive patent pending status. Until the patent issues, your product remains in the public domain and anyone may legally make, distribute, and sell it.

If your invention idea, enthusiasm, potential profit margin, and likely market are great enough, you may decide that you want to try for a patent. Only you can make that judgment call.

Are All Patents Equal?

A patent is a patent is a patent, right? Wrong! All patents are not equal. There are strong and/or broad patents, but there are also weak and/or narrow patents. Which type you get, if you are able to get one, depends on how skillfully your patent application is written and on the prior art that may limit the scope of your patent. The type of patent can also make a difference in its strength: Utility patents are generally considered to be stronger than design patents in discouraging competition.

ESSENTIAL

Anyone, anywhere in the world, can apply for a U.S. patent. You are not required to be a U.S. citizen to file for a U.S. patent. Additionally, there are no age requirements on who may and may not file for patent protection. Children as young as five years old have been listed as co-inventors of patented products.

The coverage area of a patent is also important. When you apply for a U.S. patent, your patent protection extends to all of the United States and U.S. territories. Although you cannot assert your U.S. patent outside of the United States and its territories, you can assert your U.S. patent to stop importation of infringing goods from other countries into the United States and/or its territories.

Foreign patents may be applied for directly in each individual country or an inventor may choose to file a Patent Cooperation Treaty (PCT) application in which he may choose up to seven countries (or groups of countries) to include in his application for foreign patent coverage. Interestingly, the United States can be selected as one of those countries. The European Patent Office (EPO), which can include any of twenty-four member countries, can also be selected. Not all countries are PCT-contracting states;

exceptions include Taiwan, Thailand, and Malaysia. There are five regional filing systems available: one for European countries that are members of the European Patent Convention (EPC), one for the English-speaking African countries that are members of the African Regional Industrial Property Organization (ARIPO); one for the French-speaking African countries that are members of the African Intellectual Property Organization (OAPI); one for the several countries in the Gulf region of the Middle East (GCC); and one covering the several former states of the Soviet Union (Eurasian Patent), which permits a single filing and uniform examination in the Eurasian Patent Office in Moscow.

The cost of filing international patents can quickly become prohibitive for the average inventor. It is better to carefully select the country or countries that would be the most likely lucrative market for your product. An inventor has exactly one year from the filing date on her U.S. patent in which to apply for international patents. If she does not apply within that year, she forfeits all rights to ever file for international patent coverage. Also note well that most foreign countries will not grant patent protection if you have publicly divulged your invention before the filing of your U.S. patent application (or PCT application, if you file that first and include the U.S. as one of the designated countries). So always properly use a nondisclosure agreement whenever you discuss your invention with anyone other than a patent attorney to preserve your foreign patent rights.

Types of Patents

According to the USPTO, there are three basic types of patents:

- Utility patents
- Design patents
- Plant patents

Utility Patents

The USPTO says that a utility patent "may be granted to anyone who invents or discovers any new and useful process, machine, article of manufacture, or composition of matter, or any new and useful improvement thereof."

You may be asking yourself what exactly that means. It means that a utility patent covers the useful features of an invention. In order to receive a utility patent, your invention must have a utilitarian or useful purpose. In simple terms, a utility patent protects how an invention works. The protection granted under a utility patent is based on the function of the item rather than the form or ornamental aspects (i.e., how the item looks). It is often said that *anything* can be patented unless it is a law of nature or a principle of mathematics. There are different classes of claims that can be used to describe the various categories of inventions that can be protected by a utility patent. You can claim:

- An apparatus or machine
- A method or process (including business methods)
- A product that is the result of performing the steps of a method or process
- An article of manufacture
- A composition of matter

Utility patent protection now lasts twenty years from the date on which the application is filed. Utility patents issued prior to June 8, 1995, have a term of seventeen years from the date the patent issued. Filing fees change every few years so it is best to check the USPTO Web site for the current fees. If you are an independent inventor who has fewer than 500 employees, you may qualify to file for your patent with "small entity" status. This will reduce most PTO fees by half.

FACT

The filing date of a patent application is the date that it is actually put in an Express Mail envelope and officially received by the U.S. Postal Service or personally delivered to the U.S. Patent and Trademark Office in Washington, D.C., not the date the Express Mail envelope is received at the patent office. From the moment your application is deposited into a U.S. mailbox or into the hands of a U.S. Postal Service worker, you may legally describe your invention as "patent pending."

Design Patents

Design patents protect only the way an item looks. There is absolutely no protection on how an item works or the process by which it is made. Design patents grant protection based on the form of an object rather than its function. In some cases, design patents can serve the same function as a trademark, or "trade dress"—they protect an appearance that indicates a trusted or popular source of goods. Thus, a design patent can be a valuable form of protection. For example, design patents on the shape of a product container can be valuable, just as a trademarked logo on the container can be valuable. Hypothetically, a very distinct container, such as the shape of a Coca-Cola bottle, would probably have qualified for a design patent if the Coca-Cola Company had chosen to patent it years ago. If they did patent it, then any other bottling company would have infringed their patent if they used the same bottle design while the patent was in effect.

Design patents also are granted on something as simple as a flower painted on a chair back. Patents such as those are severely limited in their value. Unless a particular design or flower is so unique and so special that it would be in demand above all other images of flowers, that design patent would be very easy to circumvent. All that would be required would be to have a different flower or a different image of the same flower. Obviously, a manufacturer would not be interested in licensing a patent that offered so little protection.

The duration of patent protection coverage varies according to the type of patent protection that has been granted. Both utility patents and plant patents offer protection for twenty years from the *filing date*, while design patents offer protection for only fourteen years from the *date of issuance*.

Plant Patents

A third category of patent that is granted by the USPTO is the plant patent. These are patents on living plants. The USPTO defines it in this way: "The law also provides for the granting of a patent to anyone who has invented or discovered and asexually reproduced any distinct and new variety of plant, including cultivated sports, mutants, hybrids, and newly found seedlings, other than a tuber-propagated plant or a plant found in an uncultivated state."

"Asexually propagated plants are those that are reproduced by means other than from seeds, such as by the rooting of cuttings, by layering, budding, grafting, inarching, etc." Obviously, few if any independent inventors apply for patents upon plants they have invented; therefore, plant patents are outside the scope of this book.

Provisional Patent Applications

Provisional patent applications (PPAs) are *not* a type of patent but have been included here because of the confusion surrounding them and because they can sometimes be useful to independent inventors. Many novice inventors, upon learning of PPAs, mistakenly assume that they are applying for and receiving a provisional patent. No such thing as a provisional patent exists. Although it is called a provisional patent application, it will never be looked at by a patent examiner or result in a patent unless you follow up with a regular patent application within one year of the filing date of the provisional.

If you need to obtain patent pending status quickly on an emergency basis—to preserve your foreign rights or to establish an early filing date, for example—you may want to file a PPA instead of filing an application for a regular utility patent. A PPA can be prepared more rapidly than a full regular patent application, because it does not need to include all the usual parts of a patent application, such as the abstract, the background, the claims, and the summary.

FACT

The PPA is very attractive to some inventors because it allows the inventor to have as early a filing date as possible and it allows him to list his product as patent pending. This gives the inventor one year in which to find a company to license his product without going to the expense of filing for a utility patent.

So, why bother to get patent pending status if it will never result in a patent? Because you can legally claim patent pending status very inexpensively for a full year while you find out if there is a market for your invention. If you get it licensed during that year, your licensee will likely take over all the expenses related to applying for and obtaining the utility patent, which will be issued to you! If you find that you can indeed build a business around it, you can apply for a utility patent at that time, as long as you're within the one-year filing deadline. If you find that you cannot market or license the invention, you have greatly limited your losses.

PPAs can be written by you, the independent inventor, without the help of an attorney. Note, however, that a PPA must satisfy the very same disclosure requirements as a regular utility patent application. A well-kept secret about PPAs is that you may include *more than one invention* in a single PPA! If you have multiple inventions in progress at the same time, you may include them all in one PPA for one fee. Unless you plan to file for international patent protection in the future, there is no need to even write a single claim in a PPA. If you do plan on seeking international patent protection, it is recommended that you write one very broad and general claim to be included in your PPA.

Within one year after you file your PPA, you must file for a regular utility patent or lose the advantage of the earlier filing date. You may file a second PPA on the same invention, even sending the exact same application in again, but you would forfeit the earlier filing date of the previous PPA.

ALERT!

Although a PPA is not as formal and complete as a regular utility patent application and is not required to have a claims section like a utility patent application, it is crucially important that it be written with the utmost care. The wording of your provisional application could affect the filing date and the claim scope of your eventual utility patent application.

When filing a PPA it is essential to include every possible embodiment and feature of your invention. Even though you may not be including claims in your PPA, it is still vital that you make it as detailed as possible, even including photos if you wish. There is no limit on the length of your application. If you choose to write your own PPA, you should take advantage of all available help in order to do the best job possible. Stim and Pressman's *Patent Pending in 24 Hours* can give you the exact help you need. It is recommended that you get a copy from your local library or bookstore. You may also want to consult with a patent attorney. PPAs are filed away immediately upon receipt by the patent office and are not even looked at by the examiners, unless the filing date becomes important during the prosecution of the patent application or during patent litigation.

Who May Write, File, and Prosecute Your Patent?

There are three categories of people who may write, file, and prosecute patents before the USPTO. (The process of seeing your patent application all the way through the USPTO review process and rewriting claims or answering questions as necessary is called patent prosecution.)

Of course, a patent attorney or a patent agent can write, file, and prosecute a patent application, but it is also possible for you, the independent inventor, to write, file, and prosecute your own patent application. When an independent inventor writes her own patent application and represents herself during the prosecution of the patent, it is referred to as a *pro se* application.

Patent Attorneys

Patent attorneys, sometimes referred to as intellectual property attorneys, are licensed to practice before the USPTO. They must pass two bar examinations: at least one state bar exam, as all attorneys must, and the patent bar exam. Often they have been professional engineers or scientists, but this is not required. What is required is that they have a combination of technical education and legal academic qualifications that uniquely prepare them for the challenging job of being a patent attorney. They are required to have done extensive study in the sciences and/or engineering, such as in physics, biology, chemistry, electrical engineering, or computer science, in addition to holding a law degree and state legal license. Intellectual property attorneys are trained to advise and represent you in anything relating to intellectual property of any kind, such as patents, trademarks, copyrights, and trade secrets.

Many inventors rush to a patent attorney when they first have their great idea. This is a mistake. You are not ready to see a patent attorney, or patent agent, until you know how you are going to actually make your invention. Thus, an invention consists of both the conception of the idea and its reduction to practice.

ALERT!

If your patent is infringed or its validity challenged, or you find that you are inadvertently infringing someone else's patent, you could find yourself in court, needing representation. In any of these cases, you would need an attorney to represent you. A patent attorney can do this.

When choosing a patent attorney or patent agent, it is important to find the right fit. Just because they are patent professionals does not mean that they have expertise in the field of your invention. It is important to find a patent professional who understands your invention completely. You may have to interview several before you find the right choice for you.

Patent Agents

Patent agents, like patent attorneys, are licensed to practice before the Patent Office. They take the same patent bar exam that the patent attorneys take to practice before the Patent Office, and they are also qualified to write, file, and prosecute patent applications. They are not attorneys, however. They work only with patents and practice only before the U.S. Patent Office. They do not take a state bar examination, and therefore they are not allowed to practice before the Trademark Office. Like patent attorneys, many patent agents have also been professional engineers, though this is not a requirement. They are required to have either a technical bachelor's degree, such as electrical engineering or physics, or a minimum of forty credit hours in engineering and the hard sciences. Since they have not been legally trained, they may tend to pay more attention to the technical issues in preparing a patent application than to some possibly important legal issues.

Since patent agents are not also attorneys, their fees are usually considerably less than those of a patent attorney. The only negative to hiring a patent agent rather than a patent attorney is that since they are not attorneys, they could not represent you in court should the need arise. This is something that is easily overcome. If you should need legal representation you could hire an attorney at that time. In the meantime, you have saved yourself a considerable sum on your patent. It is a personal judgment call.

If you employ a patent attorney or a patent agent to write and file your patent application, he will be working on your behalf. All correspondence regarding your patent application will be sent to him. You, the independent inventor, are not allowed to speak to the patent examiner alone if you have a patent agent or a patent attorney representing you. You can, however, have a conference call with the patent attorney and the patent examiner if that becomes necessary.

Write It Yourself

It is perfectly legal and acceptable for you to write, file, and prosecute your own pro se patent application. Is it wise? Not if you can help it at all. The USPTO is very strict in its guidelines regarding how an application must look and exactly how it is to be submitted. Patent attorneys and patent agents are highly trained in writing patent language. It is not really another language, but at times it might seem to be. Writing patents is a minefield for the untrained. The poor choice of *one word* can make the difference between getting a strong patent with broad coverage that will be difficult for anyone to get around and a weak patent with narrow coverage that is easy to circumvent.

E ALERT!

Possibly the most common mistake made by inventors who are writing their own patents is that they fail to follow the standard patent application forms. When they rearrange items, it makes it more difficult for the examiner to do her work. This could defeat your hopes of establishing a cordial relationship with the person who has the power to grant your patent or to reject it.

If you absolutely cannot find a way to hire a patent attorney or patent agent and you face the choice of doing it yourself or not doing it at all, there are resources you should avail yourself of that will help you do the best job that you can. Consider the following three options:

- **Self-help books:** The book that has become the bible for pro se inventors, those who are writing their own patents, is *Patent It Yourself* by David Pressman. Pressman is a patent attorney and his book, now in its eleventh edition, is the standard by which other patent-writing books are judged. A second book that is also extremely helpful for those who are writing their own PPAs is *Patent Pending in 24 Hours* by attorneys Richard Stim and David Pressman.
- **Write-it-yourself software:** There are at least three software programs designed to help the independent inventor write his own patent application. Two of them, Patent Pro and Patent Ease, are designed to guide you through a regular utility patent application, which includes writing claims. The third, Patent Wizard, was prepared specifically to help you write a PPA. Patent-writing software is available through the United Inventors Association bookstore and other independent inventor–friendly Web sites.
- **The hybrid approach:** There is a middle ground between doing it all by yourself and hiring a professional to do it for you. You can write it yourself and then take it to a professional, either a patent attorney or a patent agent, and have him look it over and make suggestions about how you might improve it before you drop it in the mail. Many patent attorneys and patent agents provide this type of review and coaching service for very reasonable fees.

After you have written the patent, including making any changes suggested by a patent attorney or patent agent, you file and prosecute the patent yourself. You will correspond directly with the patent office and speak or write to the examiner assigned to your application. You also will be responsible for responding to any forthcoming office actions, unless you choose to employ a professional to help you at that point. This is advisable, since correspondence concerning patent office actions can be even more arcane and time-consuming than the patent application.

What's Included in a Patent Application?

If you were to look through the USPTO database at the utility patents that have been issued, you would notice that all the patents follow the same format and include the same information in the same sequence. There is the abstract, the references cited, the claims, the description, a brief description of the drawings, a detailed description of the preferred embodiments, and the drawings.

Abstract

The USPTO says that the abstract portion of a patent should be a brief (150-word) statement of the technical disclosure, including the major benefits of the invention. For example, the abstract might tell concisely what the invention does and how it does it.

References Cited

This section of the patent application includes a list of all the patents that have been found, during both your patent searches and the examiner's patent searches, that might in any way be relevant to this patent application. It is extremely important for the patent applicant to list any and all possibly relevant prior art that is known to the inventor or his representative (patent attorney or patent agent).

Claims

The claims portion of a patent application consists of a series of one-sentence paragraphs at the end of a patent application or patent that define the boundaries of the invention. Each claim is the object of the phrase "I claim" or "What is claimed is." The claims represent the invention for determining patentability both during examination and after issuance if validity of the patent is challenged. Claims also determine what constitutes infringement.

A claim typically recites a number of elements or limitations, and will cover or *read on* only those products (or processes) that contain all such elements or limitations, or their equivalents. Effective claims must be neither too broad (i.e., cover prior art or matter not adequately described in the specification) nor too narrow (i.e., fail to cover significant embodiments of the invention). An applicant may include a reasonable number of claims of varying scope. The standard filing fee of $500 covers the cost of twenty claims. Additional claims can be added if needed for additional cost.

ESSENTIAL

The wise inventor familiarizes himself with the components of a patent application whether he is hiring a professional to do the work for him or he does it himself. Knowledge is power, and the more the inventor knows about patents the better able he is to communicate his vision of his product and his desired patent protection.

Description

This section of a patent application is divided into five subheadings:

- **Field of the Invention:** This section is a single sentence that describes the general category into which the product falls. For example, a patent on an improved poster board might read, "This invention relates to poster boards, and particularly relates to an improved poster board that may be used to create posters, signs, and other displays of visual material."
- **Background of Invention:** The description portion would include what is called the background of the invention. This describes the problem that the invention solves, prior solutions to the problem, and shortcomings of the prior solutions.

- **Summary of the Invention:** The summary of the invention tells in a very brief and general way what this invention does, or how it works. It often includes a summary of the claims, and the benefits of the invention.

- **Brief Description of the Drawings:** This section briefly describes what each of the drawings shows—typically one sentence per figure. A more detailed description of the drawings, labeling each drawing and describing the features of each drawing, may follow. Patent drawings may be informal until the notice of allowance—the formal letter you receive from the USPTO stating that your patent will be granted—is received. At that time, formal drawings must be submitted to the USPTO before the patent issues.

- **Detailed Description of Preferred Embodiments:** Although one of the goals of your patent is to show a variety of ways your product may be made in order to give you the broadest patent coverage, in this section you will describe what, in your opinion, is the very best way to make your invention.

Now What?

It's been a long road to move your invention from the initial idea to the writing and filing of your patent application. At this point, you have reached a milestone. Your patent application is in the mail and you may legally say that your product is patent pending and label it as such. Now the waiting begins.

Your patent application may take two to five years to move through the examination process depending on the category of your invention. Some areas of the Patent Office have huge backlogs of inventions that the examiners who work in that classification are working their way through. For example, golf inventions are abundant and inventors of golf accessories are experiencing a longer than average wait for their patent applications to be evaluated by the examiners.

As your patent progresses through the examination process, the patent examiner will communicate with you, if you are a pro se applicant, or with your patent professional. Usually there are one or more office actions before the patent issues or is denied. Each office action will require a response. If you have an attorney or agent representing you, each time you receive a communication from the examiner there will be charges for his professional services. When all is said and done, by the time your patent finally issues you will probably have spent between $6,000 and $15,000 on your patent.

FACT

It is possible to track the progress of your patent application through the USPTO. Before the patent application is published, the clerk of the category of your invention can report the status of your application. Just call the switchboard and ask to speak to the clerk who works in the classification of your invention. Also, once the application is published, you can track it yourself on the USPTO Web site.

Chapter 12

Not Patentable? Other Options

Some great ideas are just not patentable, but this doesn't mean you should forget about them. There are some other forms of legal protection for intellectual property besides the patent. However, before pursuing other options, you will first need to assess why your idea is not patentable. This information will provide the direction you will need to discover how best to protect your idea for marketing.

Figure It Out

If it is determined that your invention idea is not patentable but you still wish to pursue it, you may be able to do that as long as you understand your options and your limitations. First, look at the reasons why an invention might not be patentable to see which marketing direction might work best for you. Consider the following possibilities:

- The invention has an unexpired patent on it. You cannot patent this idea or even pursue it in its exact form.
- The invention has a patent but it has expired. You may produce and sell the product but you cannot obtain patent protection for it.
- The invention has been seen in public but has never been patented. You can probably pursue the idea but you cannot patent it.
- The invention does not fit the USPTO guidelines for patentable ideas. You may be able to obtain limited protection with a trademark.

Trademarks

According to the USPTO, a trademark is defined as a word, phrase, symbol, or design, or a combination of words, phrases, symbols, or designs, that identifies and distinguishes the source of the goods of one party from those of others. It can even be a sound, a smell, or the distinctive shape or color of a specific product. A trademark will not protect an invention, but it will identify a particular invention and protect the name.

Trademarks can be extremely powerful and immensely valuable. Consider the trademarks for Microsoft, Apple, or even Coca-Cola. The names alone conjure up images of excellence and dependability. Coca-Cola is not even a patented formula. The name alone brands the product with such a strong market impact that the Coca-Cola Company has been able to market many different types of related items with the Coca-Cola logo and thereby enhance their perceived value. Go into any antique or resale shop and you will find every imaginable item, from salt and pepper shakers to blankets, branded with the Coca-Cola trademark. Coca-Cola branded collectables are a whole industry unto themselves.

It is a little-known fact, but you may establish your rights to a particular mark simply through the legitimate use of the mark, without ever registering the mark nationally. How do you do that? Simply place the little ™ or ℠ designation on the mark each time you use it. This alerts the public to your claim on that name or mark, and it is legal.

If simply placing the designation on the name or design you have chosen gives it trademark status, why should you bother to obtain a federally registered mark? There are several good reasons for doing so. A federally registered trademark allows you to:

- Claim the exclusive right to use the mark nationwide.
- Bring action concerning the mark in federal court.
- Use the U.S. registration as the basis to obtain registration in foreign countries.
- File the U.S. registration with U.S. Customs to prevent importation of infringing foreign goods.

A working knowledge of trademarks will be helpful to you whether you decide to file for a federally registered trademark or simply to use the ™ or ℠ symbol on your invention or business.

FACT

A *service mark* is the same thing as a trademark except that it identifies and distinguishes the source of a service rather than a product. The terms *trademark* and *mark* are used interchangeably for both goods and services. If your product is not federally registered, you may legally use the symbols ™ or ℠ for your product or service.

Trademark Searching

Trademark searching can be done, for free, on the USPTO database. Just look for the link to the trademark database on the USPTO's home page. Unlike the patent database, all trademark filings, both registered and pending, are available for searching. By utilizing the different methods offered, it is possible to do a fairly thorough search on your own, particularly if what you are searching is a word, phrase, or some combination of words.

Professional trademark search firms have specific software that allows them to perform a more thorough search than you ever could. In addition, their years of experience have taught them tricks to searching that those of us not trained in searching would never know to do. If you have any doubt about the thoroughness of your own search, it would be wise to invest in a professional trademark search. You may especially need some professional help if you are searching for logos or drawings.

When you are searching a name, an important thing to remember is that trademarks are often distinguished by the way that they sound, rather than how they are spelled. For example, if you are searching for a trademark using the word *clean*, you will also need to look for unusual spellings that could sound exactly the same, such as "Kleen," "Klean," or other variations.

You may notice on the trademark database that there is often more than one live trademark with exactly the same name. How is this possible? If the trademarks are on products or services that are obviously not similar, they may both be awarded the same trademark name. An example of this would be the words *hand gliders*. You will find at least two live trademarks for those two words in combination. One trademark is for a dental instrument and the other is for a miniature kite. These two categories are so obviously different that there is no chance of mistaking one for the other. So they are both allowed to use the exact same trademark for their very different products. If there were any similarities between the two, one trademark would have been refused registration.

FACT

In the online trademark database, you can now view the actual trademark documents in full color. This can be very helpful in distinguishing exactly what is trademarked. All you need is the U.S. serial number that is provided right on the database. You will need Adobe Acrobat Reader, a free software program, in order to view the PDF version of the document.

When Is a Trademark Available to You?

When you are searching for names, if you find the exact name that you want to trademark, first look to see if the listed trademark is *live* or *dead*. If a trademark has been abandoned, it may or may not be available to you. If you find the name you want to use and it is shown as being *live,* read it carefully to see if the product trademarked is similar to your product. If it is not, you may still be able to obtain that trademark for your invention.

ALERT!

Trademarks remain active and in force as long as they are used continuously in commerce. If a trademark has been registered but abandoned—that is, not used in commerce—It is not available unless the registrant officially notifies the Trademark Office that he is abandoning the mark or legal action is taken to have the mark declared abandoned.

If you have any question about whether it is available to you, print the information and take it to an intellectual property attorney for a professional opinion. There are also trademark companies that provide all of the services related to trademarks, including searching, filing, and even assisting in selecting good trademark names.

You may file for a U.S. federally registered trademark at the USPTO. If you are granted a U.S. trademark, your protection extends to all of the United States and its territories. If you wish to file for international trademark protection, you may do that also through the USPTO under the Madrid Protocol. The Madrid system offers a trademark owner the option of having his trademark protected in several countries by simply filing one application directly with the U.S. Trademark Office. The forms are available on the U.S. Trademark Office Web site using the Madrid Protocol Forms page of the TEAS (Trademark Electronic Application System) at ✍*http://teasi.uspto.gov.*

An international mark so registered is equivalent to an application or a registration of the same mark made directly in each of the countries designated by the applicant. If the trademark office of a designated country does not refuse protection within a specified period, the protection of the mark is the same as if it had been registered by that office. The Madrid system also greatly simplifies the later management of the mark, since it is possible to record subsequent changes or to renew the registration in a single step. Additional countries may be designated later.

Copyrights

Copyrights protect the authors of original works, including literary, dramatic, musical, and artistic creations. The U.S. Copyright Office is separate from the U.S. Patent and Trademark offices. It provides protection for intellectual property of a different sort than inventions. Copyright protection begins from the time you create the work in some type of fixed form.

QUESTION?

How can I claim my copyright without registering it?
You can claim the copyright on eligible materials by simply labeling your work with your name, the word *Copyright*, and the year. This is most often listed at the end of the work. Each eligible item of your work should be marked in this way.

In other words, if you create a dance but you make no effort to record it, or you make an extemporaneous speech and do not write it down, it is not copyrighted material. But if you have recorded or written that information, it is copyrighted. With certain exceptions relating to work that is created for hire, the copyright is immediately the property of the author of the work. For example, if you create a work within the scope of your employment or as something that is specially ordered or commissioned, the copyright on that work likely belongs to the person or persons who ordered the work.

Your copyright protection is in place even if you choose not to federally register your material. So why would you want to bother with registration of your work? If you are very prolific and have a large body of work, you might not want to obtain registered copyrights on everything. Nevertheless, there are some reasons why you might elect to register certain materials that you create.

Federal copyrights, unlike patents and trademarks, are simply a legal formality that establishes ownership of original work. As such, they are neither expensive nor difficult to obtain. Some reasons you might wish to federally register your copyright are:

- The copyright establishes a public claim to your ownership of the material.
- A federal copyright is necessary if you wish to file an infringement suit.
- If registration of the work is made within three months after publication and prior to an infringement for a published work, or prior to the infringement for an unpublished work, a court has the discretion to order an infringer to pay your attorney's fees, and to award you statutory damages as an alternative to an award of your actual damages and profits.
- If your copyright is federally registered, you can register with U.S. Customs to prevent infringing foreign copies from entering the country.

You may register your materials at any time within the life of the copyright. Your copyright becomes effective immediately on the date that the copyright office receives your completed official registration, which consists of the following three elements:

- A properly completed application form, which you can get from their Web site
- A nonrefundable filing fee, which is less than $50
- A nonreturnable copy of the actual work being registered

FACT

Copyright protection on any work created after January 1, 1978, lasts until seventy years after the death of the creator of the work. Materials published or registered before that date last a total of ninety-five years.

Trade Secrets

Sometimes a company or an inventor decides to forgo any type of patent protection for an invention. They may prefer to simply keep the information secret. Often it is advantageous to protect intellectual property in this way, since patents are eventually published, revealing the details of the product or method. There are many examples of trade secrets in American society today. Some examples of trade secrets are the recipes for popular foods and beverages, such as Coca-Cola, and the exact ingredients and methods for making some products. One manufacturer of craft kits has elected to use trade secrets to keep his competition from determining exactly how his special adhesive works. If he had obtained a patent on this adhesive, he would not be able to keep the secret once the patent published.

If you decide to follow the trade secret course with your product or method, what are your rights? If you are careful to protect the secret by judiciously using nondisclosure agreements whenever you must share the knowledge, you do have recourse under the law if your secret is obtained by theft or espionage. Stealing trade secrets is a crime for which there are heavy penalties, even if the theft occurred outside of this country.

However, if the person who has the secret can prove that she came up with the knowledge independently, you will have no legal recourse to collect damages. If your product is something that could be reverse engineered to determine the secret, you could not sue for damages since reverse engineering is not illegal.

If you have something that is unique and marketable but you are unable or unwilling to obtain patent protection for it, a trade secret may be the best option for you. The only thing you have to do is simply keep it confidential. Once the secret is out, your protection comes to a screeching halt.

Expired Patents

Once a patent has expired, that product is said to be in the public domain. This means that the technology for that product now belongs to the public and anyone can make and sell it. If a product has been promoted during the lifetime of the patent with strong branding, the known brand (trademark) may still amass the lion's share of sales simply because it has become trusted for quality. However, the product is available for competing manufacturers as soon as the patent expires. Certain branded products become so much a part of the vernacular that consumers continue to refer to all similar products by the trademarked brand name. One example of this is Kleenex. One often hears similar products referred to as Kleenex rather than as facial tissue, whatever brands they happen to be.

This is one huge advantage of trademarks. Even if you are unable to obtain patent protection for your product, if you can brand it with an easily recognizable name that belongs to you and saturate the market before your competition can get out there, you may have a viable way to gain and keep a good share of the market.

Patented but Not Marketed Products

If you visit a PTDL and browse through the patent database, or even through the USPTO's online database, you will find that there are literally millions of issued patents on products that never made it into the marketplace. There are many reasons for this. Many of the patents shouldn't see the light of day! Some of them are so bizarre that they are comical. And some products are patented in forms that are immediately made obsolete by other, better designs. But you will also find patents on viable designs that would make good, marketable products. Sometimes it is simply a case of an inventor who wanted to get a patent but who has no ability to get the product on the market.

Whatever the reason, if you find your invention already patented, you may still be able to pursue your idea. If you do find your exact invention already covered by a recent patent, or even a design that is too close to yours to make your design worth fighting for, you can contact that inventor and perhaps work out something, such as a license agreement, to still get a piece of the action. First, look on the front of the patent to see if it is shown as being *assigned*. This may tell you if something is being done with it. The inventor's name and address are listed right on the front of the patent. If an attorney was used to file and prosecute the patent, that is often the best way to locate the inventor. Often the attorney will have inside information regarding the disposition of the invention. If the patent attorney or agent knows that the inventor has been unsuccessful at marketing the patent, he is usually more than willing to share contact information for the inventor since it might prove worthwhile for his client.

If you are able to work something out with the patent holder, you may still be able to cash in on a good thing. That patent owner may be delighted to learn that there is someone who so believes in her idea that they would be willing to help her market it for a share of the profits. Or she may believe her idea is worth a fortune and expect you to pay an extravagant amount to either buy the rights to the patent, license the patent, or share in the marketing of the invention. Either way, if you truly believe in the idea, it is worth finding out whether or not there may be an opportunity for you.

ESSENTIAL

Keep an open mind as you peruse the USPTO database. If you are unable to patent your invention, you may find something else that is already patented that is of interest to you, even in a different category from your original idea. Many patents are recent but uncommercialized and can be purchased or licensed from the original owners.

It is surprising to discover how many independent inventors have developed and patented their inventions with the mistaken notion that they would have to do nothing more except wait for the right manufacturer to contact them. This could be your opportunity if you are unable to patent your own idea.

You are obviously a creative person or you would not have come this far. If you have to get creative in a different sense in order to follow your dream, you may be able to take advantage of the work someone else has already done by utilizing an existing patent. Depending on what the patent holder wants to do, you may become a collaborator, an assignee, or a licensee as well as an inventor.

Chapter 13

Funding Your Invention

You have had a great idea for a new product that you would like to develop and eventually see on the market, but you realize that there are expenses involved in developing, protecting, and marketing an invention. If you are like most people, you do not have a surplus amount of expendable income just lying around waiting to be spent on your invention idea. This chapter addresses how to move forward with your product if you do not have a pile of ready cash on hand.

On a Shoestring

There are ways to make your dream come true even on a limited budget. While it is true that the total expenses of developing, protecting, and marketing a product can be significant, the good news is that you are not required to have all the money available at the onset of your inventing project. Operating on a shoestring budget is not the fastest and most direct route to getting your product on the market, but it is a great alternative for those with limited funds. It may take longer, but if you are able to get your product to market, the result is just as rewarding as if you had had unlimited funds to finance your project in the beginning.

Your Checking or Savings Account

The very first steps cost primarily time with only a small amount of cash outlay. You can't beat that! When you first have your idea you can start your inventor's journal. A notebook for this journal can be purchased for as little as $3. The two witnesses to your written notes are free. The preliminary market and patent search can be done for only an investment of your time and effort, no money at all! Unless your product is a high-tech device of some kind, you can probably make your initial prototypes using inexpensive materials available at local stores.

While you are moving through these initial, virtually cost-free stages of product development, you should be planning ahead and stashing away funds for your more substantial expenses. When the time comes for you to have a professional patent search done, be a wise shopper. While it is true that you can get a professional search done through a patent attorney, it may not be the most cost-efficient route to take. You can go directly to the professional search firms rather than using an attorney as an intermediary and get the same search, with a legal opinion of patentability, for a fraction of what it would cost to have it done through an attorney. This should cost somewhat less than $500.

The first major expense you will encounter is when you go to a patent attorney or patent agent and ask them to file either a provisional patent application or a utility patent application on your behalf. Prices for attorneys and agents vary, but expect it to be more than $2,000 and less than $12,000, depending on the complexity, for them to write and file the application initially. This will be the first payment toward your patent. Most attorneys and agents do not require an additional payment until the first office action from the USPTO is received. Unless you are among the very lucky few who get your patent application approved on the first filing, the first office action will require a response from your attorney or agent in an attempt to overcome the patent examiner's objections. Most patent attorneys or agents will require another payment for the work they do in answering the office action at that time. The good news, if you can call it that, is that it will probably be a year or more between the time you first file your application and the time you receive the first office action. This means that after your patent application has been filed but before you receive the first office action, you have a window of time during which to accumulate the money that will be required.

Each time the patent attorney or agent sends a response to the USPTO, you will be required to pay for their services. Responses from the USPTO are generally fairly slow. The lag times between responses will allow you to save the money you need for the next step. When you finally receive your notice of allowance, you will have approximately three months to gather the issue fees before your patent actually issues.

ALERT!

The professional marketability evaluation of your product is another expense for which you must plan and save. Again, there are professional marketability evaluations available for a wide range of prices. Choose wisely. If it is important to you to get the best and most thorough marketability evaluation possible, then save for it. If you can make do with a less expensive marketability evaluation, then do so. Just don't skip the professional marketability evaluation as a way to save money.

Credit Cards

Rather than actually saving the money to fund your invention as you go, there are a few other options. First, if you have good credit you can charge some of your invention expenses on your credit card. If you are one of those people who keep your credit cards maxed out or very near to maxed out, this, obviously, would not be an option for you.

Do not charge significant sums to your credit card unless you know that you will be able to pay it off without causing undue hardship to yourself or your family. Do not assume that your invention will generate the income to pay off the credit card debt accumulated during the inventing process.

If you do charge some of your inventing expenses to your credit card, keep in mind that the credit bureaus are watching and recording your payment history on your credit report. They know whether you pay the credit card companies in a timely manner and whether you pay more than you are required to each month or only make the minimum payments on each account. If, in the future, you decide that you wish to become the manufacturer of your product, you will undoubtedly require a loan for the start-up capital. Keeping your credit rating impeccable will make it much easier to get that all-important loan when the time comes.

Life Insurance

If you have a permanent life insurance policy, sometimes called a whole life policy, for which you have been paying for years, you may have accumulated a substantial cash value that can be borrowed at low interest rates. Check with your insurance company to see if your life insurance policy has a cash surrender value and what the requirements are to receive a loan based on the cash surrender value.

Most whole or permanent life insurance policies have set limits on how much money you can withdraw from your policy without reducing its face value. Do not jeopardize your family's security by diminishing the value of your life insurance. Your insurance agent can guide you through the process while protecting this asset.

Be certain that you know the time frame for repayment of the loan and that you will be able to comfortably repay the loan without undue hardship. Loans based on the cash surrender value of life insurance policies are most often used to finance college but can be used for anything.

Signature Loans

Signature loans are exactly what the name implies. They are bank loans that do not require any collateral, only your signature. These loans are generally granted only to customers who have had a good relationship with the bank for several years. A good relationship means that you have been a good customer, having few, if any, bank overdrafts or other problems with your accounts. Signature loans are generally for relatively small amounts, usually only $2,000 or $3,000. A signature loan may be enough to let you hire a professional prototype designer or hire a patent attorney to write and prosecute your patent application. You may be able to finance the rest of the cost out of your checking or savings account.

Friends and Family

Getting money from friends and family is dangerous territory but it can be achieved if you approach them with a business proposition rather than a request for a loan based on nothing more than their affection for you. Money is money. People are funny about it. They do not want to lend it to anyone, even their favorite relative, without a fair amount of certainty that they will see their money again at some mutually agreed-upon future date.

Everyone, however, is interested in a business proposition that stands to make a good return on an investment. Friends and family are no different. Before you approach friends and family and ask them to invest in your invention idea, you may want to form a company, even going so far as to incorporate it. Now, rather than asking them to just invest in your invention, you can actually sell them shares in your company. Explain that if you are able to make your invention into a source of income either by actually manufacturing and distributing it yourself or by licensing it to a manufacturer, the profit will be shared among all the stockholders in the company. It is important for them to understand that all inventions are considered to be high-risk investments; even though your invention is the greatest thing since sliced bread, there is the possibility that they may lose their money. Couching your request in these terms can help to eliminate misunderstandings and hard feelings later on.

FACT

Before you ask anyone else, even friends and family, to invest in your invention idea, you need to invest in it yourself. You invest in it with your personal money and your sweat equity. If you have not demonstrated that you have enough faith in your idea to invest your resources in it, it is extremely unlikely that anyone else will want to.

Bank Loans

If you need more money than you have access to, it is time to think about applying for a loan from a bank. First, it is important to understand that banks are very particular about what they will lend money for, and risky invention ideas (all invention ideas are risky, including yours) are probably at the very bottom of their list. If you need a substantial loan, say more than $3,000, but you plan on licensing your product for royalties rather than building a business around it, banks will only lend you money if you put up collateral such as your home or property. This is a very serious proposition, and you should analyze your situation carefully before allowing your home or property to be collateral for a loan for your invention. If you do not make your loan repayments in a timely manner, the bank will seize the collateral and sell it to recoup their money. There are no guarantees of profitability even with the greatest of inventions.

The Small Business Administration (SBA) will guarantee loans for qualified applicants who are building a business out of their invention. SBA-guaranteed loans are usually for amounts between $10,000 and $150,000. They usually require that the business be in production or preproduction of the product with orders for sales before they will approve the loan. Your bank actually lends the money but the SBA guarantees it.

FACT

Even if you put up collateral, banks also will require that you have a formalized business plan before agreeing to lend you money. How to write and get help with your business plan is addressed in Chapter 15, "Building a Business Around Your Invention."

Partners

Another way to finance your invention is to seek out contributing partners. Contributing partners are not partners you choose for their monetary contribution, although they may contribute financially. Typically, contributing partners bring their expertise, knowledge, skills, and sometimes equipment and services to the project. Contributing partners can be anyone along the way. They may be prototype designers, patent attorneys, marketing specialists, etc. You give a contributing partner a share of your potential profits in exchange for their work and expertise in moving the product forward. If you are an entrepreneurial inventor—that is, if you are making a business from your invention— you would give the contributing partner shares of stock in your company. He would then be entitled to share in any profits made by the company. If you are an inventor who wishes to license your product, the contributing partner would receive a share of your royalties in exchange for his contribution.

For independent inventors who have limited financial resources, enlisting the partnership of contributing partners in a planned and strategic manner can make the difference between success and failure. Contributing partners may make it possible to see the process through to a profitable conclusion for all involved. Although many inventors hate to give up even a small share of ownership of the profits from their idea, they must keep in mind that a smaller share of *something* is far superior to all of *nothing*.

Prototype Designers as Contributing Partners

An inventor will often invite a prototype designer to become a contributing partner in exchange for his services developing and refining the prototype to a virtually market-ready state.

ESSENTIAL

It is highly unlikely that a prototype designer will see your product idea and decide that he wants a share of the potential profits in exchange for his services. He makes his living by providing prototyping services. His income would be very unsteady if he signed on to participate in inventions rather than being paid for his services. While it is possible that your prototype designer would be the exception, not many are willing to do this.

On rare occasions a prototype designer will agree to become a contributing partner. It does not usually happen spontaneously when he is overwhelmed by the tremendous potential of your product, however. If you wish to get your prototype designer to become one of your contributing partners, you must approach him as you would approach any potential investor or banker, with facts, figures, and a business plan.

Determining how many shares of your company must be given in exchange for services is a delicate balancing act. You want to give enough so that the partner does not start out the relationship feeling he has been treated unfairly. On the other hand, you do not want to give away any more shares than you absolutely must. Shares once given are difficult, if not impossible, to get back.

Patent Attorneys or Agents as Contributing Partners

When the independent inventor meets with a patent attorney or patent agent for the first time, she is often stunned to learn the cost of writing, filing, and prosecuting a patent application. The first response of many inventors is to suggest that, since the idea is such a fantastic one, the patent attorney or patent agent should do his work in exchange for a share of the potential profits. Patent attorneys and agents seldom agree to work in this manner. They see invention ideas all day, every day and know what an uphill battle it is to get a product to market, no matter how terrific the idea is. They also know the potential pitfalls in filing for patent protection—e.g., unpublished applications for identical inventions, prior art that would prohibit the granting of a patent. They know there is no guarantee that a patent will actually be granted just because an application has been filed.

Occasionally, a patent attorney or patent agent will suggest to the inventor that he work in exchange for a share of the rights to the invention. This is rare indeed. When this happens, consider yourself fortunate. In addition to you receiving typically a 10 to 50 percent discount on legal fees, your patent attorney also now has a stake in your success, and will therefore be more motivated to help you succeed so as to make his investment in your invention pay off. A reasonable share can be anywhere from 5 percent to 33 percent. The terms of the deal are negotiable between you and your patent attorney.

If your patent attorney does not suggest this arrangement, he may be waiting to see if you have the creative initiative to suggest it on your own. Do not be surprised if he also wants to see your business credentials, and a business plan. After all, you are asking him to become an investor in you as well as in your invention, and as a prudent investor, he will also do his due diligence to ensure that his investment in you is a wise one.

Market Specialists

A third category of potential contributing partners is that of market specialists. These may include anyone who would be involved with the distributing and selling of the product, such as an advertising agency or a product publicist. This type of contributing partner would be more appropriate for the inventor who wants to directly manufacture and sell a product that embodies the invention, rather than the inventor who intends to license her invention.

Product publicists usually work for advertising agencies, but their specialty is in promoting and getting publicity for specific products. They send out press releases and appear on television and radio shows to talk up specific products. Their services are not inexpensive, and if you can enlist a product publicist as a contributing partner, you are lucky indeed!

Investors

Many first-time inventors have the mistaken notion that all they have to do is tell people about their great idea and investors will be lining up to hand over the money necessary to develop the invention. That is not going to happen. You may be able to find investors—also called venture capitalists or investment angels—who are willing to invest in your invention idea, but you need to have made significant progress in the development of the invention (e.g., working prototype built, market and patent searches done as well as a patent application in the works) and developed a business plan before you approach anyone for funding.

Venture Capitalists

To be sure, there are venture capitalists but they are not likely sources of funding for independent inventors unless the inventor has a medical innovation or an innovation in a highly technical field. Before venture capitalists invest in an invention, they require an actual business to have been established with a team of highly skilled professionals on board as the guiding forces of a very formalized business plan. The small-time independent inventor could lose his voice in this process. Venture capitalists expect a high return on their money within a fairly short period of time. Most independent inventors are small potatoes to them; they are not interested in investing in such highly speculative propositions with people who may or may not have business experience.

Investment Angels

Investment angels are a possible source of funding for independent inventors. There are two types of investment angels, those you know and those you do not know. You don't know any investment angels? Don't be so sure. Anyone who has disposable income and has a bit of the gambler in her could qualify.

Investment Angels You Know

Most often the investment angels that you know, but didn't know you knew, are professionals that you encounter in your day-to-day life. It could be your doctor, dentist, CPA, stockbroker, or business-executive friend. Perhaps they have not done well in the stock market or are just looking for an investment with a little excitement. Anyone you know might be an angel investor if the circumstances were right. If you are looking for funding and seeking an angel investor, look first to the people whom you know and who know you. They may never before have made an investment like this and it probably never occurred to them to call themselves angel investors. Present your request for funding as a business proposition. Explain both the positives and the negatives of investing in your invention idea. Be certain they understand that their investment is highly speculative but that it could bring a significant return on their investment.

Investment Angels You Don't Know

There is an abundance of angel investors in this country. Jeffrey Sohl, Director of the Center for Venture Research at the University of New Hampshire, estimates that there are 400,000 angel investors who invest more than forty *billion* dollars a year in start-up businesses.

There are a couple of ways to locate angel investors. The first is to let them find you. They are looking for you as you are looking for them. If your newspaper allows classified ads soliciting investments, this is a way that could work. The laws from state to state are different. Your local newspaper will know whether they allow such ads.

QUESTION?

What should a classified ad seeking angel investors say?
Make it short but to the point and say something like "Start-up business seeking financial partner. Relatively small investment required. Patent-pending product. Call (214) 555-0000 for business plan and details."

Another way to locate angel investors is by using the Internet. Using a search engine such as Google, you can locate thousands of links to potential investment angels by typing in a variety of key words. A few suggested key words for your Internet search for angel investors are: investment angels, financial angels, angel finance, angel organizations, seed money, and seed finance. Be sure to enclose the term in quotation marks in order to exclude listings for the words individually.

When doing an Internet search for angel investors, you will find many legitimate listings and some who are opportunists offering services to put you in touch with angel investors. Searching for angel investors is one area that you will be well advised to handle yourself. Firms that offer to locate your angel investor could be unscrupulous. It is difficult to determine who is legitimate in this line of business. Unless the offer to locate these investors is made by someone you know and trust, you are much better off doing your own research and contacting the investors on your own. It may take some time and effort but you can find potential angel investors yourself without the help of a middleman.

Chapter 14

Your Ultimate Goal

When that wonderful idea first occurred to you, you probably thought how great it would be to get that new product on the market and available to the public. If you have not given some thought to exactly how you plan to get this accomplished, now is the time to explore your options. This is one area where one size fits all does not apply. The choice of creating a business around your product, licensing it for a royalty, or selling it outright is a very personal decision.

Choosing to Sell Your Patent

The perfect disposition of your patented or patent-pending invention will depend on your needs and your plans for your life. There are solid reasons for selling the rights to your invention if that choice best fits your circumstances. Here are some reasons why you might wish to sell your invention outright:

- You desire a quick return on your investment.
- Your invention is likely to be a fad item.
- Your needs at this stage of your life require selling your invention.

Selling outright is probably the fastest way to make money from your invention. If a manufacturer likes your invention enough to want to include it in his product line, he might be willing to purchase your patented or patent-pending product. If you need to get your invested money back quickly, this could be the option for you.

While it is generally not the best marketing choice, if your invention is something that is a fad type item, selling outright might be a good option since its shelf life is not likely to be a long one. It is easier for a manufacturer that is already making and selling similar items to add your item than it would be for you to gear up to produce it. It is conceivable that it would cost you more to promote it than you would make from a fad invention.

QUESTION?

Should I sell all rights to my fad invention?
If you know that your invention will have a short shelf life, you will come out ahead by selling it to a manufacturer who can saturate the market quickly and make the most of the invention. It can be costly to launch an item that will not last.

Some inventors' life situations dictate that the best disposition of their invention is to sell it outright. Among the reasons for this decision are advanced age and/or poor health. Another reason could relate to the need for a fast cash return, since licensing can take a longer time than selling outright. Even such passive income as royalty involves some bookkeeping and regular auditing of your licensee and perhaps starting a corporation for tax and litigation protection. If you are at a place in your life where you do not want to deal with the details involved in having a licensed product, perhaps you will want to sell the rights to your invention.

Choosing Not to Sell Your Patent

Some reasons why you might not wish to sell your invention outright are:

- You intend to create a business around the invention.
- You expect the invention to be a lasting product.
- You prefer to receive regular royalty payments.
- It is unlikely that you would receive its true value in a lump-sum payment.
- Your product is an artistic item that you reproduce and sell.

The decision to build a business around your invention and actually become the manufacturer is a big one, but for some inventors it is the right choice. If you have wanted to operate your own business and you have determined, through research and the development of a business plan, that your business would be profitable, this could be your big opportunity. Perhaps industry downsizing has taken your job and you are seeking to create your own job security. Perhaps you want to provide jobs for others in addition to yourself. Just be certain before you make such a commitment that you will have the ability to get your product on the retail shelves if that is the way you elect to market it.

If your invention is something that is likely to be purchased on a regular basis by a large segment of the population, it is almost certain that you would not receive the full value of the patent by selling it outright. Manufacturers are usually unwilling to pay millions for a product for which it would take many years to recover their investment.

If your invention is something that will be popular and lasting (not a fad), licensing could give you an income on a regular basis for which you expend no further effort. Novice inventors often believe that manufacturers will pay them millions of dollars for items that are untested in the marketplace. While some manufacturers may be willing to buy patent rights for a lump sum of money, you can be sure that most manufacturers will not be willing to pay a huge amount of money for something that may not return their investment. If you decide to sell your patent outright, keep in mind that you will probably receive *far less* than you would receive in the long run if you opted to license it and receive royalty over the length of the patent, or longer. Many times the lump-sum payment for the patent will equal one or two years of royalty.

If your invention appears to be something that could become a staple purchase and would be on the market for years, it is very difficult to predetermine its value. It may be worth millions, but there is always the possibility that a new product could come along and render it obsolete. Even if that does not happen, your chances of getting full value for your invention are highly unlikely if you sell it outright.

FACT

While manufacturers are generally reluctant to pay the full perceived value of your patent by buying it outright, they will often readily sign a license agreement and pay royalties for the lifetime of the patent, or even longer if the product has a trademarked name.

Choosing to License Your Patent

Some reasons why licensing your invention might be the right decision for you are:

- You want the income from your invention without the work and expense of creating a business around your invention.
- The difficulty of marketing a single product to retailers is daunting.
- You want to continue your present career and receive regular royalty payments from your invention.
- You do not want the responsibility of enforcing the patent.

Many independent inventors choose to license their patents because they want to make money from their inventions but they have no desire to handle the manufacturing and selling of the products. Creating a business around a product is a huge undertaking, no matter how simple the product might be. The financial requirements can be daunting. If the inventor is not already a business owner, particularly in the retail area, it can be almost impossible to get a new product on store shelves as an independent item.

FACT

The single most difficult task facing the independent inventor who attempts to wholesale her invention to retailers is getting the retailers' buyers to work with her. Almost universally, they will not buy from a single-product vendor. She may have to start out with a product representative until her product is established.

Licensing the product for royalties effectively avoids these problems while providing a regular income stream for the inventor without further effort on his part. When an inventor licenses a good product to a manufacturer that is already making and placing similar items with the large retailers, the income realized by the inventor in the form of royalties can often be greater than the amount he would have realized if he had undertaken the whole project alone.

Independent inventors who go out to market their inventions to the large retail chains immediately encounter an obstacle that is almost impossible to overcome: These large retailers refuse to deal with single-product vendors. The buyers for these large chain stores insist on seeing a select few representatives who can show them an entire line of products from which to choose. The competition among wholesalers for retail shelf space is strong and it is almost 100 percent assigned to these wholesalers, making it extremely difficult for someone with only one product to gain shelf space. Retailers are also wary of placing orders with an individual who may not be able to deliver the product on time or as ordered. Licensing places your product in the hands of the very wholesalers who already have the coveted shelf space and the attention of the buyers. Problem solved!

You may be a professional whose invention relates to your work. The fact that you have developed a great new product does not make you want to abandon your career. Even if your invention is not career-related for you, it is still not likely that you will want to leave a career in which you have a substantial investment to begin a new career in manufacturing. Licensing is a way to see your invention marketed while you continue to pursue your career.

Inventors come from all lifestyles. Among them are homemakers, retirees, professionals, and even children. Many of them cannot or simply do not wish to spend their time working with their inventions. Licensing their inventions allows them to continue their lives uninterrupted while receiving a steady income from their achievements.

Saved for last is one of the most important reasons why many inventors choose to license their patents. While your government-issued patent gives you exclusive rights to your invention for a period, what your patent guarantees you is the right to stop another person from making or selling your product during that period. *It is your responsibility to enforce your patent.* In other words, your patent guarantees you the right to sue another person for infringing your patent; the government will not automatically seek out infringers and enforce the patent for you without some legal action on your part. The litigation connected with patent enforcement can amount to hundreds of thousands or even millions of dollars. A standard inclusion in most exclusive license agreements is that the licensee will be responsible for enforcing the patent. This is one of the major benefits of licensing for independent inventors.

There is one option for overcoming the formidable task and expense of enforcing the patent yourself, if you elect to be the manufacturer of your product. You may purchase patent insurance. The cost of this insurance depends upon the insurance company's assessment of the strength of your patent and its claims. Your local insurance agent should be able to direct you to a source of patent insurance.

Make sure that your license agreement contains the provision that your licensee will be responsible for enforcing your patent. The lack of this clause could spell financial disaster for you as the licensor, since an infringement lawsuit can cost one million dollars or more in legal fees to initiate and prosecute.

Choosing Not to License Your Patent

While there are compelling reasons for the independent inventor to license his patent, there are some equally compelling reasons why licensing might not be the best choice for you. Here are some of those reasons:

- For reasons of age or health, you wish to have a sense of closure.
- You do not want the responsibility for overseeing your licensee.
- Your invention fits with your existing business.
- You wish to start a business with your invention.
- Your invention is faddish in nature and is likely to burn out quickly.

Some of you may be in a personal situation that requires you to take the money and run. In other words, your best option is to sell your invention outright in order to recoup your investment and, if possible, to make a good profit. If your situation makes it desirable to be finished with the project entirely, this could be your best bet. If you have an urgent need that requires you to make whatever you can on a quick sale, this is an option for you.

Some of you will not wish to be bothered with the record-keeping and regular auditing involved in overseeing a licensee. While the time commitment is minimal with licensing, it will require some attention to royalty reports, product quality control, and annual auditing of your licensee. In most cases, this annual audit of your licensee's sales of your product will be your financial responsibility, also.

Some of you lucky inventors have invented a product that fits right in with your present business and you can simply add the product to your business. If you are in this enviable situation, you presumably already have a built-in consumer base for the new product. This is probably the easiest way to present a new product to the public and the way that it can be accomplished with the least amount of difficulty.

If you have invented something that, by its very nature, will be short-lived, licensing may not even be an option. Sometimes it is not even a good idea to pursue patent protection for it because of the time involved with patent prosecution. Inventions that must be marketed quickly in order to ride the crest of a fad are usually better handled by selling them outright and allowing a manufacturer to saturate the market.

You may not currently have a business that is compatible with your invention, but if you wish to create a business and you have a wonderful product and the financing and ability to carry it off, it can be the solution to your problems. If you need to create a new career, then you may not wish to license your patent but to become a manufacturer.

Choosing to Become a Manufacturer

If you wish to give your full attention to making a business from your inventions, it can be lucrative if your inventions and your business savvy are good enough. Here are some reasons why you might want to create a business around your invention:

- Your invention is so innovative that it will create and sustain a good share of the consumer market.
- You want to (or have to) make a career change at this time in your life and you have the necessary funding to start the business.
- You already have a business into which the new product will fit.
- You wish to build a business and create jobs in your community.
- You believe that you will make more money from your invention if you manufacture it yourself.

Sometimes an invention comes along that makes a major impact on the buying public. When this happens, it can be very lucrative for the lucky inventor to create a business around the invention. A product does not have to be highly technical or expensive to be such an item. It can even be a toy as long as it is one that will endure. Examples of toys that have stood the test of time are the Hula Hoop, Barbie, and Hot Wheels. While these toys were licensed to toy manufacturers, they could probably have become just as popular through the efforts of an individual manufacturer, assuming that the funds were available to get them before the public.

You may be facing a career change at this time due to industry downsizing or other reasons and for you this is the perfect time to start a new business. If your invention is sufficiently good and enduring to support a business and you have the funding to launch it until it is self-sustaining, this could be the answer to your career dilemma.

If you are considering giving full time to building a business around your invention, be sure to get a professional marketability evaluation of the invention to be certain that the market for the invention is big enough and lucrative enough to support a business. Avoiding that expense could be a costly savings!

If you have come up with a wonderful accessory item within your present business, this is the easiest way to introduce your new product. Without a major disruption of your life, you can simply add the new product and build sales while continuing your normal daily routine. More importantly, unlike many inventors who create something in an area in which they have no experience, you are already familiar with and have a customer base for your new product.

If your plan is to start a new business and create jobs for yourself and others in your community, your invention may well be the seed for growing a great new moneymaking organization. If you foresee spending a number of years in building the business or if you only plan to build it up and sell it, your invention can give you the product around which to build it.

If you have the time, the business savvy, and the funds to create a business around your invention, it is possible to make more money in that way than by licensing your patent. It will take a terrific product, good business connections, and great business instincts, but it is possible to build a bottom line that will equal or beat that of licensing. If you are up for the challenge, this may be your best option.

Choosing Not to Become a Manufacturer

Some reasons why you might not want to become a manufacturer of your invention are:

- You lack the funds to start and build a business.
- You lack the knowledge and contacts to market your product successfully.
- You do not have the time to devote to such an undertaking.

Many inventions can be developed, protected, and licensed on a shoe-string budget, but to start a business around a brand-new product can be so expensive as to be out of the reach of most independent inventors. All of the expenses of starting up a new business can be substantial, but they pale in comparison to the amount of funding needed to launch a new product and make it pay its own way. Before considering taking this route with your invention, it is a good idea to visit with someone at your local SBDC to get a realistic idea of what you may be facing.

When you first conceive your innovative idea, it seems simple to present it to retailers and get them to buy the product from you. However, by now you know that buyers for retail chains will not even give an appointment to single-product vendors. Thus, you will find it difficult if not impossible to get in to show your new product to the buyers for those stores. Your best bet in this situation is probably to place your product with an independent product representative who already has regular set appointments with these buyers. These reps can at least get your product before the buyers. You will have to pay a percentage of your sales to the rep and that will trim your profits, but it is the only feasible way to ensure that your product gets seen by the buyers.

If, for whatever reason, you do not have the time to devote to launching and building the momentum for your product, it is not a good idea to attempt to build a business around the product. If you have other obligations that take a great deal of your time, success is likely to be elusive. Look carefully at your lifestyle and at what you are willing to change before making this decision.

Where to Get Guidance

By now, you can see that the idea that seemed so simple in the beginning has raised some issues that must be resolved before you can make the most of your invention. Obviously, your choices will hinge on your lifestyle and your goals for the future. Your invention can become the focus of your days or it can take a peripheral position in your life. Either way, it can substantially change your life for the better if you make your decisions wisely at this point.

If there are others who will be affected by your decisions, it is wise to include them in your discussions of what your approach will be. Some people you might wish to consult for assistance in determining your path are family members, partners in the invention, financial advisors or accountants, legal advisors, or spiritual advisors.

Family Members

Your invention and the way in which you choose to promote it will affect your immediate family, so they should be included in discussions of how your family lifestyle could change. If there are financial issues that will change the way your family lives, this should be your most important consideration. If you and your family feel that the end goal is worth the sacrifice, you may choose to move in that direction, but it should be a mutual decision as to the approach.

Partners

Obviously, if you are in this project with a creative partner or an investor partner, that person will be a key decision-maker as to how you proceed with marketing. Most likely, this decision-making process will have been ongoing throughout the developmental and protective process.

Financial Advisors

You may wish to schedule an appointment with your financial advisor or accountant to learn of the impact of this new source of expenditure or income. You may be advised to set up a corporation even if you will be gaining passive income, as in a license agreement. There are financial implications to your new venture, regardless of how you elect to proceed, and it will benefit you to have made your decisions in advance and with good guidance.

Legal Advisors

By this point, you have already been involved with a patent attorney and have received advice on the handling of your patent application. Now you will be wise to seek counsel from attorneys in other specialties of the law. For example, if you plan to license your patent to a manufacturer or to sell it outright, you will need the services of a contract attorney to guide you through the writing of the licensing contract. You can be sure that the company you deal with will be using attorneys for their best interests, so do not go into these negotiations without an advocate on your behalf.

ALERT!

Be sure to visit with your legal advisor or your accountant before signing a license agreement. For tax purposes, you will need to know beforehand to what entity your royalty checks will be written—whether to you as an individual, a corporation, a partnership, or some other arrangement.

Some attorneys have more than one specialty. For example, quite a few patent attorneys are also contract attorneys. This is a great combination in the legal field: someone who can get you through the patent process and then see you through the licensing as well. It may be that your patent attorney is not also a contract attorney, or perhaps you have not been dealing with an attorney at all up to this point. Whatever the case, the time for working out the disposition of your invention is no time to cling to nickels and dimes.

Spiritual Advisors

Some of you will feel the need to confer with your spiritual advisor at this point. If this is the sphere in which you receive your most trusted guidance, then by all means, go to that person now. The point here is to get whatever help you need as you enter this uncharted territory. When you make the decision that will affect your future and the futures of those closest to you, it is vital that you make your decisions armed with as much information as possible.

Chapter 15

Building a Business Around Your Invention

If you have decided to create a business around your invention, you probably have a large collection of questions about how to proceed. What do I need to know in order to get started? What do I need to get started? Where can I find help? What are the steps and in what order do I take them? Your ultimate success depends on how prepared you are to face the hurdles involved in starting up a new enterprise. This chapter will be your guide through the challenges ahead.

Setting Up Your Business

The first things you will need to consider, even before the basics of actually setting up the company, will be your personal issues. These issues are at the top of the list because they can make or break your efforts to create a business. Unlike licensing your invention or otherwise disposing of the responsibility for the product, owning your own business will affect every area of your life, positively or negatively.

There are three main considerations when assessing your new endeavor from a personal point of view. The first issue will be the financial risk involved. You will need to make sure that you have sufficient capital going in, realizing that every mistake will cost you money. It will help you to seek cost-effective resources, discussed later in this chapter, to help you in your start-up. This type of help can replace expensive consultations in some areas of getting started in business.

Your next issue to consider is your personal risk. It will be necessary to understand the commitment required and to obtain the support of your family. As Alan Beckley, business consultant with the SBDC of Plano, Texas, puts it, "If your family doesn't have the conversation beforehand, six months later there will be an ugly conversation." You will need to find that essential balance of business and family needs. You will need to adjust your priorities as necessary to maintain harmony in your personal life while giving your business the attention it requires.

The last personal consideration is in the area of legal risk. Unfortunately, lawsuits are a part of business. Effective legal counsel will be important over time.

Resources

It is in the early days of the formation of your business when you are likely to need the most help. Fortunately, help is available through several sources right in your area and much of it is entirely free.

Small Business Development Center

Your local SBDC, with over 900 offices across the United States, exists for one purpose: to assist small business owners. They are known for providing a variety of free and low-cost services, some of which are:

- Low-cost training classes on a variety of business topics
- Free counseling with business consultants
- Business plan development and assistance
- Information on SBA-backed loans

Your local SBDC can also assist you with referrals to CPAs, attorneys, banks, and other financial resources that are small business–friendly. They can direct you to all of the resources that are available in your area.

Service Corps of Retired Executives

Another excellent resource for individuals starting a new business is the Service Corps of Retired Executives (SCORE), a resource partner with the SBA. This organization consists of a national network of 10,500 retired and working volunteers who are experienced entrepreneurs and corporate managers or executives.

If you are starting a new business, why reinvent the wheel? These folks have been there and done that. SCORE offers free, confidential face-to-face and online business counseling. They will answer business questions online for you through their Web site. You will also find templates on their Web site to help you develop your business plan, create financial statements and balance sheets, and figure start-up expenses, profit projections, and cash flow statements.

Public Libraries

Public libraries are invaluable free resources to help you start and grow your business. The reference librarians are familiar with all of the directories, trade journals, and other materials that can be of immense help to you in determining your market. The in-depth knowledge you can gain from this free resource can help to give you an edge over your competition. Some of the reference sources that you find in your library, such as the Thomas Register, are also available online.

FACT

Public libraries offer online resource databases that you can access from home if you have a library card with them. You will find ReferenceUSA, EBSCOhost, GALENET (including the Business and Company Resource Center), Facts on File, and numerous other helpful resources. Check with your librarian or your library system's Web site to find out what is available in your area.

Trade Associations

Joining industry associations can keep you abreast of current trends and statistics that will affect your bottom line. Industry magazines and trade journals published by the trade associations will be a good source of even more trend information and additional resources through their articles and advertising.

Mentors

You will need to create a team of mentors to help ensure your success. Among these mentors will be your CPA and your attorney. Because tax laws change frequently, your CPA can help you avoid expensive mistakes. He can represent you during a tax audit if necessary. Either of these professionals can counsel you in choosing the legal business type (sole proprietorship, partnership, LLC, type of corporation, etc.) for your business. This decision will be important to you for legally minimizing your tax burden on business profits and for reducing your personal financial risk from lawsuits. Your patent attorney will also assist you with contracts and the handling of any intellectual property. You will also need an insurance agent to insure your business risks. These professionals will help you plan an effective path for the growth of your business.

Your Business Identity

One essential for anyone who is contemplating starting a business is the creation of a business plan. If that sounds intimidating, there is help in almost all of the previously mentioned resources for handling this task. To begin a business without a business plan is what Alan Beckley calls the wing and a prayer plan, and that is exactly what it is. It is like starting on a long journey without a road map. Your business plan is your road map. You will need it to plan and manage your business. A business plan will be required if you intend to obtain a small business bank loan. You will find a business plan form, provided by the SBDC, in Appendix D of this book.

The name that you select for your business is your DBA. This acronym stands for *doing business as*. A DBA allows you to legally operate your company under a name other than your own. If you are using your own name but you are adding something to it, such as *Tom Smith Auto Parts*, that would be a DBA. Declaring your DBA is a simple matter of going to your local county clerk's office and paying a small fee, usually under $100. Before you can register your DBA, you will need to do a name search to be certain that the name you intend to use is available to you. Even if you plan only to operate your business within your local area, doing a national name search is a good idea. Although you are not required to do a national search before applying and your county may accept your application, if the name you select is registered nationally, you could eventually be challenged and have to give it up after investing time and money.

ESSENTIAL

In working with templates to develop your business plan, you will answer many questions in order to determine your exact situation as a start-up business. Then you will refine the information down to a form that is easily readable and something that you can use for a guide to operating the business and for obtaining advice and assistance.

Financial Needs

Money is one of the biggest concerns of anyone starting a new business. The general rule of thumb is that you will need enough to run the business for six months. Obviously, you will need that amount in addition to the amount you need to live on. Only you can determine what those amounts are, but you will need to do that in order to have some sense of security as you start out. Your business plan and your business mentors can help you.

As for where to get money, that is the most difficult part of starting a business for any entrepreneur. There are sources for funding, depending on what your invention is and how you plan to promote it. The SCORE Web site has basic information on obtaining money for new businesses, and Jack Lander has an excellent new book, *How to Finance Your Invention or Great Idea*. If you go to Jack's Web site *www.inventor-mentor.com*, you can read the entire first chapter to determine if it will be helpful to you.

You will also need to set up a company bank account. The bank representative who opens your account will walk you through the steps involved, but you will need to provide them with proof of your business status, such as your DBA documents or your certificate of incorporation. You may want to set up merchant accounts in order to accept credit cards such as VISA or MasterCard for purchases of your product. Your bank can help you set these up.

FACT

Nielsen, the company that tracks the popularity of television programs, also tracks retail sales through the UPC bar codes. It is possible to get reports showing sales of most products in several ways: regionally, type of retail establishment (mass merchandisers or specific product category), and specific products within a product line. Manufacturers often use these reports to track their competition.

UPC Code

If you plan to place your product with retailers, you will need to obtain a UPC code. The UPC acronym stands for Universal Product Code. This is the little bar code that you see on retail products. It is a group of lines of varying length and width and the numbers represented by those lines are directly beneath them. There are twelve numbers in a UPC code, one-half of them representing the manufacturer's identification number and the other half representing the individual product. GS1 US, the organization that assigns the codes for the United States, has recently joined with European Article Number International (EAN) to provide codes that can be read in any country in the world.

The GS1 US provides information on their Web site regarding how to get set up to use UPC codes. In order to get a UPC code for your company so that you can place UPC bar code symbols on your products, you will need to obtain a membership in the GS1 US for your company. You may apply online at their Web site, *www.gs1us.org/gs1us.html*. Your application generates the amount of your membership fee based mostly on your answers to the following questions:

- What is the current or projected sales revenue for your company?
- How many products will you be identifying with UPC symbols?
- How many locations might you be identifying with a Global Location Number?

Using the answers to these questions, the council will determine your membership fee. You can go online to their Web site and go through the application process up to that point to determine what your fee will be. You do not have to complete the application at that time. Once you have obtained the membership and been assigned your company's identification number, you can take that to companies in your area that specialize in creating bar code labels, stickers, and other UPC materials.

You will only need to use UPC codes if you plan to offer your product through retailers. If you intend to sell exclusively through the Internet, through catalogs, or through your own storefront, you will not be required to use bar codes and will not need to join the GS1 US.

Distribution Channels

Before you can begin distributing your product, you need to be able to store it. Warehousing your product will be your responsibility, mainly because only you know how much product you will need to store and how much space it will take. You can most likely handle this chore with a few phone calls and perhaps some networking with business associates to find out what is available.

Research is necessary to determine the best and most economical way to get your product marketed. There are a number of ways to market a product when you are the manufacturer. You might use one or a combination of these ways and change methods as the market dictates.

Internet Marketing

It is relatively inexpensive to set up a Web site and a shopping cart account to sell your product via the Internet. Your biggest obstacle with this method is how to drive the traffic to your Web site. With millions of Web sites on the Internet, it will take some special marketing ingenuity and perhaps some paid assistance to get enough traffic to the site to make sales. Even Web sites with lots of traffic do not have large sales numbers unless they have something truly unique that the public considers a special bargain. You can set up a shopping cart account through a company such as PayPal.

Direct Response Marketing

Infomercials are a great way to introduce a new product and they often result in spectacular sales numbers. This is referred to as direct response marketing. There are two basic ways to get your product into an infomercial. The first is to pay all of the up-front costs to have a professional commercial filmed and then pay for the television airtime. If you have lots of money to get your product before the public, this is a great way to get it out there quickly. Consumer education is one of the biggest hurdles facing new products, and infomercials do an excellent job of presenting new products. Infomercials can be as short as one minute or as long as thirty minutes or more. If you have the money to create your own infomercials, there are companies that will take care of all the details for you, including writing, casting, and filming the commercial, booking the airtime, and setting up fulfillment houses to handle shipping. You can find them through Internet search engines or by contacting your local television stations.

The second way to get your product into an infomercial is a good way if you do not have the money to have an infomercial made. It won't cost you any money up front. There are companies that will create your infomercial, book and pay for the airtime, and handle fulfillment house and shipping details for a percentage of the profits. Even if it is a relatively high percentage, if the product sells well you will make money and create a demand for the product. These companies are very selective as to what products they will promote. You can locate these companies in the same way that you locate the previously mentioned companies, through local television stations or the Internet. If you look for them on the Internet, be very careful to check them out thoroughly as there are some crooks operating in this area. Be sure to get references and check them to see that they followed up on their promises. If they are legitimate, they will not ask you for any money at all since they take their money from the proceeds after the infomercial begins airing.

Once the product moves from television to store shelves, you will have a chance to really profit from your invention. Be sure to have it clearly stated in your contract with the infomercial company that the aftermarket belongs to you.

QUESTION?

What is a fulfillment house?
The place where the phone calls from an infomercial are answered by trained sales people who take the orders and arrange for shipping the merchandise from their warehouse.

Television Shopping Channels

Another way to get your product jump-started is to get it on the TV shopping channels. The people who select products for these shopping shows have a good feel for what will sell in that forum and are extremely selective in their choices of products. If you are fortunate enough to have your product selected for one of these shows, you will need to have a large amount of product ready to ship to them. The television shopping networks usually require a minimum initial amount of $20,000 to $25,000 per individual item at its wholesale cost. They will buy the product from you, but it is your responsibility to have it individually packaged, labeled, and shipped to their warehouse in accordance with their guidelines. It can then be up to a year before the product airs on television. If you are interested in checking with any of these shopping channels, including some that are strictly Internet shopping sites, just go into any search engine on the Internet and use the key word *shopping*. This will bring up links for all of the television shopping channels as well as the Internet sites. Each of the individual sites contains links leading you to information on how to submit your product.

Catalogs

Placing your product in catalogs is probably the easiest way to get it before the public. Just as the shopping channels do, catalog companies have rules for placing merchandise with them, but it is generally easier to get a product with a catalog and some inventors continue to place more and more products this way for years. Some catalogs do not even require that you have your product patented. Almost all catalogs are online now, so you would have your product represented both in print and on the Internet.

Each catalog company has its own guidelines for submitting merchandise, so just go to a search engine and type in *catalogs*. This will bring up numerous links. When you find the catalogs that fit your invention, visit their individual Web sites and check out all of the links. They usually have a place on their sites giving preliminary information for making product submissions. If the one you are interested in does not have such information on its Web site, go through their contact information and send them an e-mail or phone them.

Distributors and Sales Reps

If you wish to get your product into the retail stores but you do not want to fight the battle of getting appointments with the buyers, you have two other choices. There are distributors that maintain warehouses where they have merchandise from a number of manufacturers and they distribute to specific segments of the market. For example, there is a distributor in Dallas, Texas, that handles school and office supplies and they cover several states, distributing those supplies to small office supply and school supply stores. They have both catalogs and sales representatives to get their merchandise in the stores. A manufacturer simply wholesales the product to them and they take care of placing it in the stores. To find a distributor of products in your category, check with some of the smaller stores that sell merchandise in your category, then ask their management for the name and contact information for distributors.

If you wish to engage individual sales representatives to represent your product to retailers, including the larger retailers, contact any store that carries products similar to yours and ask them for the name and contact information for the product representatives who stock their shelves.

Trade Shows

There are trade shows for every type of product where manufacturers can buy booth space to show and sell their products. If you wish to follow this path, go into a search engine and type *trade shows*. This will bring up links for trade show associations as well as individual trade shows. Explore these links and you will find the exact trade show you are seeking. The individual trade show Web site will give you information on dates, places, booth rental, and hotel prices.

Trade shows offer a method that manufacturers often use when they are introducing a new product. Most of them do not use it as the only way of marketing. A trade show allows the new product to be seen by a large target market of potential buyers who are there specifically to see new products, a special advantage.

Offshore Manufacturing

A major decision, if you have decided to have your product manufactured, will be whether you will make the product in the United States or offshore. Domestic manufacturing for most products is too costly and you may find that you will obtain greater profits by having your product made in China.

Getting your product manufactured in China can be an excellent way to cut your costs, but there are some key things you will need to know before you begin that can save you some headaches and perhaps a great deal of money as well. The first thing you need to know is that you must do it through a trading company.

Trading Companies

Why do you need a trading company? Why can't you just go to China and handle it all yourself? There are some compelling reasons *not* to take that course of action. In order to export from China legally, you *must* use a certified trading company. While many Chinese factories own trading companies, there is overhead associated with that and you will likely pay for it in your product pricing, whether you know it or not. Some factories may tell you that they are only dealing directly with you when you actually may be dealing with two or even three different trading companies before you are done and all of this is made transparent to you. Some Hong Kong trading companies have been known to entertain U.S. clients, telling them that they are factory direct when in reality they are contracting the job out to a mainland China trading company for all of the sourcing work. Not only are such clients paying for layers of which they are unaware, the communication gets weaker with each layer, resulting in more problems and greater expense.

E ALERT!

If you choose to manufacture in China, you need to take Chinese custom and tradition into account. Even if you can get directly to a factory that can export through its own trading company, chances are that a local trading company could negotiate a better price and better value for you than you can on your own. A good trading company will provide value through the entire process—development, manufacturing, quality control, and even logistics.

When you are experiencing the challenges of sourcing, manufacturing, and shipping products from China for the first time, you will want to find a company that can provide a high level of service to small to midsize companies. How do you find such a company? Mike Clarke, a Dallas, Texas, jeweler, is a partner in one such company, Silver Dragon Enterprise, Ltd., and he offers some advice for finding a good trading company.

What to Look for in a Trading Company

Mike says there is specific information you need to know to be certain that the trading company you select can give you the assistance and service you need. Here are the questions he suggests you should ask:

- Does your company have some English speakers?
- How much experience do the American partners have in this business?
- Does the trading company have its own quality control (QC) people in the factories?
- Do you trust them?

If the company has its own QC people, how often are they there during the process of manufacturing your product? What are their QC procedures? Do they understand your key quality components (KQCs) and how have they measured the production against your product's KQCs? Ask these questions up-front.

Just as in any business arrangement anywhere in the world, you must develop trust to have a good working relationship. How do you determine if there is trust? This is a difficult matter and it varies greatly depending on the individuals involved, but one thing you can do is take notice of their interest in you and your product. Are they asking enough questions about your product? Are they asking enough questions about *you*? Do they seem genuinely interested in learning about your company?

Mike also notes that if you do go to China on your own and plan to hire a translator to assist you at the factory, be aware of the things that can happen. If you have no clue about the Chinese language, what is to stop a translator from actually demanding that the factories treat him as a broker, right in front of you, without your knowledge? This happens. Now you have another layer you are unaware of and you will pay for that layer, too. He suggests that you try to find a trading company you can communicate with very well and use them to handle your factory visits.

Risks for Business Owners

Be certain that you go into this venture with your eyes wide open. Be aware of the risks involved in manufacturing so that there will be no nasty surprises. These risks are present in two general areas, manufacturing and distribution.

ALERT!

Retailers require proof of product liability insurance in amounts based on the perceived danger of the product. Even the most innocuous product can be a danger to someone, if it is used improperly. Even with warnings and disclaimers on the packaging, it can be expensive if you have to defend the product in court.

Manufacturing Risks

When you are the manufacturer, the liability of consumer injury through improper usage of your product is an issue that you must deal with in order to place your product in stores.

Another risk issue to consider is that of errors in your initial prototypes or your first runs of the product. If you are creating a new product that requires injection molding, a mistake can cost thousands of dollars. Haste in getting through this step can destroy your budget.

Obtain the help you need to be certain that you have your final and best design before investing in expensive molds. You may be able to utilize one of the rapid prototyping methods to work out all of the bugs in your design before going into full production.

Even though you can cut your costs by making larger quantities, manufacturing errors in the beginning can put you out of business. A warehouse full of product that you cannot sell can deplete your financial resources.

Distribution Risks

The actual distribution of your product is one of the most important areas of your business planning. It will be necessary for you to understand the distribution risks from the retailer's viewpoint.

- Shelf space is valued at hundreds of dollars per inch.
- The risk of single-product vendors is high.
- Large retailers prefer to work through manufacturers' representatives.

Be sure that you have a scalable manufacturer who can cost-effectively manufacture a few hundred as well as many thousands of units of your product. Starting small will help you to mitigate financial risk while determining your market. Better to spend a bit more for a small initial run than to overproduce and tie up your funds.

Many retailers work within a very small margin of profit. Product display space in retail stores is highly coveted by wholesalers. This retail display space is worth hundreds of dollars per inch to retailers. In most cases, a product must be removed in order to place a new product on the shelves, making it very difficult for a new vendor to obtain space.

An individual or a small company with just one product may be unable to ensure that sufficient product will be available to keep the stores stocked in the event of manufacturing, financial, or shipping difficulties.

Even if your goal is to offer your product in the large chain stores, it might be worthwhile to consider working with smaller retailers initially since they are more likely to be receptive to new products from individuals. This also allows you to reduce your warehouse requirements and manufacturing runs.

Starting small can be very helpful in the beginning while you are getting on solid financial ground. Once you are established with small retailers, it is usually much easier to get your product into the large retail chains.

Large manufacturers have their own sales personnel who make regular visits to the retail buyers, and many of them use independent representatives to help in covering the territories. If you want to utilize one of these independent representatives, there are several ways to locate them. One way is to check with your reference librarian for a trade journal of an association in that industry. Often such trade journals will have information or advertising for these individuals. You can also contact the trade association in your product category and ask for names and contact information for product representatives.

The business and technology section of your public library has manufacturers' directories for most categories; these directories sometimes have a section of listings for product distributors. Another way is to go directly to the management of a local store that sells similar merchandise and ask them for the name of the individuals who rep such products to them. You can also find product representatives in booths at trade shows.

Chapter 16

Finding a Licensee

You have come a long way! You have developed your great idea and protected it or at least applied for patent protection on it. You have decided to license your invention to a manufacturer. You will find licensing to be immensely easier if you carefully match your product with the manufacturers who could benefit from its addition to their existing lines. This chapter will deal with the many places to find your licensee.

Existing Products

One of the first things to do when you have your great idea is go out to the stores and check to make sure that the product you want to pursue is not already on the market. This is the very beginning of the market research for most inventors. In the case of most inventions, because your idea is an improvement on one or more products that are currently offered for sale, you will see those similar products in the stores. This will be your first opportunity to see who is manufacturing this type of product.

Make a list of your targets (potential licensees) as you do your market research. You will find these companies listed on product packaging, on the Internet, and in catalogs. As you obtain new information on these companies, you will begin to prioritize your list as to which would be the best fit or the most lucrative for your product.

Be sure to conduct your product search at every store that could conceivably offer a product such as yours. If yours is a specialty item, such as a golf accessory, after you have checked the golf specialty stores you will want to check general sporting goods stores as well as any store that might carry golf items. You will find that while the large retailers generally carry the same well-known brands, they often carry different items within that brand. An example of this is in the area of electronics. Often you will find several models of video recorders in one of the large electronics stores. An examination of the similar equipment offered by that retailer's competitor is likely to reveal several video recorders of the same brand, but slightly different models. The buyers for these retailers have a large number of models from which to choose and no retailer is likely to carry every model made by each manufacturer. It is important for you to see everything out there that is similar to your invention.

ALERT!

Do not overlook smaller manufacturers in your search for licensing targets. Often these companies will take a new product and give it prominence within their product line that you would never get from a large manufacturer. This can be the boost that makes your product a contender in the marketplace.

Trade Shows

Trade shows are probably the best way to get a look at all of the manufacturers of products in your category in the shortest amount of time. Most if not all categories of products have trade associations to which the manufacturers belong. The associations are vital to manufacturers because, among other member benefits, they sponsor the trade shows for their products.

Trade Show Basics

Some product categories have more than one association to which those manufacturers belong. When this is the case, sometimes there are two distinctly separate markets for the product. One such product category is school supplies. In addition to the retail market that includes the stores where individuals would go to buy supplies, there is the education market that sells exclusively to schools and institutions through catalogs and Web sites. This could mean two entirely different license agreements for the inventor who has an item desired by both markets. Moreover, each license would be an exclusive for that market. It is possible to find more than one market in the same trade show, so keep your eyes open to the possibilities of each company that might be a fit for your invention.

ESSENTIAL

Become familiar with every possible market for your invention. If yours is a *crossover* product that appears in two or more different markets, you may be able to obtain two separate exclusive licenses and increase your royalty income from that product. Be sure you know this information before signing an exclusive agreement.

While most manufacturers have sales personnel that stay in contact with the buyers for the retail stores, it is at the trade shows where the situation is reversed and the buyers come to the manufacturers. This gives the manufacturers an opportunity to display and highlight everything in their product lines. It also allows plenty of time for company employees to visit and discuss products with buyers in an unrestricted way. It is an opportunity for manufacturers to demonstrate and explain their new products.

Trade shows are also an excellent opportunity for you, the inventor, to find most products that are at all similar to your invention and the manufacturers who are the closest match for your product.

How to Get In

So how do you gain access to trade shows? Most trade shows are exactly that, product shows that are produced specifically for the manufacturers of products within that particular category. There are several purposes for these shows, such as ongoing education for the manufacturers within the association and updates on product trends. But the main purpose for trade shows is to allow the manufacturers to showcase their products, old and new, for the retail buyers and to make sales.

Trade association shows have no admission charge, but they do have rules about who can attend. These associations have Web sites that provide information on their trade shows, often including the criteria for admission. The easiest way to qualify is to have a membership, but you will need to fit within one of their membership categories to join the association. Generally, in addition to manufacturers and buyers, there will be an associate membership category. This is sort of a catchall category for other interested parties, including licensors, consultants, media, and suppliers of products such as packaging. These associate memberships are usually far less expensive than regular memberships, and if they are not too expensive, this is the easiest way to become an instant industry insider.

What to Do Once You're In

There is one cardinal rule for product developers about trade shows. *Do not attempt to visit with manufacturers on the first day of the show!* These shows usually run for two or three days, and on the first day the manufacturers are deluged with buyers from around the country. While they appear to be just chatting and showing off their products, this is very serious business for manufacturers. They have spent thousands of dollars setting up their booths and sending personnel to work those booths. This is when they are earnestly trying to make sales to these retail buyers. They will not look kindly upon anyone who wishes to take their attention for any other purpose on those days that are so important to their bottom lines. Instead, spend that first day just walking around and familiarizing yourself with all of the booths and with which manufacturers will be your targets.

FACT

Membership in a trade association is often the key to open communication with manufacturers. Associate or consultant memberships are often far less expensive than full memberships. Any type of membership is effective for getting the attention of decision-makers and it sometimes makes the difference in whether you get an appointment.

If you have spent this time well as an information-gathering time, it will make your return visit on the last day of the show much more advantageous for you. By the last day of the show, you will find that most of the buyers have handled their business and gone home. The manufacturers' representatives who are working in those booths are usually very bored by this time, clock-watching and drumming their fingers. They are just waiting to tear down the booths and leave. At this time, they will be happy to visit with you and to hear what you have to say. Remember to leave your business card and pick up theirs as well.

Always ask them if their company licenses from outside product developers. Some companies work exclusively with their in-house product developers. If you run across one of these, just remain pleasant and then make a notation on the back of their card that this is a company you will avoid. Do not take your prototype or product with you and do not attempt to make an actual appointment at this time. This is just a time for opening the door so that you can contact them later and they will be receptive to you.

FACT

Manufacturers often have scanners in their trade show booths where they create a permanent record of your business card. This eliminates the loss of a card and it allows the information to be kept and shared with the entire product development department. It also serves as proof to the manufacturer that you really were at the trade show.

Let Them Find You

This instruction to "Let them find you" does not suggest that you just sit there and do nothing to promote your invention. Thanks to some good Web sites on the Internet, there are ways that you can display your invention in the hope that a potential licensee will see it.

Companies That Promote Inventions

Some of these companies, such as InventionHome.com and Market-Launchers.com, actually build Web pages for you. They are in contact with manufacturers, product scouts, etc., to direct them to the new inventions that are available for licensing. Some also offer other services to help you with marketing, such as animated virtual prototypes that show prospective licensees how the invention works.

These companies offer choices of pricing structures based on the needs of the individual inventor. Be cautious in your choice of an Internet service to do this for you. There are charlatans out there who make such offers but they have no plan for driving the traffic to the Web site. The obvious result of this is that you are paying for the publicity but the right people still do not see your invention.

The best way to determine whether or not you are dealing with a legitimate company is to check with the FTC (*www.ftc.gov*) to see if there have been any complaints or actions against the company or check on one of the "good guy" Web sites, such as *www.inventored.org* or *www.uiausa.org* to see if they have any comments about the company. Your local inventor group may be another source of references for legitimate licensing companies. Still another way is to ask for references from other independent inventors who have used their services. Be aware when doing this, however, that they may only refer you to their satisfied customers.

Advertisements in Trade Publications

Still another way to let them find you is to run advertisements in trade association newsletters, magazines, or journals. Most of these publications accept advertising. The beauty of this method is that the publications are targeted to the specific types of companies that might be interested in licensing your product. The obstacle to this approach is that advertising is not cheap and in order to get noticed by the appropriate people you may need to run your ad repeatedly. If you can afford the cost of the ads, however, it may be an effective way to get your product noticed by the right people. If you write well and can write an article describing the problem that is solved by your invention and how it is solved, submit that and you may get some great free publicity sent to your exact target market.

Establish Your Own Web Site

A final way to let them find you is to establish your own Web site for your product. This is probably the most ineffective and inefficient way to attract potential licensees, because it is easy (though not always inexpensive) to set up a Web site but very difficult to drive traffic to it. The cost of getting your Web site ranked high on the various search engines can be prohibitive. Most importantly, however, creating your own Web site is a real hit-and-miss approach. The likelihood of the right person from the right company happening across your Web site is fairly slim, though it's not impossible. Overall, this approach is not a cost-effective way to get your product noticed.

Licensing Agents

If you have an outstanding invention and you are willing to give up a portion of your royalty, some legitimate licensing agents will market your invention for you. You already know that the airwaves and the print media are full of advertising for such services. You also know that if you see them advertised, even on respectable television networks or in respectable magazines and newspapers, this is not an indication that these companies are worthy of your trust. So, how do you go about finding the agents who can really get your product marketed for you?

Because the industry that offers services to independent inventors is still in its infancy, there is little regulation of the companies offering these services. The Internet, completely unregulated, is fertile ground for swindlers. It is vital that you know who you are dealing with in order to find legitimate help if you want someone else to take over the marketing for you. Legitimate licensing agents are not the charlatans discussed previously. Legitimate licensing agents are agents who generally work within specific sectors of the market and are known and trusted by manufacturers. Manufacturers often rely on them to bring them new and innovative products. The fact that they are known in the industry makes it easier for them to present and license products than it is for Joe Blow, the inventor.

Some suggested ways to find legitimate marketing agents are:

- **Ask the manufacturers.** Call the manufacturers that are your licensing targets and ask for names and contact information for the agents with whom they work.
- **Find advertising in trusted media sources.** Look for advertising from a source that is specifically for independent inventors, such as *Inventors' Digest* magazine or the United Inventors Association Web site, *www.uiausa.org*.
- **Contact Licensing Executives Society (LES) for referrals.** This group is composed of over 5,000 members who are involved in marketing intellectual property. Not all of the members are actually licensing agents. Members of this organization are lawyers, business executives, consultants, corporations, and even universities. Learn more on their Web site, *www.usa-canada.les.org/aboutus*.
- **Get word-of-mouth referral from satisfied customers.** Consult someone you know and trust, such as your patent attorney or your local inventor's club or association, for a referral.

Library Resources

Your local reference librarian is an excellent resource for finding potential licensees. The librarians in the reference department are well versed in what directories are available for all types of information relating to businesses. One of the best-known directories of information on all business categories is the Thomas Register. This resource in print form is a set of twenty books containing current information on over 165,000 U.S. and Canadian manufacturers. Updated annually, these books have the information listed in several ways so that you can find them by company name, product category, or SIC code. They have complete contact information for all of these companies and their subsidiaries, as well as annual sales figures and number of employees. The Thomas Register is also available on the Internet. The actual books at the library have more complete information, so you may want to check them out first.

FACT

Most, if not all, public libraries are online now and many of them offer online databases such as ReferenceUSA and GALENET through the library's computers. You can also access them from your home computer if you have a current library card from which you can input your card number.

Another good resource for information on big companies is the D & B Million Dollar Database. This is the same type of information as that of the Thomas Register, but it is advisable to check both to make sure that you do not overlook a good possibility—you may find some in the D & B Database that are not in the Thomas Register, or vice versa. This database is also available online.

In addition to these general directories, every trade association has membership directories. Membership directories often contain more information about the companies and their product lines than the general ones. Some of these can be found at public libraries in the reference departments and some may be available online at the trade organizations' Web sites.

Internet Searches

On the Internet, you can do key word searches that will bring up manufacturers of any imaginable product. But there is another, little known way that is a good method of finding companies that license patents. This method is in the USPTO online patent database. If you did any online searching for your invention, you undoubtedly saw, right on the first pages of the patent under the inventor's name, that some patents were listed as having been assigned to a manufacturer. Sometimes such patents have been obtained by employees of the company and are automatically assigned to the company under the terms of the employee's contract. However, sometimes the assignment is from an outside inventor.

When you find patents that have been assigned to a manufacturing company, that company is a potential licensee for your invention. The patent lists only the company name, city, and state where it is located. This is a starting point for locating the company. You may be able to find them simply by picking up the telephone, calling Information, and asking for the listing for the company in that town. If you are able to reach them, the receptionist will be able to give you the physical address as well as the mailing address. She may also be able to give you the name of the person heading the new-product division of the company and the telephone extension for that person.

If you are unable to get the manufacturer's phone number from the telephone company's information operator, it may be because they are actually in a suburb of the town listed. In that case, try finding them on the Internet by just typing the company name into any search engine or by using Switchboard, the national Yellow and White Page directory that is available free of charge at *www.switchboard.com*.

Chapter 17

Getting the Word Out

No matter how revolutionary your product may be, in today's fast-moving world you will have to make a creative effort to get it noticed. You will need to find a way to stand out from the crowd. The consuming public looks at what is right in front of it, and then only for a moment unless something about the product captures its fancy. Manufacturers are busy running their businesses and they simply do not pore over patent registrations looking for new products.

Publicity

Publicity is a catchall term that can refer to many different ways to vie for attention. Even if you have never liked the idea of boasting or being in the public eye, you will have to get creative in order to bring your invention before the targets you plan to market it to. The shyest of inventors often finds that he loves publicizing his inventions. After all, who better to explain the benefits of a great new product than the inventor himself?

Become familiar with the ways that you can promote your product. Many of the ways are entirely free and take only a bit of your time and some creative thought. You have been actively involved in the process up to this point and your active involvement now will ensure that you get your product seen by the right people.

Free Publicity

While you can hire a product publicist, you will probably do a better job on your own if you will devote the necessary time and effort to the project. It is possible to get yourself and your product featured on television and radio and in print media for no cash outlay at all with just a little ingenuity on your part.

Very few inventors come up with great new products because they sat down and said to themselves, "Hmmm, I wonder what I can invent today." Almost all inventions come about because someone recognizes the need for the new item. Unless you work as a professional product developer, there is a story behind your invention. Telling the story of how you happened to think of and develop your invention can be an excellent opportunity to get the word out about your new product.

Jeff Crilley, an Emmy award–winning reporter for Fox 4 television in Dallas, Texas, has written a great book called *Free Publicity*. Jeff's book, written by one who works in the newsroom of a busy metropolitan television station, is the real deal from an insider. *Free Publicity* tells you what makes a story newsworthy according to someone who is in the business of reporting. He gives the elements of a good story as having the following qualities:

- It is timely.
- It impacts people.
- It is unusual and sometimes controversial.

Jeff says that the timing of when you choose to pitch your story to the media is of major importance. Knowing when the slow news days and times are will help you get your story selected for use on the air or in print media. For example, if you select a day immediately after a big holiday, your chances of getting your story covered are much better because reporters are often looking for something to cover at these slow news times.

How you tell your story is a factor in making it rise to the top of the stack of stories that newsrooms receive in large numbers daily. Your story will have to meet the "Who cares?" standard by which most reporters judge interest level. What is the angle to your story that makes it something to which others can relate? Did something weird happen to you that pushed you to create a solution? Perhaps it is some unusual challenge you overcame during its development. It might be who *you* are: your age, sex, or lifestyle. Is your invention something that is unusual coming from someone like yourself?

In order for your story to be newsworthy, it must be unusual. As Jeff says, "We don't cover the ordinary, we cover the extraordinary." If your story has some controversy attached to it, all the better. As long as you are secure in your position, the fact that you are swimming upstream can add the interest factor necessary to make the news reporters want to cover your story.

FACT

A story about you carries a much bigger impact than any advertising you could buy. Paid advertising is actually you talking about yourself or your product. While the public sometimes casts a jaundiced eye at paid advertising, they will readily accept as true and believable something that the media says about you and your invention.

Sometimes, if your story is of wide interest, the wire services will pick it up and you will get nationwide newspaper publicity. The same thing can happen with television coverage. In that case, the news feed picks it up and all of the networks use it. A story that originally aired in your local area may be shown again and again all across the country, a real publicity bonus for the lucky subject. Increase your chances of getting lucky with your publicity by learning from those who know the publicity industry.

Other Publicity Ideas

Other ways to get publicity for your invention involve paying close attention to the time of the year, holidays that might have a tie-in with your product, or events for which you can create a tie-in to your invention. Mike Clarke, the inventor of the Jewel Jet home steam jewelry cleaner, took his product to a kiosk in a mall in January and February for a Valentine promotion. Jewelry is a traditional gift for Valentine's Day, so he set up an area where he offered free jewelry steam cleaning and each purchaser of a Jewel Jet was entered in a drawing to be held on Valentine's Day for a heart-shaped diamond ring. He practically caused a riot at the mall and received far more publicity than he could have purchased in advertising. While this was not an entirely free stunt, since Mike did have to rent the kiosk and give away a diamond ring, his sales figures far exceeded his expenses and the publicity introduced his product with a big splash.

FACT

If your story and your product have a natural connection to a particular time, season, activity, or event, it can make a good news story. If the story is interesting enough, it may run several times. Seize the opportunity to create your connection to anything that seems appropriate. You could get a lot of free publicity.

Look for occasions when you can just show up at a place where the media will be and get a share of the attention because you created a natural tie-in to the event. This would be free publicity and could get you television airtime, a newspaper article, or both. Keep an eye out for upcoming holidays or events that could be opportunities for you to display your invention.

News Releases

News releases are not just for the media. They are a great way of announcing your invention to the exact group that you want to reach, such as specific manufacturers if licensing is your goal. You can send the same release to manufacturers that you would send to the media.

News releases can be a very effective means of getting free publicity, but here again, you must know how to write something that the recipient will give more than a cursory glance. Jeff Crilley says that the best press releases are the ones with a bold, clever headline, such as you might see on the front page of a newspaper.

Pay special attention to the headline of your press release. It will not matter how interesting the information is that appears in the body of your release if no one reads that far. Grab the readers from the first line to make sure that they will continue reading. Use a pun, alliteration, or something with shock value as an attention getter.

News releases all have the same basic format. The secret to making your release rise to the top of the heap is in the careful attention that you give to every part of the document. Every line is important. The six basic parts are as follows:

1. Banner head (title)
2. Dateline
3. Contact
4. Headline
5. First paragraph
6. Second and possibly additional paragraphs

The parts of a news release are the same, though there is latitude in the exact placement of some elements. Your release should be on 8.5-by-11-inch paper, double-spaced except for the dateline and contact line. The important thing is to think of it as if you are writing an article for a newspaper or for broadcast media. You will want a headline that will immediately garner enough interest to make the reader continue reading. This is where Jeff Crilley's special angle comes into play. You can boast a bit here as long as you are truthful. If you can create a play on words that might have some shock value, all the better.

Your first paragraph will contain the information that answers the who, what, when, where, how questions. Even though it is information-packed, try to write it in an interesting, readable style. Your second paragraph will continue with information, and a quote is helpful here. A quote from a credible source, such as a manufacturer of similar products, gives substance to the claims in the release. If you need additional paragraphs or more than one page to complete the necessary information, you may do that, but remember to keep it as brief as possible. If you do use additional pages, be sure to number the pages.

Proof of Marketability

If you are making and selling some of your product, even in a small way, you are creating a record of accomplishment that can prove the marketability of your invention. Keep careful records of sales so that you will have proof that the product will sell and an indication of the price it will bring.

If your product is something that is inexpensive enough to make, you can give some of it away to your target market and, in return, get your recipients to fill out questionnaires. In the questionnaires, you will want to know such things as:

- What do you like about the product?
- What *don't* you like about it?
- How would you change it?
- If it were available, would you buy it?
- What would you be willing to pay for it?

Doing this simple survey, which should cost very little if your product is inexpensive enough to make, creates a *focus group study*. This is something that manufacturers do before introducing a new product to the public. They test the product on the exact consumers who are the target market for it.

This is information that will be invaluable to you, whether you plan to market the product yourself or to license it. When a user is particularly fond of the product, get a written testimonial from her and add this to your collection of materials that add strength to your case for marketability.

Displaying at Trade Shows

There are many opportunities to display your product via trade shows if you wish to rent a booth and use that method. All categories of products have their associations and the large trade shows that the associations offer once or twice annually. While these trade shows are usually a place for the large manufacturers to display their wares and take orders, any manufacturing member of the organization could rent a booth in most of these shows.

ALERT!

Be sure to have your patent protection in place by filing a patent application before displaying your product in public venues such as trade shows. Some attorneys advise against such a public disclosure even while your invention is "patent pending," so as to protect any trade secrets embodied in the product. Since the correct course of action depends on the nature of your invention and the product itself, a good rule is to check with your patent professional ahead of time.

Many smaller trade shows also offer display opportunities. Inventors' seminars, held in different cities across the country, often have booths available for displaying your product and the cost is usually very reasonable. These shows are always open to everyone to attend and to participate in booths and workshops. Manufacturers who could be potential licensees often attend these shows to see what is new.

Small distributors sometimes hold annual trade shows to display the products that they sell. The buyers for specific markets attend the shows of interest to them. Check with distributors in your product category or small, independent store managers to locate such opportunities. Many larger cities host home and garden shows, vehicle shows, etc. If your product fits into a category that hosts such shows, you could get a large audience for your invention, as these shows are generally well attended.

Participating in these shows will also give you a chance to meet manufacturers of similar products, which can be helpful if you wish to license your patent. It is also an opportunity to meet product representatives who may wish to add your product to their lines if you are manufacturing it.

The Phone Call

If you elect to contact manufacturers directly to show them your product for licensing, it is important that you call the right person and that you handle the call very professionally. Even if you have never done this kind of thing before, knowing a few secrets can help you to make the right impression from your first phone call.

Whom Do I Call?

If you have attended a trade show of products similar to yours and picked up business cards from the booths, you will have the name and contact information for the right person to call. If you have not done that and you are contacting a small to midsize manufacturer, ask for the president of the company. You may reach that person! If you do not, simply ask for the person who is the head of new product development. If you are contacting a large manufacturer, you should ask for the new product development department rather than the president.

What Do I Say?

Whether you reach the president or some other person, you should first introduce yourself and state that you are a product developer and you have a patented (or patent pending) product that is a perfect fit for their product line. If you have met them at a trade show and are calling from their business card, tell them that immediately. Knowing that you attended their trade show gives you a bit of an inside track psychologically.

You will say something like this: "Hello, Mr. Jones. I'm Jennifer Smith, a product developer from Wichita, Kansas. I met you at the XYZ trade show last month. I'm calling because I understand that your company licenses products from outside product developers and I have a patented product that is a perfect fit for your line. It just *looks* like a Brighton Enterprises product and I would love an opportunity to show it to you!"

ESSENTIAL

When you make that important phone call to schedule an appointment to show your invention to a manufacturer, be enthusiastic, but do not exaggerate. Say only what is true about your product. If you oversell the product in the beginning, you will lose any opportunity you may have had with that manufacturer.

At this point, the person to whom you are speaking will probably ask you what you wish to show him. Do not tell him exactly what it is. Rather, tell him that it is an *improved widget case.* Alternatively, you can tell him what problem your product solves, rather than what it actually is. For example, "We have a product that solves the problem of cams slipping in widgets." This should spur his interest enough that he will want to know more about it.

Be sure to tell him that it will take only a few minutes of his time and you believe that it will be worth his time to look at your product. Then listen carefully to what he says at this point. His comments here will let you know whether you will need to speak with another person or even whether to continue your efforts with this company.

ALERT!

Most large manufacturers have new product ideas pitched to them constantly. They are acutely aware of the danger of litigation from independent inventors over possible theft of an idea. They will likely require you to complete and return their submission documents acknowledging that they may have already seen your idea before they will look at your invention.

If a manufacturer asks you to sign submission documents, be aware that you have no choice if you wish to submit to them. These documents are weighted heavily in their favor, saying such things as they may have previously rejected the same idea or that they may actually be developing a similar product. If they state that one of the above situations is the case, they have no obligation to prove the claim to you. In this situation, as in many business relationships, an element of trust is necessary. It will be up to you to make the decision to continue with your disclosure or to abort this licensing attempt when the time comes. If you are presenting a patented product, that decision should be an easy one.

What Shouldn't I Say?

Even though you are the inventor of your product and you are rightly proud of that fact, one thing you should never do on this important phone call is describe yourself as an inventor. Many people have preconceived notions about inventors and they are not always flattering. A more professional way of describing yourself is to state that you are a product developer.

Another thing you should not do is use a lot of superlatives in your conversation. It is very off-putting to hear someone doing a lot of boasting about their invention being the greatest product ever invented, utterly unique and unprecedented. The fact is that there is almost nothing truly unique. Most inventions are improvements on earlier products. Even if you do have something that you feel is unique, soft-pedal the superlatives if you wish to develop a relationship with a manufacturer. If she feels that it is unique, let it come from her.

Finally, get the appointment or the agreement to send your information and get off the phone. Don't overstay your welcome, on the phone or in person.

Product Publicists

If the idea of doing your own publicity for your product is just abhorrent to you, it is possible to hire a product publicist. Product publicists are useful to the inventor who is building a business around his invention and needs help in getting publicity or generating a "buzz" for the product. Rather than paying for advertising for your product, which is always less effective than free publicity since the public is always a little suspect of an advertisement, product publicists concentrate their efforts on making your product newsworthy and getting free publicity in the form of newspaper articles, magazine articles, and mentions on television and radio programs. This is not an inexpensive way to go, but if you wish to do it and you can afford it, these companies will create the publicity around your product for you.

Most product publicists work on a contract basis and you will usually pay for a year in advance. Depending on the type of product, they will work to get mentions in newspapers and magazines, and on television shows. They will basically do the same thing that you would do for yourself, except that they are working to publicize several products at the same time. If your product has some unique or unusual aspect to it, they may be able to get air-time on national network shows such as *Good Morning America*, the *Today Show*, or other talk shows where they can show and discuss the product.

If you would like to check out product publicists, go to a search engine and type in the keywords *product publicist*. You will find several links that will tell you about these services and give you contact information for them.

Chapter 18

Presenting Your Invention for Licensing

P resenting your invention for licensing to potential licensees is a critical point in the inventing process. You may have the greatest product ever but if you blow it when presenting your product to manufacturers, all your hard work may be for naught. There are specific things you should do when presenting. This chapter will lay out a winning method for presenting your product and maximizing your chances of obtaining a license for it.

Who Is Your Target Customer?

In order for your product to succeed in the marketplace, it must solve a problem and be a value for the money. Consumers must welcome it. You know all this, so now it is time to shift gears. Your customer is the manufacturer, and your presentation to manufacturers must give them compelling reasons why your product will make money for them! They want the product to be accepted in the marketplace, but the bottom line for them is whether or not it fits in with their product line and whether or not it will make money for them. Therefore, as you prepare your product presentation, remember who your audience is—the manufacturer!

The Importance of Your Presentation

Before you call a manufacturer to make an appointment to show them your invention, you must prepare a professional-looking presentation that explains what your invention is and why it would be advantageous for them to license it. Even if you are going to meet with them personally it is important to leave a presentation with them that they can have to refer back to or to show to other key decision-makers in the company. Your presentation must be compelling enough to explain the value of your invention to that company even if you are not there! It must speak in your behalf and sell them on the worthiness of your product.

In order to *sell* them on your product it must answer all of their questions completely, accurately, and honestly. It must explain why your invention is a logical extension of their line of products, and it must explain how your invention will make money for them. That is the bottom line.

ESSENTIAL

Think of your written presentation as a dynamic representation of you that will say the things you would like to say about your product to whomever happens to read it. It is a way to make all of the important selling points in a form that will last beyond your meeting.

Every product presentation should answer the following questions:

- What exactly is your product?
- How does your product work?
- What will it cost to manufacture your product?
- How will your product benefit the manufacturer?
- How will consumers benefit from your product?
- What is the market for your product and how large is that market?
- What can your product be sold for at retail?
- Where should your product be sold?
- How should your product be packaged?
- How should your product be displayed?
- Why do potential licensees needs your product?

In order for your presentation to have any chance of succeeding, you must be *completely* truthful. Keep in mind that the manufacturer knows that industry better than you do. If you state something that is inaccurate, they will probably know it and then dismiss the entire presentation as unreliable. So know your facts before you begin. Spend all the time you need in thinking about each item in your presentation. Remember, it will be speaking for you long after you have left the meeting—and if you are unable to meet with the prospective licensee in person, it is doing *all* of the speaking for you. The importance of a first-rate presentation must not be underestimated.

When preparing your presentation, keep in mind that short lists are best. Your presentation should not be a report consisting of page after page of prose about your product. A report will most likely be set aside to be read when they have the time, but that time will probably never come! Long reports are too much like work. A presentation that consists of short, easy-to-read lists *will* be looked at, and that is what you want! You want them to look at the salient points about your invention. You will find a sample presentation in Appendix D at the back of this book.

Putting It Together

As you reference the sample presentation in Appendix D, you will notice that some of the questions you are answering appear on more than one page. There is a good deal of redundancy. That is done on purpose. It would be great if your potential licensee read each and every page of your presentation carefully, but that is unlikely. Therefore, the redundancy will ensure that they will get the major points you are trying to make even if they only give the presentation a cursory glance or two.

Your first step is to create a cover page. Don't forget this part! Once that is done, proceed with the steps that follow.

What Is Your Product?

The first item in your presentation should answer the question, "What is your product?" That page should consist of no more than one or two short paragraphs. It should be a succinct description of exactly what your product is, as you would explain it to someone who has never heard of it. After all, the manufacturer *has* never heard of it!

How Does Your Product Work?

On the next page, you should answer the question, "How does your product work?" Again, this does not have to be a long, detailed description of how your invention works, just a couple of sentences or a short paragraph. Describe how it works as far as the consumer is concerned. Be careful not to reveal any trade secrets, and if you need to reveal details of how your invention works (this is rarely necessary), make sure that nondisclosure agreements are signed. Also, get the technical disclosure approved by your patent attorney, to ensure that the technical disclosure is kept to a minimum. Keep in mind that one of the main goals of the presentation is to be quick and easy for the manufacturer to read and comprehend. If the potential licensee sees an entire page of fine print, it is unlikely that he will read it at all. Keep it short!

What Will It Cost to Manufacture Your Product?

In order to answer this question, you must do your homework. The manufacturer will *know* if you just make a wild guess. Do your best to get an accurate estimate of what it will cost to manufacture your product. Research the cost of the materials that your product is to be made of. Go to the suppliers of the raw materials and ask. You can do a great deal of this research at your public library or on the Internet.

If you absolutely *cannot* find out the probable cost of manufacturing your product, you can get an in-the-ballpark guesstimate by doing the following: Go to a store that sells similar products, or even dissimilar products that are made of the same raw materials in approximately the same quantities that your product will be made. Make note of the retail selling price and divide it by four. If you use this very rough way of estimating the manufacturing costs, you should make it clear in your presentation that this is only an approximate cost.

Every manufacturer will want to know what her tool-up costs would likely be to manufacture your product. That question should be answered in this section. If a plastic injection mold will be required, tell her. If a new piece of equipment will be required to manufacture your product, then you need to explain exactly what that might be and an estimated cost of it.

What's in It for the Licensee?

On the next page of your presentation, you will answer this question. Here you should list how the potential licensee will benefit by manufacturing and distributing your product. Ideally, one of the first things you would list here would be profit. You can explain further benefits later, but the very first benefit they are looking for is a product that will increase their bottom line. Profit is the name of the game.

Explain also how and why your product will attract customers. Describe any special features about your product that will entice customers to buy it. If there is more than one use for your product, describe it here. Can your product be expanded to include a whole line of products? If so, tell them about it! Finally, if your product is patented or "patent pending," mention that! Point out that if they elect to receive the "exclusive" license on your product, they will be the *only* source of the product in the marketplace.

Who Will Benefit from Your Product?

On the next page, you finally get to answer the question you have been thinking of since you first had your brilliant idea. You tell them who will benefit from your invention. Now you get to talk about the end users and how much they, the consumers, will love your product. List all the categories of people who would welcome your product and whose lives would be made easier by it. How will the product help them? Also, what is the market for this product and how large is that market?

What Can Your Invention Be Sold For?

When answering the question, "What can your invention be sold for?" do your homework. Do not just pull a figure out of thin air, for it will surely be wrong. Inventors often have an inflated idea of the value of their inventions. You must keep in mind that the potential selling price is not its perceived value in your mind, but what the marketplace will bear.

The general rule of thumb when pricing your product for the retail market is that it will sell for four to five times the manufacturer's cost. For example, if it costs $1 to manufacture, it will probably retail for $4 to $5.

If you have actually sold your product and you *know* that the consumer will actually be willing to pay ten times the manufacturing cost or more, then, by all means, report that here. That would make your product even more attractive to potential licensees. If this is the case, however, you must explain and document how you reached this conclusion. For instance, if you have actual sales records or invoices that show what your product sold for in the marketplace, reproduce them to attach to the presentation.

Where Should Your Product Be Sold?

In this section, list all the possible outlets that would be likely to carry a product such as yours. If these are outlets that your potential licensee already markets to, all the better! They will see that they already have the distribution channels in place for this product and it would be an easy addition to their product line.

How Should Your Product Be Packaged and Displayed?

This is the prerogative of the potential licensee, but if you can make suggestions for inexpensive yet attractive and eye-catching ways to package the product, it will demonstrate your understanding of their business. The more they see you as looking out for their interest, the more seriously they are likely to take your invention.

Five to Ten Reasons the Potential Licensee Should License Your Product

You should include a page listing a number of compelling reasons why the potential licensee needs to license your product. There should be five to ten reasons. Fewer than five reasons and your case as to why they need your product looks weak; more than ten and it gets too tedious to read and take seriously. Don't just put something in to fill space. Make sure it is a valid reason.

ESSENTIAL

If your product has a federally registered trademark, be certain to put the ® after the product name each time it appears in your presentation. If you do not have a federal trademark, then you should put ™ after your product name each time it appears.

Summary and Documentation

Next, make a summary page where you list the three or four main ideas you wish to impress upon the potential licensee. Finally, include any supporting documentation you may have. This would be the place to include surveys, market studies, or pictures of your product. If you have a video of your product in action, include that with your presentation.

Presenting Your Product

When the time comes to present your product to manufacturers for possible licensing, you have several possible courses of action. You can present it yourself in person, you can hire an agent to present the product and negotiate any license agreement, or you can mail the presentation if time, distance, or monetary concerns prevent you from traveling to the potential licensee.

Make the Appointment

When you are ready to present your product, we would encourage you to call the manufacturers and make an appointment to meet with them in person. Meeting with them in person is *far* superior to merely sending them a sample of your product and a written presentation. You know your product better than anyone else does. You understand why it is needed and you can explain it with more enthusiasm than a paid agent ever could. That is not to say that there are not a few *legitimate* agents who will do their best to represent you with enthusiasm and integrity. There are not that many, however, and you can usually represent your product better than anyone else ever could.

Employ an Agent to Represent You

If you are paralyzed with fear at the very thought of walking into the office of a president of a company or to an appointment with the head of the new product division of a company, employing a *legitimate* agent to represent you is the best choice. Keep in mind that it is not uncommon for people who are agonizingly shy to blossom when the time comes to promote their product, their baby! Being shy in social situations and being shy when explaining the benefits of their terrific product are two entirely different things. Most people are so enthusiastic and animated when talking about their invention that it is difficult to shut them up!

Tell Your Story

Every invention has a story behind it. Whether you meet with the manufacturer in person or simply send the presentation and prototype to them, your presentation is incomplete without the story behind your invention.

How did you happen to come up with it? What common problem does it solve? If you have the opportunity to meet with the prospective licensee in person, begin your presentation by telling your story. Let them see how your invention solved a problem for you that is undoubtedly a problem for thousands or millions of other people too. Telling your story allows them to understand the human need behind an invention. Who knows—it may even solve a problem they have encountered themselves.

If you are not able to meet with them in person, then write your story in a letter that will accompany the presentation. If you mail your presentations, send them out by Federal Express or U.S. Express Mail. A FedEx or Express Mail package gets attention. It gets delivered to the intended recipient when a regular U.S. Mail letter or package may get set aside as unimportant. Not only does it get delivered to the intended recipient, it will get opened, too.

Who Should You Send the Presentation To?

Finally, if you are dealing with a small to midsize company that does not have a research and development (R & D) department, you could send the presentation directly to the president or vice president of the company. If the company does not have an actual R & D department but there is a new-products person, you may want to try to contact her first. You can always try contacting the president or vice president if you get no response from the new-products person. This is a personal judgment call.

ALERT!

Don't ignore the smaller companies in favor of the larger ones. While larger companies generally make excellent licensees, it can take one to two years to get through the red tape of licensing with them. Smaller companies, on the other hand, usually work faster. In many cases, you can deal directly with the president of a smaller company.

If you are submitting to a large manufacturer that does have an R & D department, it is very important to submit your product through them. If you go over their heads to the president or vice president of the company, the chances of success with that company are somewhere in the slim-to-none range. They will resent that you have gone over their heads and will find some rationale for rejecting your product. You must play the game and nurture a relationship with someone in the R & D department to maximize your chances of success.

Know What You Want

Before you meet with the prospective licensee, you need to know exactly what you want from them. They will undoubtedly ask you what you have in mind. This is no time to stutter and stammer. If you want to sell the rights to the patent, then say so, and have what you consider to be a fair price in mind. If you want to license your patent for a royalty, then come prepared with an idea of what would be a fair royalty. It is even a good idea to have a filled-out license agreement with you. You can give it to them and explain that it is a starting point for your negotiations. The license agreement that you give them must be fair to all parties. If it is lopsided in your favor, they may decide that you will be too difficult to work with and give up then and there. If, on the other hand, it is fair to both sides, they will see that you are a reasonable person and it would probably not be too difficult to work out a fair agreement with you.

If they indicate some interest in licensing your product but are reluctant to begin the negotiation process, you may suggest an option agreement. An option agreement (a sample of which can be found in Appendix D of this book) gives them a limited amount of time, usually about sixty days, in which to evaluate whether or not they would like to proceed with licensing. During that time, you agree not to show the invention to any other manufacturers for licensing. In exchange for this concession on your part, they agree to pay you a sum of money, usually $1,000 or $2,000. If they do go on to license your agreement, then the sum they paid you for the option agreement would be credited against future royalties.

Follow Up and Prepare to Wait

Licensing is not a speedy process. Your invention may be the most important thing in the world to you, but you can be sure that it is not the most important thing to your potential licensee. They were busy dealing with their day-to-day business before you showed up and they will be busy long after you have gone. You and your invention may be of interest to them but are unlikely to be their paramount concern. They must fit you into their already full and busy schedule. If you are lucky, they may say that they will get back to you within a couple of weeks of your visit with them. However, don't take it personally if they do not get back to you within that time frame.

Always make a follow-up call to jog a potential licensee's memory. Be cordial and friendly. You want to keep nudging them to move forward but you do not want to annoy them. It is a process of waiting . . . and then waiting more. Hopefully, your patience will pay off with a signed license agreement. Ask them when you may get back in touch with them and then do so. It is reasonable to give them two to three weeks before calling and requesting an update on the status of your submission.

If you experience several months without response, it is time to move on to your next potential licensee. Remember, if you are unsuccessful with your first potential licensee, it only means that you were unsuccessful with them. You simply have not found the right manufacturer who sees the profit potential of your invention. Persistence is the name of the game. Keep trying until you find the right manufacturer or until you have exhausted all your possibilities.

Chapter 19

Your License Agreement

Would you like to have others making your money for you? Welcome to licensing! John D. Rockefeller said, "I would rather earn 1 percent off of 100 people's efforts than 100 percent of my own efforts." Most people are not as rich as Rockefeller was, but inventors can experience the reality of his statement through licensing their inventions. In most endcavors, thc incomc stops when the worker stops. For the licensor, the income continues as long as the product is viable, even after the inventor has gone on to other pursuits.

What Is a License Agreement?

The simplest definition of a license agreement is that it is a contract giving someone the legal right to use an invention that is the subject of a patent, a patent application, and/or a trademark. The important point here is that what you are conferring is the right to use the invention that is the subject of the patent, patent application, and/or trademark. The ownership of the patent and/or trademark remains with you, the original owner.

If the patent on your invention has already been issued, your rights to the invention are secured and licensing becomes easier to accomplish. Some license agreements are negotiated while the invention is still patent pending. When a licensee obtains the exclusive rights to use a patent or trademark, it is routine for that licensee to take over the legal fees involved in the prosecution and/or maintenance of that intellectual property.

FACT

If a manufacturer is willing to license an invention without absolute assurance that the patent will issue, the inventor can often get the licensee to pay for the legal costs of the patent prosecution beginning at the point of signing the agreement. This can represent a savings of several thousand dollars by the time the patent issues.

One of the variables in license agreements can be the territory that is licensed. You may choose to offer exclusive licenses in several defined territories. This obviously is not a good choice if you are licensing to manufacturers who market to national retailers. But it can be a good choice if you license to smaller manufacturers who have clearly defined and distinct marketing territories. You may also choose to define territories in your agreement if you have applied for and/or obtained foreign patents.

Another possibility is licensing your invention exclusively to more than one market in the same territory if the product undeniably fits into more than one market. To do so, it would need to be sold in very separate types of markets so that under no circumstances would it ever appear in stores marketed to by both manufacturers. An example of this situation would be a computer mouse pad that looks like a basketball. That mouse pad would be sold in office supply stores and any store where computer supplies were sold. It could also be sold in toy stores, gift stores, or even sporting goods stores. The manufacturers who wholesale to the computer aftermarket would not be selling to the toy or sporting goods markets. So that would represent two separate markets for that product.

If your product is something that lends itself to branding, it can mean a much longer lasting income stream if you obtain a trademark and then license the trademark together with the patent. With a lasting product, your trademark can prove to be more valuable than the patent since your royalties can continue beyond the expiration date of the patent.

Another variable is the term of the licensing period. Generally, the license agreement covers the life of the patent and it can go beyond that period if you have obtained a trademark for your invention and you license the trademark along with the patent. Patents have finite lives, but trademark coverage goes on for as long as the trademark is in continuous use.

Exclusive Versus Nonexclusive License Agreements

There is a place in today's business market for both exclusive and nonexclusive license agreements, although the case for exclusive agreements for independent inventors is a compelling one. Nonexclusive agreements are most often seen in cases where the property being licensed is an image, such as cartoon characters or likenesses of famous people. Artists also sometimes license their artwork in this way.

Exclusive Agreements

When you have something that is truly innovative to offer to the buying public, an exclusive license with the right manufacturer can create an income stream that will continue and even grow for years. The right manufacturer for your product could be the largest manufacturer of products in that category. It could also be one of the smaller manufacturers. Finding the right manufacturer for your product will require some due diligence on your part. Sometimes the larger manufacturer will agree to try the product in a limited market while the smaller manufacturer will go all out and give the new product a major push in the market. In some cases, the new product is the catalyst that brings the smaller manufacturer into the larger marketplace by gaining entry into markets that were previously unavailable. When all of the manufacturers, large and small, offer the exact same products, retailers do not feel the need to allow shelf space for each manufacturer. It is usually the larger manufacturers who have the advantage in this situation.

ALERT!

Once you license your patent, your licensee will have the right to license to other companies. This is called a *sublicense* and what you receive from the sublicense is determined by how your original license agreement is written. Be sure that your sublicense income and your rights regarding that licensee are clearly spelled out in your license agreement.

If you are able to license a new product exclusively to a smaller manufacturer, this gives that manufacturer a competitive edge because he can now offer the retailer a product that is only available from his company. If you are the lucky patent holder in this license agreement, your product becomes the goose that lays the golden egg for this manufacturer. In fact, this company may be the first in line for your future inventions.

Nonexclusive Agreements

If you can find a manufacturer that will accept a nonexclusive license on your invention, you can expect that your royalty rate will be far lower than what you would receive for an exclusive license. After all, the manufacturer is looking for a competitive edge in the marketplace. He will not have that edge if the same product is available from other manufacturers of similar products. However, if you are able to obtain nonexclusive licenses with a number of different manufacturers, a lower royalty rate could still result in a good income.

An additional concern is that with a nonexclusive agreement, you will be responsible for enforcing the patent. If you are willing to take on this responsibility, you will need a large amount of money set aside to cover infringement lawsuits. This is probably the main reason why independent product developers decide on exclusive licensing.

Let's Talk Royalty

Royalty, in terms of license agreements for your inventions, refers to a percentage of proceeds from sales of the product that is paid to the licensor. When you license your product to a manufacturer, your royalty will be based on wholesale sales because that is how the manufacturer sells the product to retailers. In order to really understand royalties related to intellectual property, you will need to understand some other terminology that shows up in license agreements, including advance against royalties, guaranteed minimum, and net sales.

Advance Against Royalties

Sometimes a manufacturer will agree to pay you an up-front payment at the time of signing the license agreement. They will often do this if they feel that there is competition from other manufacturers for the exclusive agreement. When this up-front payment is made, this *signing bonus* is not really a gift just for signing the agreement. What the manufacturer is doing is advancing you an agreed-upon amount at the time you sign the agreement. Your licensee, the manufacturer, will then recover this amount from your royalties. For example, if she pays you $100,000 at the signing of the agreement and then pays you royalties on a quarterly basis, the royalties will be withheld until the $100,000 has been recovered. You will receive a royalty statement detailing the sales of your product and how much of the advance has been covered.

If your product is a really good one, you may only have to wait a short time for the advance to be covered before your regular royalty payments commence. It is not always a good idea to insist on an advance against royalties, because manufacturers often have to invest a substantial amount of cash to get a new product developed and marketed. It is difficult to get an advance if you are having to convince the manufacturer to take a chance on your product. If you can get an advance, that's great. But a better way to judge the value of the license agreement is in the income stream over the long haul.

Guaranteed Minimum

A guaranteed minimum is an agreement that the manufacturer will pay you a set amount of royalty during an agreed-upon period of time, usually a year, whether or not he sells enough of your product to create that amount of royalty. For example, if he agrees to pay you $100,000 annually as a guaranteed royalty, you would receive your regular royalty percentage at each royalty payment time. If by the end of the year he has not sold enough of your product to create $100,000 in royalty payments to you, he will make up the difference at that time even though sales of the product fell short of that goal. In this case, the licensee absorbs that loss unless your agreement states that the difference can be applied to future royalties. Guaranteed minimum amounts of royalty that are to be paid to you each year are an essential part of license agreements. Be certain that your license agreement contains one.

Net Sales

It is important to have a clear understanding of this part of your license agreement. *Gross sales* refers to the total amount that the manufacturer will invoice the retailer for the products. From this figure, he will deduct the *cost of goods* to determine the *net sales* figure. What is included in the manufacturer's cost of goods? This category can include such things as advertising, sales commissions, samples given out, quantity discounts, returns, and shipping costs. Keep in mind that your royalty will not be paid on the gross sales figure.

E ALERT!

It may be necessary to place a cap on the amount of money that can be deducted from the gross sales figures for cost of goods in order to protect your royalty percentage. Make sure that each item to be deducted is precisely defined in your license agreement to avoid misunderstandings at royalty statement time.

Now that you understand some of the common terms that directly relate to royalty, how do you determine what percentage rate of royalty you should receive? This is one of the most difficult things to determine and it will depend, with some guidelines, on what the market will bear—that is, whatever you can get from the manufacturer based on the profit margin for your product and how badly the manufacturer wants the product. Royalties, from the manufacturer's point of view, are part of the cost of goods. So you will have to get realistic here and not be too greedy or you may lose the whole deal at this point.

Royalties can vary from less than 1 percent of wholesale to around 15 percent. The difference here is not in how much you can negotiate but in what your type of product can produce in net sales. As a rule, the higher end of the percentage scale is reserved for software or such well-known and bankable names as Disney and NASCAR. For most products, the average royalty is 3 percent to 5 percent. Sometimes large manufacturers will structure royalty payments on a sliding scale, taking into account the nature of a product's projected life in the market.

FACT

Sometimes it is easier to convince a manufacturer to take a chance on your new product if you agree to a lower royalty percentage for the first two or three years of the contract, until it proves itself in the market. Then, you can renegotiate for a higher royalty rate when the licensee really wants to keep the exclusive agreement.

If these numbers seem low to you, consider this. The manufacturer is taking all of the risk and doing all of the work to get the product marketed. If your product is a good one and will have lasting ability in the marketplace, your 3 percent to 5 percent could amount to a substantial income for which you exert no effort. Also, consider that with the difficulty of finding success in the market with new products, 3 percent to 5 percent of *something* is far better than 100 percent of *nothing!*

Negotiating a Contract

You have now reached that wonderful place that has been your goal since the beginning of your invention: You have a licensee on the line and it is time to finalize the deal. This is the time to pay close attention to the agreement that is being negotiated.

You may have a wonderful patent attorney who has guided you through the filing and prosecution of a good, strong patent. Remember that attorneys do specialize and your patent attorney's specialty is intellectual property. It is in the negotiating of a license agreement that using a *contract attorney* pays off. These individuals are familiar with the fine points of license agreements and with how to get the best deal for you. Whatever you have to spend for the services of a contract attorney should be considered a savings rather than an expense. Remember that the manufacturer has attorneys negotiating for him. You will want no less for yourself at this crucial time.

If you need help in locating a contract attorney, ask your patent attorney or someone else you trust, such as members of your local inventors' association, for suggestions. Occasionally a patent attorney is also a contract attorney. This is your best situation because you can be sure that this lawyer is very familiar with license agreements for intellectual property.

What Belongs in a License Agreement?

If you have engaged a contract attorney to help you get the best possible license agreement, you are in good hands. But it is still important that you understand license agreements so that you can work together with your attorney to get the best agreement possible. In many cases, the manufacturer will offer the first draft of the license agreement. You can be sure that it will be written to the advantage of the licensee. It will require some finesse at this point between your attorney and the manufacturer's attorney to come up with an agreement that is entirely fair to both parties. Read on to learn about some of the points to address in your license agreement.

Licensed Territory and Term of the Agreement

Your agreement will outline where the product may be sold under the terms of the contract. This will likely be the area covered by your patent rights. It may also detail the exact market in which the product can be sold if you have more than one market to which you can license it.

If you have obtained foreign patent rights and your U.S. licensee wants to secure those rights, do your best to be sure that he is capable of covering this market before signing it away. Determine whether he has the financial capability of entering and satisfactorily addressing that market, and place a deadline in the agreement for his doing so.

The agreement will also include the term of the covenant and the renegotiating dates. Here you will lay out the time period for the initial contract and the dates for renegotiating the license agreement. Be sure that you have a definite date for renegotiating rather than simply allowing the agreement to roll over into another license year. This will be your main leverage with the licensee for bettering your situation.

Royalty Percentage, Payment Periods, and Right to Inspect Sales Records

And now for the most important part of the agreement: the amount of royalty you will be paid, and when royalty payments are due. You will also want to detail the specifics of the royalty report that is to accompany the check. Many license agreements allow for quarterly payment of royalties, but some agreements specify that payments are to be made monthly.

It is in this part of the contract where you will state the details regarding the basis for determining the net sales figure. Your contract attorney will carefully work out what can be deducted from gross sales before your royalty is calculated. Make sure that you have a good understanding of each deduction and that it is reasonable.

Does the royalty section of a license agreement include a guaranteed minimum royalty?

Yes. This is a non-negotiable part of your agreement. You will need to have a guaranteed minimum amount of royalty that you will be paid, regardless of the sales of the product. This will ensure that the licensee will use her best efforts to get the product marketed. Guaranteed minimums are routine in license agreements.

It is also in this section of your agreement that it will state that you have the right to inspect the sales records for your product on an annual basis. This is done by means of an accounting firm that you send to their office. You must give them reasonable notice of such examination, and in most cases, the cost of these audits is your responsibility.

Time Frame for Getting Product on the Market and Quality Control

This is another non-negotiable part of the agreement. Some companies have been known to sign license agreements with no intention of promoting the product, just to keep competitors from marketing it. Requiring that the product be on the market within a reasonable time period guarantees that your licensee will indeed move forward with commercializing your invention.

The product quality control clause is worded in different ways in the agreement, but your attorney should make sure that you have some say in the quality of your product. Sometimes it is written into the contract that you have the right of approval on packaging of your product as well.

Responsibility for Patent and Trademark Maintenance

There will be maintenance fees required by the USPTO at various times during the lifetime of your patent and trademark. Since the licensee has obtained the rights to the use of this intellectual property, it is also his responsibility to pay maintenance fees. Determine who will be responsible for keeping up with the due dates for these payments. It may be that you will want to pay the fees and then get the licensee to reimburse you. This way you can be certain that it is all handled in a timely manner.

It should be in your license agreement that any improvements to your original licensed product will belong to you and any patents or trademarks filed for or obtained by your licensee on any products related to your invention will also belong to you.

Patent Enforcement and Defense Against Infringement Litigation

The enforcement of your patent against infringers is one of the most important points in your license agreement. It should be clearly spelled out that your licensee will aggressively enforce your patent against any infringement. Additionally, in the unlikely event that you would be sued for infringement, it is the licensee's responsibility to respond to that litigation.

Your Right to Terminate the Agreement

Your contract attorney will detail all of the possible circumstances in which you will have the right to terminate the agreement. These circumstances should be as detailed and definite as possible, rather than situations that are arguable, such as the licensee's lack of using best efforts to promote the product. Your attorney should give you a clearly defined way out of the agreement in case you ever need one.

FACT

Even if you have distinctly defined rules regarding what constitutes a material breach of a license agreement, be aware that if you attempt to terminate the agreement based on your opinion of a material breach, your licensee is likely to sue to avoid termination. Termination of the agreement is not automatic unless the licensee agrees to it.

Realistic Expectations

One thing that seems to be universal with inventors is the feeling that their inventions are worth millions of dollars. Your invention could well be worth a lot of money, but for purposes of licensing, you will need to be realistic. New products must prove themselves in the marketplace before they return value to the licensee or the licensor. The licensee is showing faith in the product by being willing to make a substantial investment in getting the product on the market and by agreeing to pay for the idea and the technology that you have developed and protected.

The best way for an inventor to face reality regarding licensing is to approach the undertaking from the manufacturer's point of view. If you can put yourself in the manufacturer's place, you will see that she must find ways to justify the risks that are inherent in introducing new products. The more you can understand that position, the better you will be able to work out a mutually satisfying arrangement. Think of that manufacturer as your partner in the effort to get this new product marketed. Provide everything that you can to make that job easier for her. The more cooperative you are, the more you will find that the license agreement will work to the advantage of both sides. Remember that the best arrangement is the one that is good for both parties. If it is not a good agreement for both parties, it is not good for either party in the end.

Chapter 20

Toy Inventing: A Whole Different Ball Game

Inventing products for merchandising, manufacturing, or for specific industries such as the medical industry consists of developing better, more convenient, or economical ways to solve common problems. Toy inventors, however, are not focused on solving problems, but instead aim to create items for entertainment. You can utilize any materials or technologies to create a new toy or game. There are no boundaries! For this reason, there are a few things you should know before heading down the path of toy inventing.

Throw Out All the Rules!

The total worldwide wholesale market for toys and games is estimated to be around 22 billion dollars a year, with the United States accounting for approximately 50 percent of those sales. This enormous market works on a different set of rules than those for other types of inventing.

FACT

The time span from when a manufacturer decides to proceed with a product until it appears on the store shelves can be as little as nine to twenty-four months, depending on the complexity of the toy, unlike the three- to five-year wait in other areas of inventing.

The approach for selling a toy or game to a toy company is different from selling an invention to a manufacturer. In most industries, before an inventor presents his product to a potential manufacturer or licensee, it is important that he have some sort of protection for it (a utility patent or provisional patent application). That is not the case when presenting toys or games. In fact, toys and games are almost never patented. The toy and game industry is very fast moving, and toy inventors would be left behind the trends if they waited to receive patents for their products.

Should You Patent a Toy?

Even though patent searching for toy inventions is not definitive, this does not mean that you should not conduct a preliminary patent and preliminary market search to be certain that your product does not already exist; you should. The problem with patent and market searching for toys is that most toys go to market without a patent and, as a result, patent searches can give the inventor a false impression that her toy is unique or has never been on the market. That is not to say that it would not be prudent to perform, at a minimum, the preliminary online patent search that any inventor can do for herself for absolutely no cost at all. Understand, however, that a patent search is not a definitive go or no-go when developing toys and games.

According to Mike Marra, one of the top toy agents in the industry, most toy companies do not require that a patent be obtained on items that are submitted to them for consideration. He says that if a toy company licenses a product, they often will pay the full cost of a patent or, at the very minimum, share the cost of the patent with the inventor.

One reason why patents are not filed on many toys is because it is estimated that 80 percent of the new toys that are introduced each year fail in the marketplace. As a result, many toy companies are reluctant to file for patents on each and every toy they introduce into the marketplace. On the other hand, if a toy represents a new type of technology, then a patent would be essential. As the inventor of a toy or game, only you and your licensee can make the decision as to whether or not you should seek patent protection on your product.

Unlike inventions that solve a problem or make something easier, the characteristics of a winning toy or game is that it meets the needs of the toy manufacturers. What are they looking for? They are looking for products that are fun to play with, have obvious play patterns (simple-to-understand directions and an apparent and clear objective of the play), products that encourage multiple uses (games and toys that children and adults will want to play again and again), and, of course, products that are safe. They obviously do not want toys that will represent a danger to the end user or require high product liability insurance on their part.

The toy and game industry is also different in that it is a very relationship-based industry. It takes years of developing personal relationships with the decision-makers in the various toy companies to be accepted as an insider. It is very difficult for an independent toy inventor to break into the club. Most toy companies will not meet with independent developers of toys. They have had many lawsuits from independent inventors who say that the toy company stole their idea even though the idea may have already been in development by the toy company before they ever met with the inventor.

Additionally, if the toy executives were to meet with every independent toy designer who wanted to see them, it would take up an extraordinary amount of their time. They would not have the time to get their real job done. Toy industry executives can usually determine within one to two minutes if a toy meets their criteria. Most toy inventors would be insulted to receive so little of the executive's time and would insist on trying to sell the executive on their toy. The toy executives don't have time for this and will not take the time for it. This is not to say that an individual has not or cannot be the exception. The larger the company, however, the more difficult it is to reach the product managers.

Usually, when an independent toy designer does manage to get to the decision-makers, he is referred to toy agents or brokers and asked to submit his toy or game through them—so in the end, he still must go through an agent or broker in order to get his toy seen by the toy executives. This information is not offered to discourage you, but rather to inform you of the obstacles you may face.

Do You Need a Prototype of Your Toy or Game?

Yes, you do need a prototype, but it does not have to look exactly like the product will look when it is on the toy store shelves. It should look as good as you can make it look. For example, you may want to laminate cards, if your game includes cards. It is also important that you are able to actually play the game. Have all the parts there. The more polished your prototype, the more likely it will be to sell.

FACT

Toy agents do not do test marketing on the toys since they do not sell to the consumer market. They are trying to get a toy manufacturer interested in licensing the toy. It is then up to the manufacturer to make the decision as to whether or not focus groups or market testing will be done on the toy or game.

Test your prototype before you present it to anyone. Be sure to test it with the target market to which you hope to appeal. If your game is for children, be sure to have children play the game. Watch their reactions more than their words. Did they catch on to the point of the game quickly? Did they have fun? Did they want to play longer? Children will often tell you what you want to hear. They may say, "Oh, it was great!" because they don't want to hurt your feelings. This is a case where their actions speak much more loudly than their words. If your toy or game is for children, don't make it too hard. When children play, they want it to be fun, not work.

If you plan to submit your toy idea to a legitimate toy agent to see if he wants to represent you with the toy companies, it is probably not necessary to even have a prototype at that point. Toy agents are actually only evaluating the underlying concept of your toy or game as the first step in the process. If the agent agrees to represent you, he will, at that point, request a working prototype of your toy or game. If you already have a presentable and operational prototype, the agent can begin presenting your toy or game immediately. If you do not have one, then you (in cooperation with the agent) must go through the development phase to create and fabricate the presentation materials before toy companies can be approached.

Toy Marketing

Marketing is a huge part of any inventing process, and it's no different with toys. In fact, there are certain nuances you should be aware of when looking to market your toy or game. Certain professionals, such as toy agents, can help you with this. It's also a good idea to attend toy shows and conventions.

Toy Agents

The easiest way to break into the industry is to hire an agent. Toy companies like to deal with agents with whom they are familiar. Toy agents can get the ear of the decision-makers when it is very difficult for you to do so.

Toy agents have ongoing relationships with the toy companies and make presentations in person to them throughout the year. If your toy is accepted by a toy agent for representation, it will be presented to the appropriate toy company executives at the earliest possible date.

The easiest way to find an agent is to call the company to whom you wish to sell your idea. Ask to speak to the inventor liaison. If they do not have someone by that title, they will know who you should be directed to. When you get them on the line, ask them for the name and contact information for the agent they like to work with. They will tell you! Then call that agent and see if he would be interested in representing your toy or game.

Agents are not cheap. They normally charge 50 to 60 percent of your royalty. For example, if they negotiate a 5 percent royalty (the most common rate), then they would get 2½ to 3 percent and you would get 2 percent. (Keep in mind that a small percentage of *something* is much better than all of *nothing*!) That is steep, but it is the going rate, and it gets you in the door.

Although the usual royalty for a toy is 5 percent, toy agents are sometimes able to negotiate a royalty as high as 8 percent of the wholesale price. When a third-party licensed character, such as Disney, Harry Potter, NASCAR, etc., is involved, the inventor's rate drops to between 2 and 4 percent. Many factors influence the royalty rate. A few of the key factors to consider are the wholesale price, the estimated unit volume, the distribution level, and the category of the game or toy. Most toy agents will negotiate an up-front payment for the inventor, which is an advance payment against future royalties.

One of the big advantages of having a toy agent represent you is that you can sit back and relax while your product is being presented and a license agreement is negotiated. The agent handles all of that for you. It is not necessary for you to hire an attorney, so you avoid what could be a significant expense.

Your chances of success with your toy are increased if your toy raises the bar in its category, catches a trend, or is a toy that brings play to a new level. For example, Legos have been the leading building toy for years. K'Nex and Magnitex have taken building toys to a new level.

Toy Shows and Conventions

Attend toy shows and conventions. The largest, the Toy Industry Association's American International Toy Fair, is held each February in New York

City at the Jacob K. Javits Convention Center. Each year they welcome more than 20,000 guests from more than 100 countries. Toy Fair highlights every type of toy imaginable, from classic and traditional toys to breathtaking and technologically advanced new toys. In order to attend Toy Fair you must be a qualified buyer, trade guest, or media representative.

FACT

Qualified buyers eligible to attend Toy Fair are typically retail stores such as discount toy stores, apparel stores, arts and crafts shops, bookstores, computer software retailers, convenience stores, department stores, discount chain stores, hardware stores, mass merchandise stores, supermarkets, TV shopping channels, variety stores, etc. Find the complete list of those eligible to attend on the American International Toy Fair Web site.

Independent inventors are allowed to attend Toy Fair by registering as inventors. First-time buyers and trade guests need a minimum of two of the following types of documentation in order to attend:

- Tax resale certificate or business license
- Recent invoices showing purchase of youth industry–related products
- Yellow Pages listing
- Printed materials (brochures, catalogs, sell sheets, etc.) illustrating industry-related products
- Letter of intent from a lawyer or bank on official letterhead stating your intent to start a business (*for new retailers only*)
- Company credit card or company paycheck stub
- Letter from a toy industry client on their letterhead confirming your business relationship
- Letter of referral from an exhibiting youth-product manufacturer or agent with whom you do business (*mandatory for inventors*)
- Business card listing of title, company, and address
- List of lines you currently represent (*for manufacturer's reps only*)

There is no admission fee for buyers and trade guests who register before the event, but there is a fee for those who choose to wait to register at the door.

Another large toy show is the Toy and Game Inventors Forum (TGIF) Conference for adult or strategic games, held in Las Vegas each year. TGIF welcomes guests from all over the world and is structured to be a learning environment as well as a presenting and networking opportunity. Attendees sign up for one of three tracks. Track A is for inventors and newcomers, Track B is for returning inventors and entrepreneurs, and Track C is for industry professionals. Admission can be quite pricey, even for Track A, the least expensive level. Though it is a significant investment, the contacts, networking, and learning opportunities can make it well worth the expense.

If you have a toy or game to show, wait until the last day of the fair when the exhibitors have done most of their work before approaching them with your toy or game. By the last day, they may be just passing the time until they can go home and they would be available and happy to visit with you. They may not be buying toys or games on the spot, but you can get their business cards and write to them when you get home. Remind them that you met them at Toy Fair or TGIF, etc.

Professional Associations and Magazines

If you wish to be a toy or game inventor, you should start by joining the professional associations for the industry (e.g., Women and Toys Association or American Specialty Toys Retail Association). Go to your local library and talk to the librarians. They can show you how to find the various professional associations. Subscribe to the magazines put out by the toy industry, such as *Playthings* magazine. Study them front to back, including the classified ads. As you become more familiar with them, you will begin to see the same names appear over and over. When you go to a trade show, notice the nametags of the other attendees. Because you've done your homework by studying the magazines, you will recognize names of people in your specific category of toy inventing. When you recognize these names, walk up and introduce yourself. Don't take a lot of their time, however, if they are busy. Exchange business cards. After the show, you can call or e-mail them. They will probably be receptive to your call since they met you at the show.

Representing Yourself

It is possible to present your toy or game to a manufacturer yourself, particularly if it is a relatively small toy company. Choose the companies carefully. For example, if your toy is a board game made of cardboard and plastic, choose a company that makes similar products. Don't waste the time of a company that makes nothing even remotely similar to your toy or game. Use nondisclosure agreements. Most companies will sign your version but others may ask you to sign theirs.

Ask What They Are Looking For

Ask each manufacturer you consider what they are looking for. (If your toy or game does not fit into their plan, excuse yourself and leave. Do not insist on showing them your game if they are not interested.)

Present Quickly

If you do meet with someone at the company, present your product quickly and succinctly. Don't read them all the rules; just show them how the game is played. They do not have a lot of time to spend and will appreciate it if you do not waste their time. If you respect their time, when you do have a toy or game that might be a fit for them they will listen to you.

Don't assume that the opinions of your friends and relatives are an adequate endorsement. Do realize that *your* buyer is the toy manufacturer, not the consumer. It is best to seek out a professional evaluation by a toy agent for your idea before proceeding unless you choose to be the manufacturer. In that case, you should proceed with professional focus group testing and research.

Leave a Presentation

Leave them with a description or presentation of your product that they can refer to after you've gone. (Do not leave your *only* prototype with them.)

Don't simply expect them to remember every word you say. Furthermore, making a declaration like "All the kids in the neighborhood love it" is a dead giveaway that you are a novice to the industry. Present facts and figures to back up your claims and to leave a lasting impression.

Toy Contracts

If you are lucky enough to find a company to license your toy, it is crucially important that you get a good contract. Here are a few things to watch for:

- Always get an exclusive, *not* a nonexclusive, contract.
- Describe your invention completely.
- Get a lawyer to look it over and negotiate for you.
- Carefully review what the company is allowed to subtract before paying the royalty. For example, it is common that they deduct promotion deals. However, you can request a cap on how much that can add up to.
- Get the highest royalty percentage that you can! Unlike nontoy invention licensing guaranteed minimum amounts for royalty are seldom, if ever, included in a toy license.
- Try to get as big an advance on your royalties as you can. (There are a few companies that do not pay advances.)
- Protect yourself against lawsuits. Insist on being listed on their insurance policy as an insured. Require them to send you a certificate of insurance as proof that they have done this. Also, get a statement that says you are only liable if your actual product, not its packaging, injures someone.
- Spell out the criteria that could make the contract end. You may wish to have an ending date, or you may choose not to have an ending date but rather have performance requirements determine the end of the contract.
- Be certain that the terms and conditions of the contract maintain your rights, title, and interest in your product once the contract ends.
- Strive to get international distribution for your toy or game. International distribution can double the unit volume and income!

In addition to knowing what should be in your contract, it is equally important to know what should *not* be in your contract or license agreement. You should not place any terms and conditions that handcuff the toy manufacturer by requiring specific pricing or inventory levels. Avoid anything in the agreement that curtails the toy manufacturer from swinging with market conditions.

Above all, be patient! Negotiating a contract with a toy company can be a long process. Sometimes negotiations take nine months or more. As long as you're thorough and clear about your goals, it will be worth the wait.

Take the Money and Run!

Toy and game inventors who make a living from their inventions are a very prolific group. They have to be! Since the shelf life of the average toy is less than three years, the toy inventor must always keep toys in the pipeline in order to keep her stream of income coming. Most toy licenses do not have a guaranteed minimum royalty that is to be paid to the inventor regardless of whether the product sells. As a result, when the toy stops selling, the income stops, too. They must have, at any one time, toys in various stages of the developmental process in order to constantly have new toy licenses on the horizon.

Like the toy industry in general, which is constantly changing, toy inventors must always be vigilant in following or setting trends. If they are lucky or very perceptive, they will be trendsetters.

Even if you are dealing with an agent for marketing your toys, you can call toy manufacturers to find out what's hot and what's not. It's the best way to find out the latest trends in toys and games. Ask them if they have a wish list or specific categories of toys that they are particularly interested in developing.

The wise toy inventor does not fall in love with any one of his ideas and rest on his laurels. He negotiates the best contract he can for his item and then quickly moves on to the next one. That is why the saying goes that successful toy inventors *take the money and run!*

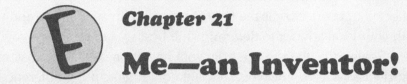

Chapter 21

Me—an Inventor!

Congratulations! You did it! You dreamed up a great idea, developed and protected it, and are now marketing your invention. This distinction sets you apart from the 97 percent of inventors who drop the ball somewhere along the way. Whether you are earning your main income from your invention or adding royalties to your regular salaried income, you have already achieved a major accomplishment. Your decisions from this point on become easier and more satisfying.

You're in the Money Now

Your immediate decisions now will revolve around your plans for your new income. If you have decided to build a business around your invention, you have already crossed that bridge. If you are taking the licensing route, you will have some decisions to make regarding your royalty payments that could affect your taxes. Now is the time to visit with an accountant and perhaps with your legal advisor to determine the best way to set up the royalty payments. Realize that the income from your invention could be substantial and your decisions as to how you are paid could make a big difference in your bottom line.

Even though as an independent inventor you may have come this far on your own, and you may have no plans to do anything more than collect your royalty checks, you should now consider yourself a business. The income stream from your invention will have an impact on your taxes. Your accountant and/or attorney can help you decide what your business arrangement will be. It will be helpful if you have some basic understanding of the different types of businesses that you may form.

Sole Proprietorships and Partnerships

A sole proprietorship is exactly what it sounds like: a business with one owner (you). You do not register with your state as a limited liability company or as a corporation. It is the easiest way to be in business because you avoid a lot of preliminary paperwork. You may have to register with your city and pay some minimum business tax. Other than that, your business exists simply because you now have an income stream. But there are drawbacks to this type of business that can cause you grief, since you are unprotected against litigation. For example, if your licensor is sued by a retailer for late delivery of product or by an end user claiming injury from your product, you will undoubtedly be included in the lawsuit. If a lawsuit is instituted against your licensor for any reason whatsoever, in fact, you will likely be included in the litigation, and your personal assets, even including your home, are at risk.

If you are a sole proprietor, legally you and the business are the same entity. If you are the business, you are responsible for all of your taxes and withholding. You are your own employer, meaning that you have to pay a self-employment tax. Employees make contributions for Social Security and Medicare that are matched by their employers. As the employee/employer, you are responsible for the entire amount. You will also need to pay quarterly estimated taxes toward your yearly federal taxes and, depending on where you live, possibly your state as well.

ALERT!

Consult with your tax professional before hiring your spouse to work for you in your business. You may find that it is better to hire her to work for you as an independent contractor, paying her own taxes, rather than to set her up as a paid employee. Having this decision made in advance can save some tax difficulties later.

A partnership is similar to a sole proprietorship in that there is no formal filing of paperwork to set up the business. You and your partner or partners just begin doing business together. However, there are some things you will want to know regarding legal responsibility in this type of business. If you have a general partnership, you will share equally in personal responsibility for indebtedness, including court judgments. If you set your company up as a limited partnership, the partner who actually manages the business will have the major financial liability. The investing partner(s) would be liable only up to the amount of their portions of the partnership. If you are considering setting up a partnership, be sure that there are no trust issues between you since there can be difficulties relating to business decisions and liabilities.

ESSENTIAL

Most states have a law known as the Uniform Partnership Act. If you do not create your own document setting out the rules for your partnership, this act will be used to settle any disagreements that end up in court. Be sure you are familiar with this act in your state before leaving dispute settlement to this method.

It is a good idea to have partnership documents between the partners even though they are not filed with the state. Additionally, the tax responsibilities pass through to the individual partners in this business arrangement, rather than being the responsibility of the company.

Limited Liability Companies and Corporations

A limited liability company (LLC) is a hybrid business, not a corporation, but with some of the benefits of a corporation. With an LLC, your personal assets are not at risk from business liabilities, but the company is not legally viewed as a separate entity, meaning that the profits pass through to and are reported on your personal tax return.

Another option available to you is becoming a corporation. Because of the liability issues related to sole proprietorships and partnerships, many independent inventors choose to set up corporations once they have license agreements. Legally, corporations are separate entities from their owners. This means that the shareholders cannot be held personally responsible for debts of or judgments against the corporation.

Two types of corporations will be discussed here: C corporations and S corporations. Professional corporations refer to a special type that is designed for business professions in which there could be malpractice suits, such as attorneys and doctors, and those will not be covered in this book.

C Corporation

A C corporation is one in which the corporation itself pays income taxes on the profits that are left over in the company after all expenses are paid. Your corporation would file Form 1120 and pay taxes on money left in the account after all salaries and expenses are paid. As an owner of the corporation, you would be paid a salary just as an employee of any company would be paid. You would file a personal income tax return on that salary and your personal taxes would relate only to the money that the company paid you. With a few exceptions, you would have limited personal liability against the debts of the business. The exceptions relate to circumstances such as your personally guaranteeing a company debt or your failing to treat the company as a corporation, thus breaking the rules that are set out for corporations.

S Corporation

If you elect to form an S corporation, you would have the limited liability status of a C corporation but you would pay income taxes as if you were organized as a sole proprietorship or a partnership. That is, the business profits would pass through the business to you and you would report those profits on your personal income tax return. Moreover, business losses also pass through to your personal tax return, and this can lower your personal taxes. Another advantage of this type of business arrangement is that as an S corporation shareholder, you do not have to pay self-employment taxes. Your S corporation would not pay corporate income taxes, but you would be required to file a form reporting each shareholder's portion of the income.

No matter what type of corporation you decide to create, you will need to follow some rules in order to keep it legal. You must file *articles of incorporation* and create some rules for running your business, called *bylaws*. You will also need to issue stock certificates to the owners and keep a record of that stock ownership.

Visit with your legal and tax advisors to determine which business arrangement will be most advantageous for you. Each type of business has different requirements for setting up, but none is difficult or expensive to accomplish and your advisors can help you with handling the details.

Don't Be a One-Hit Wonder—Invent Again!

As in so many of life's endeavors, inventing gets much easier the second time around. Although each invention is a brand-new project with some different aspects, much of the process is the same. And now you know how it is done! Creative people have more ideas than they can develop. It is simply a matter of taking the skills that you have developed and applying them to a new project.

Another wonderful perk of having achieved your first success is that you suddenly have credibility. Once you have succeeded, people view you in a new light, whether they are people related to your new business or novice inventors who seek you out for advice. If you have licensed your invention, you will find manufacturers much easier to reach for your next new product. This is true even when your new product is in an entirely different category, necessitating the opening of new marketing doors. A great deal of this is due to your new confidence. Now you know it can be done!

QUESTION?

Does a different category of invention require starting over?
Not exactly. Your next great idea may be in a completely different field than your first one, but you now have credentials as a professional product developer. You will find that the doors open more easily even if you choose a new path with your next invention.

You may already have your next great idea. If you do, get started on the steps to create success all over again. If you don't have that great idea yet, just keep your eyes open and it will come, as surely as the first one came. The important thing to remember here is that in order to succeed, your product must be one that will have a huge market. Just be sure that you have carefully looked at the potential market for each new idea before moving forward with it.

Life in the Slow Lane

Success with inventing is all about choices. When you worked for someone else, most of the choices belonged to your employer. Choices such as when and where you would work, what you would wear, and what your job duties involved belonged to your employer. Sometimes life can be pretty hectic when you are balancing your own needs with those of an employer and perhaps those of your family thrown in.

Now, with the financial breathing room provided by your success with your invention, you can rearrange your life to fit your own internal clock. Like to stay up late and sleep late? Go ahead! You know what you need to accomplish and how to do it. Like to work at home, in your pajamas? Do it! You may find that you are working longer hours than you did before, but now it is with a difference. Now you are spending your time doing what you love doing. It makes a huge difference when your schedule belongs to you and you can take advantage of opportunities that come along. Enjoy life in the slow lane. You've earned it!

Share the Wealth

Once you have attained that goal of getting your idea protected, developed, and marketed, you will find that there are others who have great ideas and who just need a little push in the right direction to succeed. Friends and relatives are likely to approach you asking for advice on how they might achieve success with their ideas. You may be one of those rare individuals who figured it all out on your own and mapped out your own success. More likely, there were people who assisted you all along the way.

This is your opportunity to pass along the things you have learned and help someone else achieve a goal. You will never do harm to yourself or your own invention by giving someone else the tools he needs to succeed. Since each invention is different and you have already achieved success with your invention, you cannot possibly hurt yourself by giving a boost to another hopeful inventor. A more likely result is that you will find that helping others helps you as well. Since inventing is a learning process, you will continue to learn by involving yourself in the inventing community. What you learn as you reach out to others could be just what you need for marketing your next idea.

There are lots of ways to reach out to others. In many cases, people who have good ideas but no knowledge of how to proceed will seek you out for advice. If you have a local inventors' club or association, this is an excellent way to reach those who are seeking help with their ideas. If you do not have such a group in your area, it is not at all difficult to start one. There are many new inventors who would love to meet and share experiences, resources, and motivation.

How can I start an inventors' club in my area?
Contact your local patent professionals (attorneys and agents) and invite them to meet with you and to share meeting information with the inventors with whom they are working. Look in the USPTO database and find people in your area who have been granted patents. These are good places to start.

You will find that area patent attorneys and agents are eager to join a local inventors' group. They enjoy visiting with creative people and they often get new business as a result of their volunteer involvement with these organizations. Local newspapers and radio stations often give free public service announcements to such nonprofit organizations. Even without free publicity, you can reach the interested people through the patent professionals and the patent database. Public libraries often have free meeting rooms available for such groups.

In addition to organized groups, you will find numerous opportunities to reach out to other inventors through the seminars and workshops that are held throughout the year in different cities around the country. These meetings are always open to the public. Additionally, you will find opportunities to spread the word about your willingness to share your knowledge in your daily life. If you write or if any of your present civic or religious organizations have newsletters, take this opportunity to tell your story. Telling your story offers two benefits to you. First, in telling your story you are spreading the word about your great invention. Any time you can get publicity for your invention, even if it has been licensed, it will only increase sales, which translates to more money in your pocket. Second, in telling your story you may provide just the bit of information or inspiration that another aspiring inventor may need to hear in order to move forward with his product.

The importance of independent inventors to the U.S. economy should not be underestimated. Every successful invention created by an independent inventor has far-reaching effects. New products create jobs for those advertising, manufacturing, distributing, and selling them at both the wholesale and retail levels. New product developers contribute to the economy by providing products that solve everyday problems for the average consumer.

Most licensees welcome publicity that the inventor is able to generate even though all rights to the patent have been assigned to the manufacturer. The publicity that you are able to get only makes their job of selling your product to the retail stores easier. After all, if there were already a public demand for your product the retailer would be foolish *not* to carry it!

In our consumer product–hungry society there is a continuous and constant demand for newer and better products. Look in any store you frequent. The products on the shelves are constantly changing. Independent inventors just like you created many of the new products on the shelves. Your intelligence, creativity, determination, and skills are making a positive contribution to our society and the world. Welcome to the wonderful world of product development!

Appendix A

Glossary of Terms

Throughout this book, you undoubtedly encountered words or usage specific to inventions, inventing, and patenting that were unfamiliar to you. This appendix lists some of the most important terms related to inventing and patenting.

Application (patent)

An application for patent can be one of four types of *patent applications* (i.e., utility, design, and plant) except provisional patent applications. A *provisional* patent application can establish the filing date but does not initiate the examination process. A nonprovisional utility patent application can also establish a filing date, initiates the examination process, and must include a specification, including a claim or claims; drawings, when necessary; an oath or declaration; and the prescribed filing fee.

Bacon's Directories

Directories listing press release contact information for television, radio, magazines, and newspapers.

Blanket nondisclosure agreement

Nondisclosure agreements that are designed to be used in a group setting such as an inventor's club.

Brainstorming

A method of shared problem-solving in which all members of a group spontaneously contribute ideas. A similar process undertaken by a person to solve a problem by rapidly generating a variety of possible solutions without judging their value or practicality until a later phase.

Claims

A series of one-sentence paragraphs at the end of a patent application or patent that defines the boundaries of the invention. Each claim is the object of the phrase "I claim" or "What is claimed is." The claims define the invention for determining patentability both during examination and after issuance when validity is challenged. Claims also determine what constitutes infringement. A claim typically recites a number of elements or limitations, and will cover or "read on" only those products (or processes) that contain all such elements or limitations, or their equivalents. Effective claims must be neither too broad (i.e., not cover prior art or matter not adequately described in the specification so as to support the claims) nor too narrow (i.e., fail to cover significant embodiments of the invention). An applicant may include a reasonable number of claims of varying scope.

Classification

The technology described in a patent is classified (organized) in the U.S. by a system using a three-digit class and a subclass to describe every similar grouping of patent art. A single invention may be described by multiple classification codes. There is a U.S. technology classification system and an international technology classification system.

Co-inventor

An inventor who is named with at least one other inventor in a patent application, wherein each inventor contributes to the conception (creation) of the invention set forth in at least one claim in a patent application.

Commercialized

A product or invention that has successfully been placed in the marketplace.

Contingency basis

Term used to describe an agreement between attorney and client where the attorney agrees to work without any monies upfront. He agrees to take a percentage portion of any award by the courts as his payment.

Contract attorney

An attorney who specializes and has extensive experience in writing and negotiating contracts for his clients.

Contractor's nondisclosure agreement

A nondisclosure agreement written specifically for use with professionals who help inventors develop their product. It states that they are working for hire only and have no proprietary interest in the invention or any improvements to the invention, even if they have contributed to those improvements.

Copyrights

Legal rights that protect works of authorship, such as writings, music, and works of art that have been tangibly expressed. Copyrights give the owner of the copyright the right to sue those who plagiarize their work. The Library of Congress registers copyrights, which last for the life of the author plus seventy years. Copyrights granted since January 1, 1978 are not renewable. They expire seventy years after the death of the creator.

Design patent

A patent that may be granted to anyone who invents a new, original, and ornamental design for an article of manufacture.

Disclosure

A written description, which the inventor is required to supply to the USPTO, that describes the invention in detail in exchange for the protection granted under a patent. In return for a patent, the inventor gives as consideration a complete revelation or disclosure of the invention for which protection is sought.

Disclosure Document

A paper disclosing an invention and signed by the inventor or inventors that has been forwarded to the USPTO by the inventor (or by any one of the inventors when there are joint inventors), by the owner of the invention, or by the attorney or agent of the inventor(s) or owner. The Disclosure Document will be retained for two years and will then be destroyed unless it is referred to in a separate letter in a related patent application filed within those two years. There is a significant difference between a Disclosure Document and a provisional U.S. patent application.

Drawings (patent)

Drawings that must show every feature of the invention as specified in the claims. Omission of drawings may cause an application to be considered incomplete but are only required if drawings are necessary for the understanding of the subject matter sought to be patented.

Embodiment

A manner in which an invention can be made, used, practiced, or expressed.

Enforceability of patent

The right of the patent owner to bring an infringement suit against a party who, without permission, makes, uses, or sells the claimed invention. The period of enforceability of a patent is the length of the term of the patent plus the six years under the statute of limitations for bringing an infringement action.

Examination

The search conducted by a USPTO patent examiner after the filing of an application for a patent. The examiner conducts a search of prior art and determines compliance with the substantive, formal, and procedural requirements of patentability. The examiner in a first office action notifies the applicant of rejection or allowance of each claim. The applicant may amend his patent application or present evidence and arguments in order to secure further examination. After a final office action, a patent may issue on any allowed claims, and the applicant must appeal any rejected claims to the Board of Appeals (or cancel the rejected claims and file a continuation application to pursue the rejected claims) in order to avoid abandonment and loss of the benefit of the original application filing date.

Examiner (patent examiner)

USPTO employee who is assigned the task of determining whether or not a patent application qualifies to be granted a patent. Patent examiners are assigned to specific categories of inventions.

Federal Trade Commission

Government regulatory agency responsible for overseeing commerce in the United States. Unscrupulous behavior on the part of invention-promotion or marketing companies should be reported to them.

First to File

Governing rule for most patent offices in the world whereby patents are issued to the first person to file for the patent regardless of whether or not they were the first to invent the product.

First to Invent

Governing rule of the patent offices in the United States, Canada, and Mexico whereby patents are granted to the person who can prove they were the first to invent the product regardless of whether or not they were the first to file for patent protection.

Hybrid search

A patent search using both key words and patent classification numbers.

Independent inventor

An inventor, sometimes called a product developer, who works on his own or in association with one or more partners. He does not invent for a company.

Infringement

The unauthorized making, selling, or using of an invention as defined by the claims of a patent. Patent infringement may take one of two forms: direct or literal infringement or infringement under the doctrine of equivalents.

Innovation

An improvement in an existing product.

Intellectual property

Creations of the mind—creative works or ideas embodied in a form that can be shared or can enable others to re-create, emulate, or manufacture them—that are legally protected in one or more ways including patents, trademarks, copyrights, or trade secrets.

International application

Allows a trademark owner to seek registration in any of the countries that have joined the Madrid Protocol by filing a single application.

InterneTIFF

Free Internet program that allows viewing of the image files on the USPTO patent database.

Invention

The word *invention* may have several different meanings. Most frequently, it refers to 1) the act of invention through original conception and reduction to practice, or 2) the subject matter described and/or claimed in a patent, patent application, or prior art reference (e.g., a product or process). In current usage, the word is used to refer to both patentable and unpatentable subject matter.

Invention-promotion companies

Companies that advertise that they can help independent inventors commercialize their products.

Inventor

One who contributes to the conception of an invention. The patent law of the United States of America requires that the applicant in a patent application must be the inventor.

Inventors' clubs and associations

Groups of people who meet to share resources and encouragement in the development of new products.

Inventor's journal

The inventor's diary of the progress and development of her invention. Entries must be recorded in a very specific way in order to be considered proof of when an idea was first conceived. Also called an engineering notebook.

Key word

Descriptive word used to search for an invention in a list or database; for example, for purposes of online searching.

License

Permission by the owner of a patent to make, use, or sell it under specific conditions, such as payment of royalties. A license may be exclusive or nonexclusive depending upon the terms of the license agreement.

Licensing agents

Professionals who generally work in one specific sector of the market to help inventors find manufacturers to license their products.

Light bulb moment

That moment when a terrific idea pops into your head.

Mailbox money

Royalty payments that come to the inventor as the result of a license agreement and without any further effort on the part of the inventor.

Maintenance fees

Fees for maintaining the enforceability of a patent based on an application filed on or after December 12, 1980.

Market size

The number of potential buyers for a specific product.

Marketability evaluation

Process of determining the likelihood of market acceptance for a specific product.

Nondisclosure agreement

A document that states that the information regarding the invention will be held in strict confidence. When a nondisclosure document is used, the showing or describing of an invention is not considered to be a public disclosure.

Nonobviousness

One of three basic conditions of patentability, the nonobviousness requirement precludes a patent if the differences between the subject matter sought to be patented and the prior art are such that the subject matter as a whole would have been obvious at the time the invention was made to a person having ordinary skill in the pertinent art. The determination of obviousness is made on the basis of several basic factual inquiries: 1) the scope and content of the prior art, 2) the differences between the prior art and the claims at issue, and 3) the level of ordinary skill in the pertinent art.

Notice of allowance

The official notice by the Patent Office stating that the application has been allowed and that the final issue fee should be paid within six months.

Office action

A letter from the patent office taking some official action upon an application. An office action may include rejections, objections, or requirements.

One-Year Rule

USPTO rule that gives inventors exactly one year from the first sale, offer for sale, public disclosure, or public use of their invention in which to file for patent protection or forfeit it forever.

Patent

A property right granted by the Government of the United States of America to an inventor "to exclude others from making, using, offering for sale, or selling the invention throughout the United States or importing the invention into the United States" for a limited time in exchange for public disclosure of the invention when the patent is granted.

Patent agent

Someone who is not an attorney but is registered to practice before the U.S. Patent Office and is authorized to represent patent applicant(s) before the U.S. Patent Office. An agent cannot render legal opinions on patentability, validity, or infringement. Also referred to as a practitioner or representative.

Patent application

A document submitted to the USPTO in order to request that a limited monopoly be granted to a person to manufacture, distribute, and sell an invention for a period of time, such as twenty years from the filing date of the patent application document.

Patent attorney

An attorney who is qualified to write and prosecute patent applications as well as represent inventors in court, should the need arise. Also called an intellectual property attorney.

Patent and Trademark Depository Library (PTDL)

A library designated by the USPTO to receive copies of patents, CD-ROMs containing registered and pending marks, and patent and trademark materials that are made available to the public for free. The libraries also actively disseminate patent and trademark information and offer Internet access to USPTO's online collections.

Patent Cooperation Treaty (PCT)

A convention, which came into force in 1978 and includes the United States and 110 other countries as members, that allows an inventor to file an international application in one member country that is also considered to be filed with one or more additional member countries that he designates. The application, after a preliminary prior art search and an optional examination, is forwarded to the patent offices of the designated countries for a determination of patentability under their domestic laws. The international filing date is the effective filing date in all of the designated countries. The Treaty does not alter any national requirements of patentability. However, it may change national requirements for drafting and filing a patent application in a number of countries.

Patent number

Unique number assigned to a patent application when it issues as a patent.

Patent pending

A phrase that often appears on manufactured items and that indicates a patent has been applied for on an invention that is embodied in the manufactured item. It serves as a warning that a patent may issue that would cover the item and that copiers should be careful because they might infringe if the patent issues. Once the patent issues, the patent owner will stop using the phrase "patent pending" and start using a phrase such as "covered by U.S. Patent Number XXXXXXX." Applying the "patent pending" phrase to an item when no patent application has been made can result in a fine.

Patent search

A search for any patent that may have a bearing on a patent application. Patent searches may be done by individuals, patent professionals, or professional searchers.

Patentability

The patent status sets forth three basic requirements for the patentability of an invention–utility, novelty, and nonobviousness. An applicant must be an original inventor (i.e., not have derived the subject matter from some other source) and must apply within one year of certain events that constitute potential statutory bars (e.g., public disclosure or public use). The USPTO determines the patentability of each claim during examination.

Person skilled in the art

The hypothetical person supposed to possess the usual or common available knowledge in his/her particular field.

Planogram

A map of a retail store's shelf space, which shows the allotment and location given to each distributor or manufacturer.

"Poor man's patent"

A self-addressed stamped envelope that contains a description of an invention and the date it was conceived. This has been ruled by the courts to be worthless as proof of ownership of an idea.

Preliminary market search

A search of stores, catalogs, and Web sites to be certain that a product is not already available for sale.

Preliminary online patent search

Also called a "knock out" search, this search is performed by an individual, not a professional patent searcher, using the USPTO patent database.

Prior art

Items similar to yours that have been previously marketed, described in a publication, or patented.

Product developer

Term for an independent inventor that does not conjure up the image of a wild-haired crazy inventor, but projects the image of a professional.

Professional patent search

A thorough patent search with a legal opinion of patentability performed by a professional search firm.

Project Mousetrap

Government "sting" operation to catch the scam invention-promotion companies providing inferior services.

Prosecution

The process of seeing your patent all the way through the USPTO review process and rewriting claims and/or advancing arguments, as necessary.

Prototype

A working model of a new invention that shows what it is, how it works, and that it does work.

Provisional patent application

A provisional application for patent is a U.S. national application for patent filed in the USPTO. It allows filing without a formal patent claim, oath, or declaration, or any information disclosure (prior art) statement. It provides the means to establish an early effective filing date in a nonprovisional patent application and automatically becomes abandoned after one year. It also allows the term "patent pending" to be applied. It must satisfy the same disclosure requirements as a regular utility patent application.

PTDL

Patent and Trademark Depository Library.

Public disclosure

Telling of or showing an invention that does not have patent protection without the use of nondisclosure agreements.

Public domain

The term used to describe publications and products that are not protected by copyrights or patents and are available for anyone to make and distribute.

Public use

A term describing an event that begins the one-year grace period within which an inventor must file a patent application. An experimental public use will not begin the one year grace period.

Rapid prototyping

Term used for a group of computer technologies that fabricate prototypes directly from CAD data sources. It is a dramatically less expensive method than plastic injection molding. Also called layered manufacturing.

Royalty

The sum of money paid to the owner of a patent, typically pursuant to a license agreement, for specified permission to use the invention.

Small entity

An independent inventor, a small business concern, or a nonprofit organization eligible for reduced patent fees in the USPTO.

State of the art

The entire available knowledge and practice existing in a particular field at the time an invention is made.

Stereolithography

Method for making rapid prototypes.

Thomas Register

A set of twenty books found in most libraries that list American manufacturers according to the products they manufacture. It is also available online at ✍*www. thomasnet.com.*

Trade directories

Books that are specific to industries and provide information on companies and key personnel of the companies as well as information on distributors of products in that industry. These directories are available in most major libraries.

Trade secret

The USPTO defines a trade secret as "any formula, pattern, machine, or process of manufacturing, or any device or compilation of information used in one's business, that is maintained in secrecy and may give the owner an advantage over competitors who do not know or use it."

Trade show

Industry event usually held over a two- to three-day time period in which manufacturers set up booths and show and sell their new products to their retail customers.

Trademark

According to the USPTO, "a trademark is any word, name, symbol, or device or combination thereof adopted and used by a manufacturer or merchant to identify his goods and distinguish them from those manufactured or sold by others."

United Inventors Association

National organization whose goal is to provide leadership, support, and services to inventor support groups and independent inventors (✍*www.uiausa.org*).

USPTO

The U.S. Patent and Trademark Office (USPTO) is an office headed by a Commissioner within the Department of Commerce. The Patent Office was created in 1793 and renamed in 1975 to reflect its dual functions as an office that reviews applications for and issues both patents and trademarks. Although the patent and trademark offices have different staffs and examiners they are a part of the same entity. The USPTO is staffed by a large body of skilled employees. It accepts and examines applications for the issuance of patents on inventions and for registration of rights in trademarks, service marks, certification marks, and collective marks.

Utility patent application

According to the USPTO, a utility patent application is "a patent application for protection of useful processes, machines, articles of manufacture, or compositions of matter."

Appendix B

Resources for Inventors

This appendix contains a list of many of the helpful books, Web sites, and services mentioned throughout the book. As always, the companies and their services are mere suggestions and you should thoroughly check out any suggested source before engaging their services.

Books

Create a Compelling Presentation for Your Invention by Mary Russell Sarao (free e-book online at ✑*www.asktheinventors. com/Books/presentations.htm*)

Free Publicity by Jeff Crilley (available in most bookstores)

How to Finance Your Invention or Great Idea by Jack Lander (available through the bookstore of the United Inventors Association at ✑*www.uiausa.org*)

How to License Your Million Dollar Idea by Harvey Reese (available in most libraries and bookstores)

Patent It Yourself by David Pressman (available in most libraries and bookstores)

Patent Pending in 24 Hours by Richard Levy and David Pressman (available in most libraries and bookstores)

Super Easy Guide to Step-by-Step Online Patent Searching by Mary Russell Sarao (free online e-book at ✑*www.askthein-ventors.com/Books/patentsearch.htm*)

The Toy and Game Inventor's Handbook by Richard Levy and Ronald Weingartner (available in most libraries and bookstores)

Web Sites

Assistance for Independent Inventors

The Academy of Applied Sciences
✑*www.aas-world.org*

The Academy is recognized nationally as an educational resource center offering enrichment programs for students, and professional development for teachers and educational administrators.

Ask the Inventors!™
✑*www.asktheinventors.com*

Great idea? What next? Are you looking for trustworthy help to get your invention developed, patented, and on the market? Run by successful inventors, this site can help you find success without being scammed by invention promoters.

Delphion
✑*www.delphion.com*

An international patent search database.

Disclosure Document Program of USPTO
✑*www.uspto.gov/web/forms/sb0095.pdf*

Federal Trade Commission
✑*http://rn.ftc.gov/pls/dod/wsolcq$. startup?Z_ORG_CODE=PU01*

File complaints here if you have been the victim of scam inventor-promotion companies.

International Federation of Inventors' Associations
✍www.invention-ifia.ch

IFIA is a nonprofit, nongovernmental organization created by seven European inventor associations in 1968. Today, its members belong to more than 110 countries. IFIA is the only organization that represents inventor groups worldwide.

Inventors' Digest Magazine
✍www.inventorsdigest.com/ME2/default. asp

This site is designed for anyone who has ever said, "I've got a great idea . . . Now what do I do?" It's also the spot for anyone who's searching for the next hot product. Check out the magazine site and then follow the links to the wonderful world of invention!

Inventors HQ
✍www.inventorshq.com

This site helps inventors from around the world get their products from the garage to the marketplace for the least possible amount of out-of-pocket money.

InventorEd
✍www.inventored.org

Education and news for inventors that can help you avoid scams.

Martindale Hubble Directory
✍www.martindale.com/xp/Martindale/ home.xml

Online version of the leading attorney directory in which you can locate attorneys according to the category of their practice and their geographical location.

Patent Café
✍www.patentcafe.com

This Web site offers a wealth of information and links for independent inventors.

Service Corps of Retired Executives (SCORE)
✍www.score.org

Small Business Development Centers (SBDCs)
✍www.asbdc-us.org

United Inventors Association
✍www.uiausa.org

The mission of the UIA is to provide leadership, support, and services to inventor support groups and independent inventors.

Membership is extended to these as well as to others who provide reputable service and support to the inventor community. The Inventors' Awareness Center is the inventor education and advocacy program of UIA and is presented in detail under the section Red Flag Warnings.

United States Copyright Office
✍*www.copyright.gov*

United States Patent and Trademark Office
✍*www.uspto.gov*

Marketability Evaluation Services

United Inventors Association Innovation Assessment Program
✍*www.uiausa.org/UIAIAP.htm*

Wal-Mart's Innovation Institute
✍*www.innovation-institute.com*

This Web site offers an inexpensive marketability evaluation service.

Wisconsin Innovation Service Center
✍*http://academics.uww.edu/business/innovate*

The Wisconsin Innovation Service Center (WISC) specializes in new product and invention assessments and market expansion opportunities for innovative manufacturers, technology businesses, and independent inventors. Since 1980, WISC has researched the viability of over 6,000 projects. Technical experts and researchers use an extensive array of resources to analyze information on technical feasibility, existing patents, market size, competitive intensity, demand trends, and other areas. WISC's research products cover product feasibility, competitive intelligence, distributor assessment, customer satisfaction, and licensing partnerships.

Toy and Game Links

American International TOY FAIR
✍*www.toy-tia.org/AITF/index.html*

American Specialty Toys Retail Association
✍*www.astratoy.org/about_astra_fs.htm*

Discover Games
✍*www.discovergames.com*

International Council of Toy Industries
✍*www.toy-icti.org*

Playthings.com
✍*www.playthings.com/index. asp?layout=front_page&webzine=playthings&publication=playthings*

Online magazine for the toy industry.

Toy Industry Association, Inc.
✍*www.toy-tia.org/index.html*

U.S. Domestic Trade Shows
www.toy-tia.org/industry/related-org/ domestic.html

Women in Toys
www.womenintoys.com

Funding Resources

About.com How to Get New Ideas Funded
http://inventors.about.com/od/ gettingthemoney

Deal Flow Venture Capital Firms and Angel Investors
www.dealflow.com

Department of Energy Inventions and Innovations
www.oit.doe.gov

On this site you will find grants for research and development of energy-related inventions.

National Science Foundation Grants and Awards
www.nsf.gov/home/grants.htm

Small Business Administration
www.sbaonline.sba.gov/hotlist/ procure.html

Student Programs for Invention Funding
http://inventors.about.com/od/competitionsprize

VFinance.com Directory
www.vfinance.com

Directory of 1,800 venture capital firms and 23,000 angel investors.

Marketing and Licensing Resources

Ask the Inventors!™
www.asktheinventors.com/process.htm

Free licensing referrals.

Bacon's Directories
www.bacons.com

Complete list of media sources such as newspapers, magazines, and television and radio networks, including contact information.

Catalog searching
www.catalogs.com
www.shopathome.com
www.yes-its-free.com
www.24hourmall.com
www.mailordercatalogs.net

Dun & Bradstreet Million Dollar Companies
www.dnbmdd.com/mddi

Harvey Reese & Associates
www.money4ideas.com

Successful inventor and invention licensing agents.

InventPro.com

✐*www.inventpro.com*

This Web site specializes in connecting inventors with various manufacturers who might wish to license their patented or patent pending ideas. Also offered are professional patent searches, virtual prototyping, online invention promoting, and marketability studies.

Lambert & Lambert

✐*www.lambertinvent.com/inventions.htm*

Invention licensing agents.

Licensing Executives Society

✐ *www.usa-canada.les.org/aboutus*

The Thomasnet.com

✐*www.thomasnet.com*

Listings of manufacturers according to the types of items they manufacture. Available in a twenty-volume set at public libraries everywhere and in a more limited version online. When you are ready to locate possible licensees, this is one of the first places you should visit.

Prototyping Services

Rapid Prototyping Services

✐*www.rapidprototyping.net*
✐*http://home.att.net/~castleisland*

Find other listings for rapid prototyping by typing "rapid prototyping" in any search engine.

Reproduce Almost Anything with Basic Silicone Mold Making

✐*www.reproduce100s.com*

Randall Landreneau, the former president of the Tampa Bay Inventor's Council, has developed an ideal method for creating plastic prototypes inexpensively. After watching his video you will be able to produce professional prototypes on your own with very basic tools and no more expertise and knowledge than that which you will learn from the video. This video is a must for every inventor!

Patent Searching

Patent Search International

✐*www.patentsearchinternational.com*

Provides professional patent searches with legal opinion of patentability for reasonable fees. Mention coupon #ATI251248 for a $25 discount.

Trademark Searching and Filing

Trademark Partners

✐*www.TrademarkPartners.com*

Provides trademark searches and filings for reasonable fees.

Appendix C

Patent and Trademark Depository Libraries

The following is a collection of all the PTDLs listed alphabetically by state in the United States. The librarians at these libraries are trained by the USPTO and can show you how to perform your own patent search.

Alabama

Auburn University Libraries (205) 844-1737

Birmingham Public Library (205) 226-3620

Alaska

Anchorage: Z. J. Loussac Public Library (907) 562-7323

Arizona

Tempe: Noble Library, Arizona State University (602) 965-7010

Arkansas

Little Rock: Arkansas State Library (501) 682-2053

California

Los Angeles Public Library (213) 228-7220

Sacramento: California State Library (916) 654-0069

San Diego Public Library (619) 236-5813

San Francisco Public Library (415) 557-4488

Sunnyvale Patent Clearinghouse (408) 730-7290

Colorado

Denver Public Library (303) 640-8847

Connecticut

New Haven: Free Public Library (203) 946-7452

Hartford: Hartford Public Library (860) 543-8628

Delaware

Newark: University of Delaware Library (302) 831-2965

District of Columbia

Howard University Libraries (202) 806-7252

Florida

Fort Lauderdale: Broward County Main Library (305) 357-7444

Miami-Dade Public Library (305) 375-2665

Orlando: University of Central Florida Libraries (407) 823-2562

Tampa Campus Library, University of South Florida (813) 974-2726

Georgia

Atlanta: Price Gilbert Memorial Library, Georgia Institute of Technology (404) 894-4508

Hawaii

Honolulu: Hawaii State Public Library System (808) 586-3477

Idaho

Moscow: University of Idaho Library (208) 885-6235

Illinois

Chicago Public Library (312) 747-4450

Indiana

Indianapolis: Marion County Public Library (317) 269-1741

West Lafayette: Siegesmund Engineering Library, Purdue University (317) 494-2872

Iowa

Des Moines: State Library of Iowa (515) 281-4118

Kansas

Wichita: Ablah Library, Wichita State Library (316) 689-3155

Kentucky

Louisville: Free Public Library (502) 574-1611

Louisiana

Baton Rouge: Troy H. Middleton Library, Louisiana State University (504) 388-8875

Maine

Orono: Raymond H. Fogler Library, University of Maine (207) 581-1691

Maryland

College Park: Engineering and Physical Sciences Library, University of Maryland (301) 405-9157

Massachusetts

Amherst: Physical Sciences Library, University of Massachusetts (413) 545-1370

Boston Public Library (617) 536-5400, ext. 265

Michigan

Ann Arbor: Media Union, University of Michigan (734) 647-5735

Big Rapids: Abigail S. Timme Library, Ferris State University (616) 592-3602

Detroit Public Library (313) 833-3379

Minnesota

Minneapolis Public Library and Information Center (612) 630-6120

Mississippi

Jackson: Mississippi Library Commission (601) 961-4111

Missouri

Kansas City: Linda Hall Library (816) 363-4600

St. Louis Public Library (314) 241-2288, ext. 390

Montana

Butte: Montana College of Mineral Science and Technology Library (406) 496-4281

Nebraska

Lincoln: Engineering Library, University of Nebraska-Lincoln (402) 472-3411

Nevada

Las Vegas: Clark County Library, Clark County Library District (702) 507-3421

Reno: University of Nevada-Reno Library (702) 784-6500

New Hampshire

Concord: New Hampshire State Library (603) 271-2239

New Jersey

Newark Public Library (973) 733-7779

Piscataway: Library of Science and Medicine, Rutgers University (908) 445-2895

New Mexico

Albuquerque: University of New Mexico General Library (505) 277-4412

New York

Albany: New York State Library (518) 474-5355

Buffalo and Erie County Public Library (716) 858-7101

New York Public Library (the Research Libraries) (212) 592-7000

Rochester: Center Library of Rochester and Monroe County (716) 428-8110

Stony Brook: Melville Library, Room 1101, SUNY at Stony Brook (516) 632-7148

West Virginia

Morgantown: Evansdale Library, West Virginia University (304) 293-4695, Ext. 5113

Wisconsin

Madison: Kurt F. Wendt Library, University of Wisconsin-Madison (608) 262-6845

Milwaukee Public Library (414) 286-3051

Wyoming

Cheyenne: Wyoming State Library (307) 777-7281

Appendix D

Forms and Samples

In this appendix, you will find samples of a license agreement, option agreement, standard nondisclosure form, contractor's nondisclosure form, business plan form, and product presentation. These are samples only, and you are advised to have an attorney review any legal form that you create for your own invention.

LICENSE AGREEMENT

_____, with principal offices located at _____ (hereinafter "LICENSOR") has given _____, with principal offices located at _____ _____(hereinafter "LICENSEE") the exclusive production and marketing rights, in the _____ market, to their intellectual property identified by U.S. Patent Serial No. _____. In exchange for these exclusive rights, LICENSEE agrees to pay LICENSOR a royalty in the amount and under the terms outlined in this agreement.

PRODUCT DESCRIPTION

_____

_____

_____

_____

1. ROYALTY PAYMENTS. A ____% royalty, based on net selling price, will be paid by LICENSEE to LICENSOR on all sales of LICENSED PRODUCT and all subsequent variations thereof by LICENSEE, its subsidiaries, and/or associate companies. The term "net selling price" shall mean the price LICENSEE receives from its customers, less any discounts for volume, promotion, defects or freight.

    Royalty payments are to be made quarterly, on or before the fifteenth (15th) day of the month following the end of each quarter. LICENSOR shall have the right to examine and audit LICENSEE'S books and records as they pertain to sales of LICENSED PRODUCT.

    LICENSEE agrees to pay to LICENSOR a guaranteed minimum royalty of $_____ annually and if the agreed upon amount is not recovered by LICENSEE through sales during the annual term, such overage in royalty payments as may occur is not recoverable from future royalty years.

2. TERRITORY. LICENSEE shall have the right to market LICENSED PRODUCT throughout the United States, its possessions, and territories,

and Canada. However, LICENSEE agrees that it will not knowingly sell to parties who intend to resell the product(s) outside of the licensed territory.

3. ADVANCE PAYMENT. Upon execution of this Agreement, LICENSEE will make a nonrefundable payment to LICENSOR of $_____, which shall be construed as an advance against future earned royalties.

4. COPYRIGHT, PATENT, AND TRADEMARK NOTICES. LICENSEE agrees that on the product, its packaging and collateral material there will be printed notices of any patents issued or pending and applicable trademark and/or copyright notices showing the LICENSOR as the owner of said patents, trademarks or copyrights under exclusive license to LICENSEE.

    In the event there has been no previous registration or patent application for the licensed product(s), LICENSEE may, at LICENSEE's discretion and expense, make such application or registration in the name of the LICENSOR. However, LICENSEE agrees that at termination or expiration of this Agreement, LICENSEE will be deemed to have assigned, transferred and conveyed to LICENSOR all trade rights, equities, goodwill, titles or other rights in and to licensed products which may have been attained by the LICENSEE. Any such transfer shall be without consideration other than as specified in this Agreement.

5. TERMS AND WARRANTS. This Agreement shall be considered to be in force so long as LICENSEE continues to sell the original product line or subsequent extension and/or variations thereof.

6. PRODUCT DESIGNS. LICENSOR agrees to furnish conceptual product designs, if requested, for the initial product line and all subsequent variations and extensions at no charge to LICENSEE. In addition, if requested, LICENSOR will assist in the design of packaging, point-of-purchase material, displays, etc. at no charge to LICENSEE.

7. QUALITY OF MERCHANDISE. LICENSEE agrees that Licensed product(s) will be produced and distributed in accordance with federal, state and local laws. LICENSEE further agrees to submit a sample of said

product(s), its cartons, containers, and packing material to LICENSOR for approval (which approval shall not be unreasonably withheld) The product(s) may not thereafter be materially changed without the approval of the LICENSOR.

8.   DEFAULT, BANKRUPTCY, VIOLATION, ETC.

   A.   In the event LICENSEE does not commence to manufacture, distribute and sell product(s) within six (6) months after the execution of this Agreement, LICENSOR, in addition to all other remedies available to him, shall have the option of canceling this Agreement. Should this event occur, to be activated by registered letter, LICENSEE agrees not to continue with the product's development and is obligated to return all prototype samples and drawings to LICENSOR.

   B.   In the event LICENSEE files a petition in bankruptcy, or if the LICENSEE becomes insolvent, or makes an assignment for the benefit of creditors, the license granted hereunder shall terminate automatically without the requirement of a written notice. No further sales of licensed product(s) may be made by LICENSEE, its receivers, agents, administrators or assigns without the express written approval of the LICENSOR.

   C.   If LICENSEE shall violate any other obligations under the terms of this Agreement, and upon receiving written notice of such violation by LICENSOR, LICENSEE shall have thirty (30) days to remedy such violation. If this has not been done, LICENSOR shall have the option of canceling the Agreement upon ten (10) days written notice. If this event occurs, all sales activity must cease and any royalties owing are immediately due.

9.   LICENSEE'S RIGHT TO TERMINATE. Not withstanding anything contained in this Agreement, LICENSEE shall have the absolute right to cancel this Agreement at any time by providing sixty (60) days written notice to LICENSOR of his decision to discontinue the sale of the product(s) covered by this Agreement. This cancellation shall be without recourse from

LICENSOR other than for the collection of any royalty payment that may be due him. This notice of cancellation does not relieve LICENSEE of responsibility for payment of any minimum royalty due for that license year.

10. LICENSOR'S RIGHT TO TERMINATE. In the event of a material breach of this Agreement by LICENSEE, LICENSOR shall have the right to terminate this Agreement upon sixty (60) days written notice and such termination shall take effect immediately if said material breach is not remedied during that sixty (60) day period.

11. INDEMNIFICATION. LICENSEE agrees to obtain, at its own expense, product liability insurance for at least $2,000,000 combined single unit for LICENSEE and LICENSOR against claims, suits, loss or damage arising out of any alleged defect in the licensed product(s). As proof of such insurance, LICENSEE will submit to LICENSOR a fully paid certificate of insurance naming LICENSOR as an insured party. This submission is to be made before any licensed product is distributed or sold.

12. NO PARTNERSHIP, ETC. This Agreement shall be binding upon the successors and assigns of the parties hereto. Nothing contained in this Agreement shall be construed to place the parties in the relationship of legal representatives, partners, or joint venturers. Neither LICENSOR nor LICENSEE shall have the power to bind or obligate in any matter whatsoever, other than as per this Agreement.

13. GOVERNING LAW. This Agreement shall be construed in accordance with the laws of the state of _____. IN WITNESS WHEREOF, the parties hereto have signed this Agreement as of the day and year written below.

_____   _____

LICENSEE   LICENSOR

DATE:_____   DATE:_____

OPTION AGREEMENT

This Agreement is made and entered into between _____ (hereinafter "GRANTOR"), located at _____ ____ and _____, a company organized under the laws of _____ (hereinafter "GRANTEE"), located at _____ _____.

1. <u>Grant of Option</u>. In consideration of payment of $_____ by GRANT-EE to GRANTOR, receipt of which GRANTOR acknowledges, GRANTOR grants GRANTEE an exclusive option to obtain a license from GRANTOR to the OPTIONED RIGHTS, in accordance with this Option Agreement.

2. <u>Definitions</u>.

   a.   OPTIONED RIGHTS means the intellectual property herein described as:_____.

   b.   TERM means that period of time which GRANTOR and GRANTEE agree shall allow GRANTEE to evaluate the OPTIONED RIGHTS. The TERM shall be from _____ to _____.

3. <u>Exercise of the Option</u>. GRANTEE may exercise its option at any time prior to expiration of the TERM by giving written notice signed by GRANTEE to GRANTOR at its address stated above. The notice must be personally delivered or postmarked before the expiration of the TERM.

4. <u>Confidentiality</u>. The GRANTOR and GRANTEE agree to maintain discussions and proprietary information revealed pursuant to the Option Agreement in confidence, to disclose them only to persons within their respective companies having a need to know, and to pledge to GRANTOR that such persons also agree to hold said information strictly confidential.

5. <u>Conditions to License</u>. In the event that GRANTEE elects to exercise its option, execution of a license agreement shall occur within thirty (30) days after GRANTOR receives notice that GRANTEE is exercising the option.

6. <u>Terms of License</u>. Terms and conditions of the license agreement will be negotiated in good faith so as to result in a license acceptable to both parties.

7. <u>Failure to Exercise Option or to Close</u>. If GRANTEE fails to exercise its option properly before expiration of the TERM or fails to meet the conditions to license and enter into a license within the time allowed, this Option Agreement shall

terminate and GRANTOR may retain the Option Payment and shall have no further obligation to GRANTEE.

8.   Assignment. This Option Agreement shall bind and benefit the parties' successors and assigns. Neither party may assign rights under this Agreement without the prior written consent of the other party.

9.   Entire Agreement; Amendment. This Agreement represents the entire agreement of the parties with respect to the transaction described in this Agreement, and no prior or simultaneous oral or other written representations or promises shall be a part of this Agreement or otherwise effective. This Agreement may not be amended or released, in whole or in part, except by a document signed by both parties.

10. Interpretation. In the event any provision of this Agreement proves to be illegal or unenforceable, the remaining provisions of this Agreement shall be interpreted as if such illegal or unenforceable provision were not a part of the Agreement.

11. Law. This Agreement shall be constructed in accordance with the laws of the State of _____.

To evidence their agreement to the foregoing terms and conditions, GRANTOR and GRANTEE have executed this Option Agreement below.

Grantor: _____   Grantee: _____

By:_____   By:_____

Signature: Signature:

_____   _____

Title:_____   Title:_____

Date:_____   Date:_____

Standard Nondisclosure Form

Confidential Disclosure Agreement
This Agreement is between
<u>(Enter name/s of recipients of information here)</u>,
hereinafter called "Recipient", and

_____,

hereinafter called "Owner".

WHEREAS Owner possesses certain confidential information concerning:

_____

_____

_____ ;

WHEREAS Recipient is desirous of obtaining said confidential information for purposes of evaluation thereof and as a basis for further discussions with Owner regarding assistance with development of the confidential information for the benefit of Owner or for the mutual benefit of Owner and Recipient;

THEREFORE, Recipient hereby agrees to receive the information in confidence and to treat it as confidential for all purposes. Recipient will not divulge or use in any manner any of said confidential information unless by written consent from Owner, and Recipient will use at least the same efforts it regularly employs for its own confidential information to avoid disclosure to others.

Provided, however, that this obligation to treat information confidentially will not apply to any information already in Recipient's possession or to any information that is generally available to the public or becomes generally available through no act or influence of Recipient. Recipient will inform Owner of the public nature or Recipient's possession of the information without delay after Owner's disclosure thereof or will be stopped from asserting such as defense to remedy under this agreement.

Recipient will exercise its best efforts to conduct its evaluation within a reasonable time after Owner's disclosure and will provide Owner with its assessment thereof without delay. Recipient will return all information, including all copies thereof, to Owner upon request. This agreement shall remain in effect for ten years after the date of its execution, and it shall be construed under the laws of the State of _____ _____.

_____   _____

Date   (enter Recipient's name/s here)

_____   _____

(Date)   (Owner)

Contractor's Nondisclosure Form

Confidentiality and Safeguard Agreement

This agreement is between _____, whose place of residence or business is _____, hereafter known as the inventor, and _____, whose place of business or residence is _____, hereafter known as the vendor.

Vendor will provide certain services as follows:

[   ]   prototyping
[   ]   design and/or drafting
[   ]   marketability evaluation and/or research and/or plan
[   ]   overall planning for development, protection, and marketing.
[   ]   other: _____

Vendor agrees to maintain all information divulged to him or her by inventor, in whatever form (written, drawn, photographed, verbal, video, or other), confidential and safe. Vendor will not transmit or divulge said information to any third person (except his or her employee who has a need to know). Vendor will not use said information as his or her own, or for his or her own advantage. Vendor will preserve as confidential and safe said information for a period of _____ from date of order, and will (   ) return to inventor, or (   ) destroy tangibles by shredding or burning after said period.

Vendor further agrees that all patentable features arising from his or her services will be revealed to the inventor as the work progresses, and become inventor's property in full at the time the vendor receives payment in amount agreed to by vendor and inventor at the time inventor's order is placed. Vendor further agrees that he/she has no claim to any intellectual property rights related to this invention.

_____Vendor _____Date

Small Business Development Center Sample Business Plan

Contents of a Business Plan

- Cover Page
- Name of Business, Address, Phone, Name of Owner(s), and Logo, if you have one
- Introduction
- Business form (corporation, sole proprietorship, etc.)
- If you are applying for financing, list how much, what funds of your own you have, and how the funds will be used
- Executive Summary
  In one or two pages, give the reader an idea of what the business does. Try to cover:
- What you do
- What will be unique or different
- Who will be your customers
- Why you will be successful
- When you plan to start
- How you plan to implement your idea
- How much money it will cost and where you will get the necessary funds

Sample Presentation: Ghostline® Poster Board

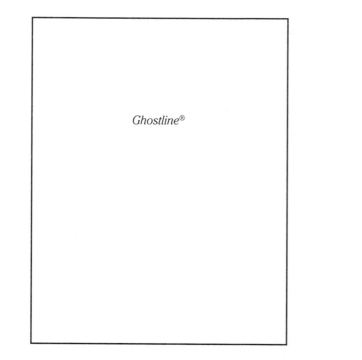

Ghostline®

What is Ghostline®?

It is the poster board with the patented "ghosted" grid. It is ready to use immediately. No measuring! No drawing lines! And, best of all, once there is writing or drawing on the board the lines seem to disappear!

It is the poster board that allows you to spend your time working on the project, not getting the poster board ready for use. Think of the time and energy it saves!

How does Ghostline® work?

- It makes lettering quick and easy because the user does not have to measure and draw lines before starting a project.

- The lines are easy to see up close for lettering or drawing but virtually disappear once there is writing or drawing on the board.

What will it cost to manufacture Ghostline®?

- The cost to apply the patented Ghostline® grid to poster board is minimal. Estimates are that it can be done for three to four cents per sheet and possibly much less with greater volume.

- There will be virtually no tool-up fees. Carolina Pad already has the equipment and facilities to manufacture Ghostline®. All that will be required is the special ink formulation and a screen of the grid for use in either offset or flexography printing.

What's in it for Carolina Pad?

- Profit!

- Customers will choose to buy their poster board from Carolina Pad in order to get Ghostline® once they have been introduced to it.

- A low-profit item can be turned into a profitable one. Ghostline® lifts poster board out of the commodity category. With Ghostline®, poster board will have brand name appeal.

- In addition to poster board, Carolina Pad can apply the Ghostline® grid to many other items such as display boards, flip charts, tablets, stationery, and art papers and enhance their value also.

- And it is patent protected! Carolina Pad will hold exclusive rights to produce Ghostline®.

Who benefits from Ghostline®?

Students
Students of all ages are able to make neat and impressive science, math, history, language arts, geography, social studies, and art projects, etc. Lines are straight and even. There is no need to draw and then erase pencil lines, smudging or ruining lettering in the process.

Parents
Parents no longer have to help their children measure and draw the lines before beginning a poster board project. Children are able to spend time on productive work rather than on the time-consuming task of preparing the poster board.

Teachers
Ghostline® is great for use in preparation of bulletin boards, teaching aids, student progress charts, customized calendars, maps, graphs, and time lines without the tedious process of drawing preliminary lines.

Businesses
Poster board is not just a school supply item. The possible uses for GHOSTLINE® in the business world are unlimited. It can be used to make employee signs, notices, duty charts, goal setting charts, comparative progress charts and graphs, customized calendars, and presentation projects, to name just a few.

What can Ghostline® be sold for?

It will sell for substantially more than plain poster board. Our retailers have told us that customers happily pay ninety-nine cents per sheet and more for the convenience of not having to measure and draw the lines. (We were right on with our suggested retail selling price. The two-pack of GHOSTLINE® now sells for $1.99.)

Where should Ghostline® be sold?

- Retail stores such as Target, Kmart, Wal-Mart, Eckerd Drug Stores, grocery stores, hobby and craft store, etc. (The list is truly endless.)

- Schools and school districts

- Teacher supply stores

- Office supply stores such as Office Depot, Office Max, and Staples.

- Any place that sells poster board!

How should Ghostline® be packaged?

Ghostline® should be packaged exactly the same way that your poster board is packaged now.

- It can be sold in bulk in the trays of the poster board display.
- It can be sold in plastic wrappers with inserts that explain why it is unique and a valuable time-saver for the consumer.
- Or it can be sold in cartons of 15–50–100 sheets.

How should Ghostline® be displayed?

Prominently! GHOSTLINE® is a great innovation. Consumers need only to be introduced to it and they will want no other. Point of purchase signs should point out that GHOSTLINE® is no ordinary poster board and list the many advantages it provides as a time-saver and a tool to make neater, more attractive projects and signs.

If the product is wrapped in packages of two or three sheets, there should be a paper insert under the wrapping identifying GHOSTLINE® as offering unique advantages over plain poster board.

Ten Reasons Why Carolina Pad Needs Ghostline®

1. Ghostline® has been awarded a U.S. patent and has an option to apply for worldwide patent protection. An application for a Canadian patent is already in progress.
2.
3.
4.
5.
6.
7.
8.
9.
10.

Summary

- Ghostline® is a great improvement in poster board that consumers will welcome.

- The process of applying the Ghostline® grid is an easy and economical process that Carolina Pad already has the equipment and facilities to accomplish.

- The Ghostline® patented grid is a perfect addition to the high quality line of products carried by Carolina Pad.

Index

The EVERYTHING Series!

BUSINESS & PERSONAL FINANCE

Everything® **Accounting Book**
Everything® Budgeting Book
Everything® Business Planning Book
Everything® Coaching and Mentoring Book
Everything® Fundraising Book
Everything® Get Out of Debt Book
Everything® Grant Writing Book
Everything® Home-Based Business Book, 2nd Ed.
Everything® Homebuying Book, 2nd Ed.
Everything® Homeselling Book, 2nd Ed.
Everything® Investing Book, 2nd Ed.
Everything® Landlording Book
Everything® Leadership Book
Everything® **Managing People Book, 2nd Ed.**
Everything® Negotiating Book
Everything® Online Auctions Book
Everything® Online Business Book
Everything® Personal Finance Book
Everything® Personal Finance in Your 20s and 30s Book
Everything® Project Management Book
Everything® Real Estate Investing Book
Everything® Robert's Rules Book, $7.95
Everything® Selling Book
Everything® **Start Your Own Business Book, 2nd Ed.**
Everything® Wills & Estate Planning Book

COOKING

Everything® Barbecue Cookbook
Everything® Bartender's Book, $9.95
Everything® Chinese Cookbook
Everything® **Classic Recipes Book**
Everything® Cocktail Parties and Drinks Book
Everything® College Cookbook
Everything® **Cooking for Baby and Toddler Book**
Everything® Cooking for Two Cookbook
Everything® Diabetes Cookbook
Everything® Easy Gourmet Cookbook
Everything® Fondue Cookbook
Everything® **Fondue Party Book**
Everything® Gluten-Free Cookbook
Everything® Glycemic Index Cookbook
Everything® Grilling Cookbook

Everything® Healthy Meals in Minutes Cookbook
Everything® Holiday Cookbook
Everything® Indian Cookbook
Everything® Italian Cookbook
Everything® Low-Carb Cookbook
Everything® Low-Fat High-Flavor Cookbook
Everything® Low-Salt Cookbook
Everything® Meals for a Month Cookbook
Everything® Mediterranean Cookbook
Everything® Mexican Cookbook
Everything® One-Pot Cookbook
Everything® **Quick and Easy 30-Minute, 5-Ingredient Cookbook**
Everything® Quick Meals Cookbook
Everything® Slow Cooker Cookbook
Everything® Slow Cooking for a Crowd Cookbook
Everything® Soup Cookbook
Everything® Tex-Mex Cookbook
Everything® Thai Cookbook
Everything® Vegetarian Cookbook
Everything® Wild Game Cookbook
Everything® Wine Book, 2nd Ed.

GAMES

Everything® 15-Minute Sudoku Book, $9.95
Everything® 30-Minute Sudoku Book, $9.95
Everything® Blackjack Strategy Book
Everything® Brain Strain Book, $9.95
Everything® Bridge Book
Everything® Card Games Book
Everything® Card Tricks Book, $9.95
Everything® Casino Gambling Book, 2nd Ed.
Everything® Chess Basics Book
Everything® Craps Strategy Book
Everything® Crossword and Puzzle Book
Everything® Crossword Challenge Book
Everything® Cryptograms Book, $9.95
Everything® Easy Crosswords Book
Everything® Easy Kakuro Book, $9.95
Everything® Games Book, 2nd Ed.
Everything® Giant Sudoku Book, $9.95
Everything® Kakuro Challenge Book, $9.95
Everything® **Large-Print Crossword Challenge Book**
Everything® Large-Print Crosswords Book
Everything® Lateral Thinking Puzzles Book, $9.95
Everything® **Mazes Book**

Everything® Pencil Puzzles Book, $9.95
Everything® Poker Strategy Book
Everything® Pool & Billiards Book
Everything® Test Your IQ Book, $9.95
Everything® Texas Hold 'Em Book, $9.95
Everything® Travel Crosswords Book, $9.95
Everything® Word Games Challenge Book
Everything® Word Search Book

HEALTH

Everything® Alzheimer's Book
Everything® Diabetes Book
Everything® Health Guide to Adult Bipolar Disorder
Everything® Health Guide to Controlling Anxiety
Everything® Health Guide to Fibromyalgia
Everything® **Health Guide to Thyroid Disease**
Everything® Hypnosis Book
Everything® Low Cholesterol Book
Everything® Massage Book
Everything® Menopause Book
Everything® Nutrition Book
Everything® Reflexology Book
Everything® Stress Management Book

HISTORY

Everything® American Government Book
Everything® American History Book
Everything® Civil War Book
Everything® Freemasons Book
Everything® Irish History & Heritage Book
Everything® Middle East Book

HOBBIES

Everything® Candlemaking Book
Everything® Cartooning Book
Everything® **Coin Collecting Book**
Everything® Drawing Book
Everything® Family Tree Book, 2nd Ed.
Everything® Knitting Book
Everything® Knots Book
Everything® Photography Book
Everything® Quilting Book
Everything® Scrapbooking Book
Everything® Sewing Book
Everything® Woodworking Book

Bolded titles are new additions to the series.
All Everything® books are priced at $12.95 or $14.95, unless otherwise stated. Prices subject to change without notice.

HOME IMPROVEMENT

Everything® Feng Shui Book
Everything® Feng Shui Decluttering Book, $9.95
Everything® Fix-It Book
Everything® Home Decorating Book
Everything® Home Storage Solutions Book
Everything® Homebuilding Book
Everything® Lawn Care Book
Everything® Organize Your Home Book

KIDS' BOOKS

All titles are $7.95

Everything® Kids' Animal Puzzle & Activity Book
Everything® Kids' Baseball Book, 4th Ed.
Everything® Kids' Bible Trivia Book
Everything® Kids' Bugs Book
Everything® Kids' Cars and Trucks Puzzle & Activity Book
Everything® Kids' Christmas Puzzle & Activity Book
Everything® Kids' Cookbook
Everything® Kids' Crazy Puzzles Book
Everything® Kids' Dinosaurs Book
Everything® Kids' First Spanish Puzzle and Activity Book
Everything® Kids' Gross Hidden Pictures Book
Everything® Kids' Gross Jokes Book
Everything® Kids' Gross Mazes Book
Everything® Kids' Gross Puzzle and Activity Book
Everything® Kids' Halloween Puzzle & Activity Book
Everything® Kids' Hidden Pictures Book
Everything® Kids' Horses Book
Everything® Kids' Joke Book
Everything® Kids' Knock Knock Book
Everything® Kids' Learning Spanish Book
Everything® Kids' Math Puzzles Book
Everything® Kids' Mazes Book
Everything® Kids' Money Book
Everything® Kids' Nature Book
Everything® Kids' Pirates Puzzle and Activity Book
Everything® Kids' Princess Puzzle and Activity Book
Everything® Kids' Puzzle Book
Everything® Kids' Riddles & Brain Teasers Book
Everything® Kids' Science Experiments Book
Everything® Kids' Sharks Book
Everything® Kids' Soccer Book
Everything® Kids' Travel Activity Book

KIDS' STORY BOOKS

Everything® Fairy Tales Book

LANGUAGE

Everything® Conversational Chinese Book with CD, $19.95
Everything® Conversational Japanese Book with CD, $19.95
Everything® French Grammar Book
Everything® French Phrase Book, $9.95
Everything® French Verb Book, $9.95
Everything® German Practice Book with CD, $19.95
Everything® Inglés Book
Everything® Learning French Book
Everything® Learning German Book
Everything® Learning Italian Book
Everything® Learning Latin Book
Everything® Learning Spanish Book
Everything® Russian Practice Book with CD, $19.95
Everything® Sign Language Book
Everything® Spanish Grammar Book
Everything® Spanish Phrase Book, $9.95
Everything® Spanish Practice Book with CD, $19.95
Everything® Spanish Verb Book, $9.95

MUSIC

Everything® Drums Book with CD, $19.95
Everything® Guitar Book
Everything® Guitar Chords Book with CD, $19.95
Everything® Home Recording Book
Everything® Music Theory Book with CD, $19.95
Everything® Reading Music Book with CD, $19.95
Everything® Rock & Blues Guitar Book (with CD), $19.95
Everything® Songwriting Book

NEW AGE

Everything® Astrology Book, 2nd Ed.
Everything® Birthday Personology Book
Everything® Dreams Book, 2nd Ed.
Everything® Love Signs Book, $9.95
Everything® Numerology Book
Everything® Paganism Book
Everything® Palmistry Book
Everything® Psychic Book
Everything® Reiki Book
Everything® Sex Signs Book, $9.95
Everything® Tarot Book, 2nd Ed.
Everything® Wicca and Witchcraft Book

PARENTING

Everything® Baby Names Book, 2nd Ed.
Everything® Baby Shower Book
Everything® Baby's First Food Book
Everything® Baby's First Year Book
Everything® Birthing Book
Everything® Breastfeeding Book
Everything® Father-to-Be Book
Everything® Father's First Year Book
Everything® Get Ready for Baby Book
Everything® Get Your Baby to Sleep Book, $9.95
Everything® Getting Pregnant Book
Everything® Guide to Raising a One-Year-Old
Everything® Guide to Raising a Two-Year-Old
Everything® Homeschooling Book
Everything® Mother's First Year Book
Everything® Parent's Guide to Children and Divorce
Everything® Parent's Guide to Children with ADD/ADHD
Everything® Parent's Guide to Children with Asperger's Syndrome
Everything® Parent's Guide to Children with Autism
Everything® Parent's Guide to Children with Bipolar Disorder
Everything® Parent's Guide to Children with Dyslexia
Everything® Parent's Guide to Positive Discipline
Everything® Parent's Guide to Raising a Successful Child
Everything® Parent's Guide to Raising Boys
Everything® Parent's Guide to Raising Siblings
Everything® Parent's Guide to Sensory Integration Disorder
Everything® Parent's Guide to Tantrums
Everything® Parent's Guide to the Overweight Child
Everything® Parent's Guide to the Strong-Willed Child
Everything® Parenting a Teenager Book
Everything® Potty Training Book, $9.95
Everything® Pregnancy Book, 2nd Ed.
Everything® Pregnancy Fitness Book
Everything® Pregnancy Nutrition Book
Everything® Pregnancy Organizer, 2nd Ed., $16.95
Everything® Toddler Activities Book
Everything® Toddler Book
Everything® Tween Book
Everything® Twins, Triplets, and More Book

PETS

Everything® Aquarium Book
Everything® Boxer Book
Everything® Cat Book, 2nd Ed.
Everything® Chihuahua Book
Everything® Dachshund Book
Everything® Dog Book
Everything® Dog Health Book
Everything® Dog Owner's Organizer, $16.95
Everything® Dog Training and Tricks Book
Everything® German Shepherd Book
Everything® Golden Retriever Book
Everything® Horse Book
Everything® Horse Care Book
Everything® Horseback Riding Book
Everything® Labrador Retriever Book
Everything® Poodle Book
Everything® Pug Book
Everything® Puppy Book
Everything® Rottweiler Book
Everything® Small Dogs Book
Everything® Tropical Fish Book
Everything® Yorkshire Terrier Book

REFERENCE

Everything® Blogging Book
Everything® Build Your Vocabulary Book
Everything® Car Care Book
Everything® Classical Mythology Book
Everything® Da Vinci Book
Everything® Divorce Book
Everything® Einstein Book
Everything® Etiquette Book, 2nd Ed.
Everything® Inventions and Patents Book
Everything® Mafia Book
Everything® Philosophy Book
Everything® Psychology Book
Everything® Shakespeare Book

RELIGION

Everything® Angels Book
Everything® Bible Book
Everything® Buddhism Book
Everything® Catholicism Book
Everything® Christianity Book
Everything® History of the Bible Book
Everything® Jesus Book
Everything® Jewish History & Heritage Book
Everything® Judaism Book
Everything® Kabbalah Book
Everything® Koran Book
Everything® Mary Book

Everything® Mary Magdalene Book
Everything® Prayer Book
Everything® Saints Book
Everything® Torah Book
Everything® Understanding Islam Book
Everything® World's Religions Book
Everything® Zen Book

SCHOOL & CAREERS

Everything® Alternative Careers Book
Everything® Career Tests Book
Everything® College Major Test Book
Everything® College Survival Book, 2nd Ed.
Everything® Cover Letter Book, 2nd Ed.
Everything® Filmmaking Book
Everything® Get-a-Job Book
Everything® Guide to Being a Paralegal
Everything® Guide to Being a Real Estate Agent
Everything® Guide to Being a Sales Rep
Everything® Guide to Careers in Health Care
Everything® Guide to Careers in Law Enforcement
Everything® Guide to Government Jobs
Everything® Guide to Starting and Running a Restaurant
Everything® Job Interview Book
Everything® New Nurse Book
Everything® New Teacher Book
Everything® Paying for College Book
Everything® Practice Interview Book
Everything® Resume Book, 2nd Ed.
Everything® Study Book

SELF-HELP

Everything® Dating Book, 2nd Ed.
Everything® Great Sex Book
Everything® Kama Sutra Book
Everything® Self-Esteem Book

SPORTS & FITNESS

Everything® Easy Fitness Book
Everything® Fishing Book
Everything® Golf Instruction Book
Everything® Pilates Book
Everything® Running Book
Everything® Weight Training Book
Everything® Yoga Book

TRAVEL

Everything® Family Guide to Cruise Vacations
Everything® Family Guide to Hawaii

Everything® Family Guide to Las Vegas, 2nd Ed.
Everything® Family Guide to Mexico
Everything® Family Guide to New York City, 2nd Ed.
Everything® Family Guide to RV Travel & Campgrounds
Everything® Family Guide to the Caribbean
Everything® Family Guide to the Walt Disney World Resort®, Universal Studios®, and Greater Orlando, 4th Ed.
Everything® Family Guide to Timeshares
Everything® Family Guide to Washington D.C., 2nd Ed.
Everything® Guide to New England

WEDDINGS

Everything® Bachelorette Party Book, $9.95
Everything® Bridesmaid Book, $9.95
Everything® Destination Wedding Book
Everything® Elopement Book, $9.95
Everything® Father of the Bride Book, $9.95
Everything® Groom Book, $9.95
Everything® Mother of the Bride Book, $9.95
Everything® Outdoor Wedding Book
Everything® Wedding Book, 3rd Ed.
Everything® Wedding Checklist, $9.95
Everything® Wedding Etiquette Book, $9.95
Everything® Wedding Organizer, 2nd Ed., $16.95
Everything® Wedding Shower Book, $9.95
Everything® Wedding Vows Book, $9.95
Everything® Wedding Workout Book
Everything® Weddings on a Budget Book, $9.95

WRITING

Everything® Creative Writing Book
Everything® Get Published Book, 2nd Ed.
Everything® Grammar and Style Book
Everything® Guide to Writing a Book Proposal
Everything® Guide to Writing a Novel
Everything® Guide to Writing Children's Books
Everything® Guide to Writing Research Papers
Everything® Screenwriting Book
Everything® Writing Poetry Book
Everything® Writing Well Book